GRE® Graduate Record Examination

All the Verbal

Seventh Edition

GRE® is a registered trademark of Educational Testing Service (ETS), which is not affiliated with Kaplan and was not involved in the production of, and does not endorse, this product.

GRE All the Verbal

Retail ISBN: 978-1-5062-9890-0
Course ISBN: 978-1-5062-9892-4
Retail eISBN: 978-1-5062-9891-7
Course eISBN: 978-1-5062-9893-1

Copyright © 2025 Kaplan North America, LLC dba Manhattan Prep.
1515 West Cypress Creek Road
Fort Lauderdale, Florida 33309

10 9 8 7 6 5 4 3 2 1

All Rights Reserved. This material is protected under International and Pan-American Copyright Conventions. No part of this publication may be reproduced, distributed, or transmitted in any form or by any means—including photocopying, recording, or other electronic or mechanical methods, now known or hereinafter invented—duplicated, resold, stored in, introduced into, or incorporated into any information storage or retrieval system, or used in any artificial intelligence analysis software, such as generative AI systems or machine learning models, without the express written permission of Kaplan North America, LLC.

GRE® is a registered trademark of Educational Testing Service (ETS), which is not affiliated with Kaplan and was not involved in the production of, and does not endorse, this product.

INSTRUCTIONAL GUIDE SERIES

1 GRE All the Quant

2 GRE All the Verbal

3 5 lb. Book of GRE® Practice Problems

SUPPLEMENTAL MATERIALS

500 Essential Words:
GRE® Vocabulary Flash Cards

500 Advanced Words:
GRE® Vocabulary Flash Cards

September 2, 2025

Hello! Welcome to **GRE® All the Verbal**.

I hope this book provides just the guidance you need to get the most out of your GRE studies. **If you have any questions or feedback, please do not hesitate to contact us at gre@manhattanprep.com or 212-721-7400.** Also: We try to keep all of our books free of errors, but if you think we've goofed, please visit manhattanprep.com/GRE/errata.

All of our Manhattan Prep books are based on the continuing experiences of both our instructors and our students. The primary vision for this edition of the book was developed by Chris Gentry and Whitney Garner. The primary authors of this edition of the book were Manhattan Prep instructors Chris Gentry and Ryan Starr, and the primary editors were Whitney Garner and Logan Smeallie. Project management, design, and quality assurance were led by Arunsanthosh Kannan, Mario Gambino, Marie Gugnishev, and Helen Tan.

Finally, we are indebted to all of the Manhattan Prep students who have given us excellent feedback over the years. This book wouldn't be half of what it is without their voice.

And now that you are one of our students too, please chime in! I look forward to hearing from you. Thanks again and best of luck preparing for the GRE!

Sincerely,

Stacey Koprince
Director of Content and Curriculum
Manhattan Prep

www.manhattanprep.com/gre   623 Broadway, New York, NY 10012   Tel: 212-721-7400

TABLE OF CONTENTS

Introduction 1
    Your GRE Journey 3
    The GRE Exam 3
    Off the Deep End: What GRE Verbal Can Look Like 5
    Verbal Question Formats in Detail. 5
    Timing. 12
    How to Use This Book. 13

UNIT ONE: Words and Sentences. 15

Chapter 1: GRE Vocabulary 17
    Learning Vocabulary Words in This Book 19
    Studying Vocabulary Effectively 19
    Two Options for Vocabulary Study 21
    Other Study Techniques 24
    When to Use Roots 24
    Specialized Vocabulary in Reading Comprehension Passages . 26
    Using Social Networks to Buttress Your Vocabulary Studies 26
    Vocabulary Challenge 27
    Answers and Explanations 28

Chapter 2: GRE Sentences. 29
    Complex Sentences 31
    Unpacking GRE Sentences 32
    Principles for Unpacking Sentences 33
    Link to Real Ideas 35
    Vocabulary Challenge 36
    Problem Set 37
    Answers and Explanations 38

Chapter 3: Text Completion and Sentence Equivalence 41
    One-Blank Text Completion 43
    The Three-Step Process for Text Completions 44
    Direction Markers 50
    Drill: Sentence Analysis 53

Sentence Equivalence..55
Sentence Analysis in Sentence Equivalence........................56
Answer Choice Analysis...58
When to Use (and NOT to Use) Answer Choice Analysis..............61
Drill: Answer Choice Analysis....................................63
What If I Don't Know the Words?..................................66
Why It Is Important to Learn Words in Context....................67
Traps in TC and SE...68
Text Completion and Sentence Equivalence Recap...................69
Vocabulary Challenge...69
Problem Set (Text Completion)....................................70
Problem Set (Sentence Equivalence)...............................75
Answers and Explanations...91

UNIT TWO: Paragraphs and Passages.............................109

Chapter 4: GRE Paragraphs....................................111
Making Connections..113
Signals and Pronouns..115
Components of Paragraphs..117
The Main Idea (and Archetypes)..................................119
The Big Picture...122
Don't Just Read, Do Something!..................................123
A Note-Taking Exercise (Sample Notes)...........................124
Common Notations..124
Vocabulary Challenge..125
Problem Set...126
Answers and Explanations..127

Chapter 5: Short Passages in Reading Comprehension...........129
Two Types of Passages...131
Scanning Ahead..132
Strategy for General Questions..................................133
Strategy for Specific Questions.................................134
Common Wrong Answer Categories..................................137
Summary of Strategies for Answer Choice Eliminations............138
Comprehensive Strategies for All Reading Comprehension..........139
Vocabulary Challenge..139
A Short Introduction to the Problem Set.........................140

    Problem Set 141

    Answers and Explanations 145

Chapter 6: Argument-Based Reading Comprehension 153

    Recognizing Argument-Based Passages 155

    Components of Argument-Based Passages 156

    Identifying the Components of an Argument 157

    Strategy for ABP Questions. 158

    Taking Notes 160

    Useful Focal Points for All Question Types 162

    Question Types 165

    Vocabulary Challenge 178

    Problem Set 179

    Answers and Explanations 184

Chapter 7: Multi-Blank Text Completion. 199

    Two- and Three-Blank Text Completions 201

    Start with the Easier (or Easiest) Blank 202

    Tricky Aspects of Multi-Blank Text Completion. 206

    More on Traps in Text Completion 210

    Vocabulary Challenge 212

    Problem Set 213

    Answers and Explanations 222

Chapter 8: Reading Comprehension Problem Set 237

    Problem Set 241

    Answers and Explanations 250

Chapter 9: Issue Essay. 271

    Essay in a Nutshell. 273

    Analyze an Issue. 275

    Style Points. 282

    Analyze an Issue Sample Essays 283

    Notes on Preparation 286

    Vocabulary Challenge 287

    Answers and Explanations 288

Introduction

In This Chapter . . .

- Your GRE Journey
- The GRE Exam
- Off the Deep End: What GRE Verbal Can Look Like
- Verbal Question Formats in Detail
- Timing
- How to Use This Book

Introduction

Your GRE Journey

We know that you're looking to succeed on the GRE so that you can go to graduate school and do the things you want to do in life. We also know that you're not frequently taking standardized tests asking you to answer multiple choice questions after reading long passages of text you're not interested in (or at least not recently).

In order to succeed, you will need to get (back) into an academic mindset, reading dense material, confronting difficult vocabulary, and answering analytical questions, all within short time limits. In other words, it's going to take hard work on your part to get a top GRE score. That's why we've put together this set of books that will take you from the basics all the way up to the material you need to master for a near-perfect score (or whatever *your* goal score may be).

In this chapter, you will learn the format of the test, with more information specific to question formats in the Verbal section of the test. You'll also see study planning advice to help you place elements of this book (and possibly the class syllabus) into a context more relevant to your personal needs.

You've taken the first step. Now it's time to get to work!

The GRE Exam

Exam Structure

The GRE has five scored sections. You will get a 1-minute break between each section. The Analytical Writing section, also known as the Essay section, is always first.

The remaining sections will include:

- Two Verbal Reasoning sections, the first containing 12 problems to answer in 18 minutes, and the second with 15 problems to answer in 23 minutes
- Two Quantitative Reasoning (Math) sections, the first containing 12 problems to answer in 21 minutes, and the second with 15 problems to answer in 26 minutes

Introduction

Section #	Section Type	# Problems	Time
1	Essay	1 Issue Essay	30 minutes
2	Initial Math or Verbal	12	21 or 18 minutes
3	Initial Verbal or Math	12	18 or 21 minutes
4	Adaptive Math or Verbal	15	26 or 23 minutes
5	Adaptive Verbal or Math	15	23 or 26 minutes

After the essay, the sections can come in any order, although Math and Verbal tend to alternate. For example, you could see:

- Essay, Initial Math, Initial Verbal, Adaptive Math, Adaptive Verbal
- Essay, Initial Verbal, Initial Math, Adaptive Verbal, Adaptive Math

Navigating the Problems in a Section

The GRE offers you the ability to move freely around the problems in a single section. You can go forward and backward one-by-one and can even jump directly to any problem from the "review list" screen. You can also mark a problem for later review. The review list screen provides a snapshot of which problems you have answered, which ones you have marked, and which ones are incomplete.

If you finish a section early, double-check the review list for completion. Do answer every problem—there's no penalty for getting something wrong. You'll get a chance to practice with the review list when you take practice exams.

The majority of GRE test-takers are pressed for time in at least some of the sections. You may find that you have time to go back to just one or two problems—or you may not have time to go back to any of them. With these points in mind, here's what we recommend:

1. In general, do the problems in the order in which they appear.
2. When you encounter a pretty-hard-but-not-impossible problem, do your best to eliminate answer choices that you know are wrong. Then choose one of the remaining answers and keep going. (What you've just done is called "educated guessing".)
3. If it's an impossible one, don't try to eliminate answers first—just put in a random guess and move on.
4. When you encounter an "I could do this but it's going to take extra time" problem, put in a random guess *for now* but mark the problem for later review. Do this on a maximum of 3 problems in the section. (If it turns out that you don't have time to get back to it, at least you've made a guess.)
5. Aim to save at least a minute at the end of the section to review the review list. Scan down: Did you leave any problems blank? If so, click into them and put in a random guess.
6. If you still have more time left, jump into one of your "marked for later" problems.

Avoid repeatedly clicking forward and backward through all of the problems, searching for "easy" ones. This will eat up valuable time. Instead, be disciplined about making the call to move on when you hit a problem that's just too hard. (And how do you know that, quickly and confidently? Via your studies. Part of the value in prioritizing your studies as you go is knowing when you want to bail on a problem during the test.)

Introduction

Getting good at navigating the test sections will take a lot of practice. Use the above advice on practice exams *and* when doing timed problem sets (even when you're doing timed sets out of a book and not on a computer screen).

Off the Deep End: What GRE Verbal Can Look Like

The tokens given by the aristocrat, while nugatory, still served as a reminder that the power of the Crown continued to be held in some esteem even in such mercurial political times.

Welcome to the marvelous world of GRE Verbal, where you too will find forbiddingly dense and frustratingly constructed, sentences, paragraphs, and passages the norm rather than the exception. The GRE both works within and directly tests formal, sometimes nearly archaic, phrasings and structures to mimic the challenges of difficult academic writing. (And yes, the phrasing of those two sentences was deliberate. This is similar to the writing style used on the GRE.)

Hopefully, the above introduction serves as a demonstration that a need exists to "learn to read for the GRE." Therefore, test takers need to follow a reading process that will address these challenges at the outset and build a study process that reinforces the necessary mental habits to implement that reading process.

Or, put in less GRE-ish terms, yes, you do actually want to study Verbal. It's not a situation of "well, I'll just try my best," hoping that repetition of problems will make you better. There is a method to the madness, and that is why this book exists!

Why Is GRE Verbal So Challenging?

There are several specific, concrete reasons for why GRE Verbal is so challenging.

- The content is demanding. GRE Verbal questions focus on specific and often unfamiliar topics in sciences, social science, history, and other humanities (literature, art, music). You might be neither knowledgeable nor enthusiastic about these fields.
- You have to read on the screen, which is physically stressful on the human eye.
- You have to read quickly, regardless of how dense the material is. Some verbal questions need to be answered in one minute; that is not a lot of time!
- You have to stay engaged, even if you do not feel you understand, or maybe even just don't *like*, a sentence or passage. So even in those situations, you need strategies to continue to work productively through the section.

Thus, this book! The following sections will address specific Verbal question formats and timing guidelines.

Verbal Question Formats in Detail

The 27 questions throughout the Verbal sections can be broken down by format as follows:

- Reading Comprehension questions ($\approx$ 5 in the initial section, $\approx$ 8 in the adaptive section)
- Text Completion questions ($\approx$ 3 in the initial section, $\approx$ 4 in the adaptive section)
- Sentence Equivalence questions ($\approx$ 4 in the initial section, $\approx$ 3 in the adaptive section)

Before going into these Verbal question types further, let's go back to the beginning of the exam: the Analytical Writing section, also known as the Essay.

Introduction

The Essays

The Analytical Writing section consists of one timed 30-minute task: Analyze an Issue. As you can imagine, the 30-minute time limit implies that you aren't aiming to write an essay that would garner a Pulitzer Prize nomination but rather to complete the task adequately and according to the directions. The essay is scored separately from the Quant and Verbal sections on a 0–6 scale.

The essay prompt will present a claim, generally one that is vague enough to be interpreted in a variety of ways and discussed from numerous perspectives. Your job as a test-taker is to write a response discussing the extent to which you agree or disagree and support your position. Don't sit on the fence—pick a side!

Check out the official GRE website (www.ets.org/gre) for example essay prompts and sample essays with scores.

Multiple-Choice Questions

In this book and in *The Official Guide to the GRE® General Test*, you will see letters at the beginning of the answer choices for multiple choice questions (A, B, C, and so on). When you're taking a test on a computer, however, there will be no answer letters, just boxes or open bubbles that you will select with your mouse.

Although the real test won't show letters on the screen, there's an important reason why you want to imagine that there are letters there: As you solve problems, you'll eliminate wrong answers before selecting the correct one—but you can't cross off answers on the screen.

Write down A, B, C, D, E (or however many letters are needed for that problem) on your scratch paper to keep track of your answer-choice eliminations as you go. The answer letters shown in this book will help you get into the habit of doing this, even though you will not see answer letters on the screen when you take the test.

Reading Comprehension Questions

Reading Comprehension (RC) questions will be associated with three or four passages that vary in length from one paragraph to several. A passage typically has between one and three questions associated with it, and longer passages typically have more questions.

Most Reading Comprehension problems will have five answer choices from which you'll choose one answer. For these, use the letters A, B, C, D, and E to keep track of your eliminations. There are also two other possible RC formats, Select One or More and Select-in-Passage.

Select One or More Answer Choices

Some RC problems will give you three statements about a passage and ask you to "select all that apply." Either one, two, or all three can be correct (there is no "none of the above" option). There is no partial credit; you must indicate all of the correct choices and none of the incorrect choices. Use the letters A, B, and C to keep track of your eliminations on these problems.

On your screen, the answer choice boxes for "Select One or More" will always be *squares*, while the standard "pick just one" multiple-choice problems will always use *circles*. The squares are a good visual reminder that you may need to select more than one choice on these problems, just as you might check more than one box on a checklist.

> *Strategy Tip:*
>
> On **Select One or More Answer Choices**, consider each choice independently! You cannot use the process of elimination in the same way as you do on normal multiple-choice questions.

Select-in-Passage

For the question type Select-in-Passage, you are given an assignment such as "Select the sentence in the passage that explains why the experiment's results were discovered to be invalid." Clicking anywhere on the sentence in the passage will highlight it. (As with any GRE question, you will have to click "Confirm" to submit your answer, so don't worry about accidentally selecting the wrong sentence due to a slip of the mouse.)

> *Strategy Tip:*
>
> Because **Select-in-Passage** questions don't have a consistent number of sentences or paragraphs, use numbers rather than letters to keep track of your eliminations.
>
> If you have a single paragraph, number each sentence. If you have multiple paragraphs, start by numbering each paragraph. Once you've narrowed down to one paragraph, number the sentences in that paragraph.

Now give these new question types a try.

> *The sample questions below are based on this passage:*
>
> Physicist Robert Oppenheimer, director of the fateful Manhattan Project, said, "It is a profound and necessary truth that the deep things in science are not found because they are useful; they are found because it was possible to find them." In a later address at MIT, Oppenheimer presented the thesis that scientists could be held only very nominally responsible for the consequences of their research and discovery. Oppenheimer asserted that ethics, philosophy, and politics have very little to do with the day-to-day work of the scientist and that scientists could not rationally be expected to predict all the effects of their work. Yet, in a talk in 1945 to the Association of Los Alamos Scientists, Oppenheimer offered some reasons why the Manhattan Project scientists built the atomic bomb; the justifications included "fear that Nazi Germany would build it first" and "hope that it would shorten the war."

Introduction

For question #1, consider each of the three choices separately and select all that apply.

1. The passage implies that Robert Oppenheimer would most likely have agreed with which of the following views:

    A Some scientists take military goals into account in their work.
    B Deep things in science are not useful.
    C The everyday work of a scientist is only minimally involved with ethics.

2. Select the sentence in which the writer implies that Oppenheimer has not been consistent in his view that scientists have little consideration for the effects of their work.

    (Here, you would highlight the appropriate sentence with your mouse. There are four sentences, so there are four options.)

To answer the first question, Oppenheimer is quoted in the last sentence as saying that one of the reasons the bomb was built was the scientists' "hope that it would shorten the war." Thus, Oppenheimer would likely agree with the view that "some scientists take military goals into account in their work." Choice (B) is a trap answer using familiar language from the passage. According to the passage, Oppenheimer says that the possible usefulness of scientific discoveries is not why scientists make discoveries; he does not say that the discoveries aren't useful. The passage quotes Oppenheimer as saying that ethics has *very* "little to do with the day-to-day work of the scientist," which is a good match for "only minimally involved with ethics." So for the Select One or More, you would select choices (A) and (C), but not choice (B).

> **Strategy Tip:**
> On Select One or More Answer Choices, write A B C on your paper and mark each choice with a check, an *X*, or a symbol such as ~ if you're not sure. This should keep you from crossing out all three choices.

For the second question, the correct sentence is the final sentence:

"Yet, in a talk in 1945 to the Association of Los Alamos Scientists, Oppenheimer offered some reasons why the Manhattan Project scientists built the atomic bomb; the justifications included 'fear that Nazi Germany would build it first' and 'hope that it would shorten the war.'"

The word *yet* is a good clue that this sentence is about to express a view contrary to the views expressed in the rest of the passage. On the test, you would click this sentence in the text of the passage with the computer mouse, highlighting it. (If you clicked on a sentence by mistake, you can just click on the sentence you actually intended to change the highlight.)

The chapters on Reading Comprehension in this book contain more detail on solving both the more standard multiple choice RC questions and these more unique ones.

Introduction

Text Completion Questions

Text Completion (TC) questions will consist of anywhere from one to three blanks spread across one to five sentences. When TCs have one blank, you will have five words or phrases to choose from for that blank, so use answer letters A, B, C, D, and E to keep track of your eliminations.

When TCs have two or three blanks, each blank will have three options, and you will select words or short phrases for each blank independently. There is no partial credit; the selection for every blank in the problem must be correct in order to get that question right. Use answer letters A through F for two-blank TCs and answer letters A through I for three-blank TCs.

Try the following two-blank example:

> Leaders are not always expected to (i) _____ the same rules as are those they lead; leaders are often looked up to for a surety and presumption that would be viewed as (ii) _____ in most others.

Blank (i)	
A	decree
B	proscribe
C	conform to

Blank (ii)	
D	hubris
E	avarice
F	anachronism

In the first blank, you need a word similar to *follow*. In the second blank, you need a word similar to *arrogance*. The correct answers are *conform to* and *hubris*.

> **Strategy Tip:**
>
> In **Text Completion** questions, do NOT look at the answer choices until you've decided for yourself what kind of word needs to go in each blank. Then, review the choices and eliminate those that are not matches.

Now try an example with three blanks:

> For Kant, the fact of having a right and having the (i) _____ to enforce it via coercion cannot be separated, and he asserts that this marriage of rights and coercion is compatible with the freedom of everyone. This is not at all peculiar from the standpoint of modern political thought—what good is a right if its violation triggers no enforcement (be it punishment or (ii) _____)? The necessity of coercion is not at all in conflict with the freedom of everyone, because this coercion only comes into play when someone has (iii) _____ someone else.

Blank (i)	
A	technique
B	license
C	prohibition

Blank (ii)	
D	amortization
E	reward
F	restitution

Blank (iii)	
G	questioned the hypothesis of
H	violated the rights of
I	granted civil liberties to

Introduction

In the first sentence, use the clue "he asserts that this marriage of rights and coercion is compatible with the freedom of everyone" to help fill in the first blank. Kant believes that *coercion* is "married to" rights and is compatible with freedom for all. So you want something in the first blank like *right* or *power*. Kant believes that rights are meaningless without enforcement. Only the choice *license* can work (while a *license* can be physical, like a driver's license, the word *license* can also mean *right*).

The second blank is part of the phrase "punishment or _____," which you are told is the *enforcement* resulting from the violation of a right. So the blank should be something, other than punishment, that constitutes enforcement against someone who violates a right. (More simply, it should be something bad.) Only *restitution* works. *Restitution* is compensating the victim in some way (perhaps monetarily or by returning stolen goods).

The final sentence says, "coercion only comes into play when someone has _____ someone else." Throughout the text, *coercion* means "enforcement against someone who has violated the rights of someone else." The meaning is the same here. The answer is *violated the rights of*.

The complete and correct answer is this combination:

Blank (i)	Blank (ii)	Blank (iii)
B license	F restitution	H violated the rights of

There are a total of 3 × 3 × 3, or 27 possible ways to answer a three-blank Text Completion question—and only one of those 27 ways is correct. In theory, these are tough odds. In practice, you will often have certainty about some of the blanks, so your guessing odds are almost never this difficult. Just follow the basic process: Come up with your own filler for each blank, and match to the answer choices. If you're confused by this example, don't worry! The chapters on Text Completion and Sentence Equivalence in this book cover all of this in detail.

> **Strategy Tip:**
>
> On **Text Completion** questions, the GRE will give you a clue to the correct answer in the text. Look for textual evidence for each answer choice you select.

Sentence Equivalence Questions

For this question type, you are given one sentence with a single blank. This looks very much like a one-blank Text Completion question, but the assignment has a twist. This time, instead of five choices, there are six, and instead of choosing one answer, you need to pick two that fit the blank and are alike in meaning. Use answer letters A through F to keep track of your eliminations.

Of the Verbal question types, this one depends the most on vocabulary and also yields the most to strategy.

No partial credit is given on Sentence Equivalence; both correct answers must be selected, and no incorrect answers may be selected. When you pick 2 of 6 choices, there are 15 possible combinations of choices, and only 1 is correct. However, this is not nearly as daunting as it sounds.

If you have six choices, but the two correct ones must be similar in meaning, then you have, at most, three possible *pairs* of choices. There may be fewer, since not all choices are guaranteed to have a partner. If you know the meaning of the words in the answer choices and can match up the pairs, you can seriously narrow down your options.

Here is a sample set of answer choices. The square boxes indicate that you are to select more than one answer.

- [A] tractable
- [B] taciturn
- [C] arbitrary
- [D] tantamount
- [E] reticent
- [F] amenable

The question is deliberately omitted here in order to illustrate how much you can do with the choices alone, assuming you have learned these words during your vocabulary studies.

Tractable and *amenable* are synonyms (*tractable, amenable* people will do whatever you want them to do). *Taciturn* and *reticent* are synonyms (both mean "not talkative").

Arbitrary (based on one's own will) and *tantamount* (equivalent) are not similar in meaning and cannot be a pair. Therefore, the *only* possible correct answer pairs are choices (A) and (F) or choices (B) and (E). You have improved your chances from 1 in 15 to a 50/50 shot without even reading the question!

Of course, in approaching a Sentence Equivalence question, you do want to analyze the sentence in the same way you would in Text Completion—read for a textual clue that tells you what type of word *must* go in the blank. Then, look for a matching pair.

> **Strategy Tip:**
>
> In **Sentence Equivalence** questions, if you're sure that a word in the choices does *not* have a partner, cross it out!

The sentence for the previous answer choice options could read as follows:

Though the dinner guests were quite _____, the hostess did her best to keep the conversation active and engaging.

Since the hostess needed to work "to keep the conversation active and engaging" due to the nature of her dinner guests, you can infer that the guests were not talkative. Thus, choice (B) and choice (E) are the best pairing.

Introduction

Try this example of a complete problem:

> While athletes usually expect to achieve their greatest feats in their teens or twenties, opera singers don't reach the _____ of their vocal powers until middle age.
>
> [A] harmony
> [B] zenith
> [C] acme
> [D] terminus
> [E] nadir
> [F] cessation

Those with strong vocabularies might go straight to the choices to make pairs. *Zenith* and *acme* are synonyms, meaning "high point, peak." *Terminus* and *cessation* are synonyms meaning "end." *Nadir* is a low point, and *harmony* is present here as a trap answer reminding you of opera singers. Cross off choices (A) and (E), since they do not have partners. Then, go back to the sentence, knowing that your only options are a pair meaning "peak" and a pair meaning "end."

Since the sentence discusses the various career points when two groups of professionals "achieve their greatest feats," the correct answer pair is choice (B) and choice (C).

Now that you have a few examples of the question formats, let's examine the timing goals for each question type. (The Essay is omitted from the following chart, as it is not scored as a section, but rather as a single response to a single prompt. Your timing goal for the Essay is direct: 30 minutes.)

Timing

One of the most pressing challenges on GRE Verbal is the timing. Spending enough time to answer the questions accurately but not so much that you lose points because you run out of time requires practice and planning.

Use the following chart as a guideline for how much time to spend answering a question. There are two things to note. First, the following are timing recommendations for standard (1x) GRE timing. If you have timing accommodations (1.5x or 2x), adjust your goals accordingly. Second, these recommendations are for time spent attempting the problem—time yourself while attempting problems, but don't time yourself when reviewing problems.

Question Type	Time Spent Reading	Time Spent in Answer Choices	Total Time
Text Completion	45 to 60 seconds	10 seconds per blank	55–90 seconds
Sentence Equivalence	45 to 60 seconds	20 seconds	65–80 seconds
Reading Comprehension	1.5 to 3.5 minutes, depending on passage length	30–60 seconds per question	2 to 6 minutes, depending on number of questions and length of passage

Introduction

You probably already notice a challenge: Reading Comprehension timing varies extensively. This is an awkward necessity due to the fact that the length of passages varies, as does the number of questions per passage. Your exact timing will vary according to your strengths, and you must take into account that your timing needs to pace you through a whole section.

While you will need to be flexible in your timing allocations for Reading Comprehension, here is a general guideline: Spend about half of your total time reading the passage and about half of your total time evaluating the answer choices for each question. The table below illustrates a typical timing breakdown for each likely length of a Reading Comprehension passage.

# of Questions	Time Spent Reading	Time Spent on Answer Choices	Total Time
1	1 minute 30 seconds	45 seconds	2 minutes, 15 seconds
2	2 minutes	45 seconds	3 minutes, 30 seconds
3	3 minutes	45 seconds	5 minutes, 15 seconds
4 (very rare)	3 minutes	45 seconds	6 minutes

These timing benchmarks are rough, especially because more questions doesn't necessarily mean a longer passage. Additionally, different question types take differing amounts of time. More detailed timing suggestions are in the coming chapters that cover each type of question you will see.

How to Use This Book

If you're using this book as part of a course, you will have a syllabus to guide you. If you are not, however, we want to offer you some additional guidance.

This book is *not* a novel, a news story, or an article on a topic that interests you; it isn't meant to be dug into and read cover to cover. However, this book also isn't meant to be used as an encyclopedia, only flipping to specific sections for reference or to look up a topic. Our recommendation is to instead see this book as a balance between the two.

The organization of material is intended to build skills in order from the briefest units of verbal text (vocabulary) to the lengthiest (RC passages). Don't confuse "brief" with easy or introductory, however. The material in the first chapters on words and sentences will set you up for some of the most advanced study and test taking strategies in the entire book. Skipping these earlier sections completely is likely to artificially limit your progress in the later sections.

That said, we understand that your needs may not lie in the order this book presents the material. Rather than skipping around, though, consider instead changing your pace as you move through the book. Dig more deeply into areas of weakness and be ready to skim or briefly reference areas of strength. If you find yourself struggling with later chapters, return to earlier sections to reinforce the micro-skills that build better performance in longer problem types.

Introduction

Top Tips for Studying GRE Verbal

Regardless of how you feel about your verbal abilities and which areas are strengths and weaknesses, all students benefit from doing the following three things:

1. **Practice vocabulary early and often.**
   - Before you do anything else, read Chapter 1: GRE Vocabulary, and choose your favorite method(s) for learning and practicing new words.
   - Commit to consistent (daily) practice. Even if you don't have time to sit down and study anything else that day, find five minutes for your flashcards or stories.
2. **Give yourself mental variety.**
   - Everyone needs a break sometimes—even if it's just studying a different component of the test.
   - Keep in mind, you can move backward to old material or forward to new material as you wish.
3. **Periodically test yourself.**
   - Periodically challenge yourself to *do* something. Whether this is a full practice test or a single problem, make regular attempts to apply your skills.
   - Use practice tests as assessments and reassessments. Your abilities will change, and you need periodic "checks" on your actual abilities versus your perception of them.

Final Notes

Keep in mind that, while some of your study materials may be on paper (including the Educational Testing Service's most recent source of official GRE problems, *The Official Guide to the GRE® General Test*), your exam will be administered on a computer. Because this is a computer-based test, you will *not* be able to underline portions of reading passages or otherwise physically mark up problems. Get used to this now. Use separate scratch paper to solve the problems in these books.

And use your available online resources. Create a free account on the Manhattan Prep website to gain access to a plethora of online resources, including a vocabulary tracker/organizer, Interact lessons, and a full practice test!

UNIT ONE

Words and Sentences

This unit provides you with a comprehensive approach to the study of the most fundamental building blocks of GRE Verbal problems: words and sentences. Included are practical techniques for developing vocabulary and grasping the meaning of complex sentences. Finally, this unit introduces two question types: Text Completions and Sentence Equivalence.

In This Unit ...

- Chapter 1: GRE Vocabulary
- Chapter 2: GRE Sentences
- Chapter 3: Text Completion and Sentence Equivalence

CHAPTER 1
GRE Vocabulary

In This Chapter...

- Learning Vocabulary Words in This Book
- Studying Vocabulary Effectively
- Two Options for Vocabulary Study
- Other Study Techniques
- When to Use Roots
- Specialized Vocabulary in Reading Comprehension Passages
- Using Social Networks to Buttress Your Vocabulary Studies
- Vocabulary Challenge
- Answers and Explanations

CHAPTER 1 GRE Vocabulary

GRE Vocabulary is one of the, if not the, first stumbling blocks students face when preparing for the Verbal section of this test. In this chapter, you will learn methods to study vocabulary that are effective and time-efficient.

Learning Vocabulary Words in This Book

Each chapter in this book will feature a few GRE vocabulary words mixed into the text. Six will be introduced at the start of the chapter; look for them as you read! They might appear in different forms— for example, from this chapter's list, "assiduous" could appear as "assiduously."

At the end of the chapter, you'll have a chance to write your own predicted definition based on the context in which they appeared, and then you'll be given the official definition.

Each chapter's list contains three words labeled (E) for essential and three words labeled (A) for advanced. The essential words are essential for everyone; study the advanced words if you are aiming for an especially high verbal score. (You can also find all of these words in our GRE Flash Cards, if you have purchased them.)

Here are your Chapter 1 vocabulary words, listed in the order in which they appear in the chapter:

> assiduous (A)
> engender (A)
> bombastic (A)
> inchoate (E)
> judicious (E)
> buttress (E)

Studying Vocabulary Effectively

The tokens given by the aristocrat, while nugatory, still served as a reminder that the power of the Crown continued to be held in some esteem even in such mercurial political times.

In that introductory sentence there are a few words that are probably unfamiliar to most English speakers; the most likely culprits are *nugatory* and *mercurial*. Can you name synonyms for these words immediately and confidently? If not—if you find yourself mentally saying "well, mercurial is kind of like when..."—then you need to study this vocabulary!

The study of vocabulary for the GRE, unsurprisingly, begins with the definition. (The following are some of the definitions published in dictionary.com.)

Unit One: Words and Sentences

Nugatory (adj.): of no real value; trifling; worthless

Mercurial (adj.): changeable, volatile, fickle, flighty, or erratic

Great! Now what?

Many students want to know *how many* words they have to learn in order to get a high score on the GRE, as though the GRE were a pure vocabulary quiz. It would be far simpler if the GRE tested you by giving you a list of words and asking you to write out the definition for each. You could memorize the dictionary definitions of 1,000 vocabulary words and regurgitate them up as quickly as possible on test day. Memorizing 500 new words (much less 1,000) in the weeks before the exam would be a substantial feat, but the GRE wants more.

The GRE is *actually* testing whether you've been reading college-level and academic writing (in English) for years, assiduously looking up all the words you didn't know in *The Scarlet Letter* and *The Great Gatsby* or researching the technical language from scientific papers when you didn't understand the meaning. And then, if you've been out of school, you've continued reading college-level material ever since. In other words, the GRE is testing whether you know these "big" words *in context:* not merely memorized, but internalized over years of study.

Simulating that level of verbal knowledge (when you haven't actually been doing the things listed above) takes some work. It can be done, but it's very important to *learn*—not just memorize—vocabulary words.

Many students make the mistake of memorizing dictionary definitions of words without really understanding those definitions or being able to comfortably use those words in sentences. Memorizing by itself is not learning; it is not flexible. If you've learned *torpid*, you can make a connection to *torpor*. If you've learned *anthropology* and *engender*, you can make some reasonable assumptions about *anthropogenesis*.

For sources of difficult material, try *The Economist, Scientific American, Smithsonian, Foreign, MIT Technology Review*, or any of the articles posted on aldaily.com (that's Arts and Letters Daily). These are also the same resources recommended for improving your reading comprehension; you can do both at the same time!

If you've ever learned a foreign language, think about the words that were easiest to learn. When you're in class, most of the words you learn (*stove, tire, classroom, grandmother*) seem equally important. But when you are actually in a foreign country, trying to speak that language, it is *very, very easy* to learn and remember words and phrases like *bathroom*, "What is the price?" and "Where is the hotel?" That is, the easiest things to learn are things that you *really wanted to know* at the time so you looked them up; the emotion or urgency of the situation told your brain that it was important to learn that word, and you did.

Similarly, if you are reading something interesting and come across a word you don't know, look up the word and consider its usage in the sentence you were just puzzling over—that's almost as good as learning the word *bathroom* when you really need to use one! It's easier to retain a new word when there's a "hole" in your knowledge that you just cannot wait to fill.

If you look up unknown words right away, you are creating an immediate, real connection between that word and some external source. You create immediate associations to the meaning of that word. It is these associations that engender the learning process! If you make this a daily habit and supplement it with tools for later review (like the flashcards we will discuss in the next section), your vocabulary studies will be immensely effective.

Finally, don't hesitate to look up or ask someone about the words you *thought* you knew but that seem to be used in novel ways. (Did you notice what just happened there? As a noun, a *novel* is a book-length work of fiction, but as an adjective, *novel* means "new, original.")

For another example, consider the use of "informed by" in the following sentence: "Her historical analysis of family dynamics in the antebellum South is informed by an academic background in feminist theory." Clearly, an "academic background in feminist theory" can't talk—"informed by" means "influenced by" in this context. Or the use of "qualified" in the sentence, "Dr. Wong could give only qualified approval to the theory, as the available data was limited in scope." ("Qualified" here means "limited, conditional, holding back.")

If you read a definition of a word—on a flashcard, in a test prep book, or anywhere else—and it doesn't make sense to you, look up the word in several online dictionaries (thefreedictionary.com, m-w.com, and dictionary.com), ask someone, and/or Google the word to see how other people are using it.

Combine the mindset of immediate gratification—"I will look up the definition of any new or unusual word *now*"—to the more long-term strategies for vocabulary studies discussed in the following sections, and you'll have great success!

Two Options for Vocabulary Study

There are two options that many people find effective: building flashcards and writing stories.

Option 1: Flashcards

Flashcards are possibly the most 'old-school' of memorization aids. Most people *want* to use them, but few want to actually *make* them and commit to studying them consistently. While flashcards allow for quick quizzing (once created), the standard "word on front, definition on back" versions slow down the process of learning the words in the first place. And even less effective are pre-made decks: With zero effort in their creation, you drastically increase the number of times you'll have to flip through each card to even start learning the word.

As mentioned before, emotion, interest, and need are huge drivers of learning and memorizing new vocabulary. To capitalize on that, you want a flashcard that allows for creativity and personalization. A good flashcard certainly has the word on the front and the definition on the back, but a great flashcard has more. A great flashcard should include multiple mnemonic devices to aid memorization: a sample sentence, a picture, a rhyme, or a reference to a person or memory connected to that word.

Do you remember what *mercurial* means? If not, that's proof that reading the definition of a word isn't enough to learn that word; if it was, then you'd know *mercurial* from the definition provided just a few pages ago. How many times do you think you'd need to review that card before really knowing the word? You might be okay if this is one of only a few words you need to learn, but this card is going to be in a deck of hundreds of new words. Learning in this way is going to be slow.

But what if, instead, you decided that you wanted to create a great flashcard for *mercurial*. You looked it up and saw that it was based on the Roman god Mercury, who is often depicted with a winged helmet. You connected wings with the idea of flying or flight, and then connected that to the word flighty (easily changeable or irresponsible). To help remind you, you didn't just write the words, you sketched an image of Mercury's helmet, wings and all. How many times do you think you'll need to see this card to remember?

Unit One: **Words and Sentences**

Honestly, you might know the word already given the research and creativity you used to make the card in the first place! Plain, boring flashcards just can't compare to richly customized flashcards.

Here is a sample flashcard that you can use as a model for making your own.

---

torpid

(adj)

Also *torpor* (noun)

> *Definition:*
>
> Slow, sluggish, lazy
>
> Usage: After a massive family dinner, Ani felt too **torpid** to even get up off the couch. "My **torpor** has turned me into a tired turtle," she said slowly.

You can find a word's synonyms by using the "Thesaurus" tab on dictionary.com, although make sure you click on a synonym and verify that it really is similar in meaning—many thesauruses will give more than 20 synonyms for a single word, but most of them won't be that closely related (and some will be quite obscure). Make sure to look at the etymologies of any words you don't know. This is how you learn the roots of words like *mercurial*!

Now that you're *making* great flashcards, what do you *do* with them? If you're most people, it looks something like this:

> Okay, here's my enormous stack of flashcards. How many is this? 500? Okay, let's start. *Synoptic* ... Hmm, I don't know, I'll look at the answer. Oh, right, okay ... Next. *Turpitude*. Hmm ... I'll flip and read. Oh that's right. Next. *Platitude* ... Hmm ...

You see where this is going: nowhere and slowly.

There's not much motivation to remember the words because your brain knows deep down that the information is already written on the flashcard, and you'll be seeing that flashcard again (and again and again). Brains are efficient but not great at memorizing—imagine if you remembered everything you saw, did, ate, etc., in just a single day! Your brain dumps well over 99 percent of the information it is presented with. You need to give it a very good reason to hang on to that specific vocabulary word.

The other problem with this approach is that you have no idea when you're done, and it rarely feels like you're making any progress. Instead, use this method:

1. Pull out a small stack of cards, perhaps 10.
2. Go through the stack one word at a time. When you get one right, *take it out of the stack* and lay it aside.
3. As you continue, the stack will get smaller and smaller. It will become easier and easier to remember the words that are left.

Now you're done. You did a set. Move on to another set if you like.

Because this exercise has an end (as opposed to just cycling through your flashcards over and over again), you get to feel a sense of accomplishment when you're finished.

Depending on your timeline and goal score, you might decide to do this once or twice per day. In fact, if you are working a full-time job and have a hard time studying on weeknights, make a vow that you can do this one thing *every* day, no matter what (if you're really tired, you can make it a 5–6 card set rather than 10, but do at least a little vocab every single day).

Option 2: Stories

A second option is to build a story with vocabulary words. Each day is a new addition to the story, and each week is the start of a new story! To use this method, take ten vocabulary words you wish to learn that day. (Ten is merely a suggested number, but keep the number of words you use reasonable.)

Take those ten words and use as many as you can to build that day's portion of the story. Any of the words that you cannot use get held over to the next day, and you will add new words to the held-over words to create a new list of ten.

Imagine that while studying, you encountered the following dense bits of text (the first you read earlier, but the other two are new):

> Example 1: *The tokens given by the aristocrat, while nugatory, still served as a reminder that the power of the Crown continued to be held in some esteem even in such mercurial political times.*

> Example 2: *Architectural cognoscenti such as Koolhaas recognized Hadid's talents early and encouraged their development. By 1977, only a few years after their initial encounter, she had perfected her heteromorphic style, inspired equally by such disparate styles as Malevich's sparse constructivism and the flowing calligraphy of her native Arabic.*

> Example 3: *The Biblical portrayal of flagitious times preceding the great deluge stands in stark contrast to the ancient Greek representation of the antediluvian past as a Golden Age from which humanity has slowly descended into godless chaos.*

Ouch. Those examples are very convoluted, and if you have concerns about how complicated they are, don't worry; you will address that in later chapters. For now, let's consider only the vocab.

Let's assume these are the words you didn't know: *nugatory, mercurial, cognoscenti, heteromorphic, disparate, flagitious, deluge, antediluvian*. Now, you create your story.

There are a few guidelines when creating stories. First, attempt to make each sentence as GRE-like as possible. This means incorporating more than one vocabulary word into each sentence. Second, give enough context in each sentence so that you are reminded of the meaning of the word from the story alone. Finally, be kind to yourself! This is a difficult exercise.

A Sample Story:

> The town's citizenry had so many **disparate** interests, many of which were so different from each other, that any attempts to satisfy all of the various desires were bound to be **nugatory**. The **cognoscenti** of the town, comprised of those individuals with the most expertise in governance, knew that the **heteromorphic** demands of the townspeople were unfortunately **mercurial**, changing in a moment from one wish to another. Because of the **deluge** of unending demands, there seemed no way to reduce the immense stress of the job…

That is the beginning of a story, and it could serve as a starting point for a week's worth of vocabulary words. Note that the words *antediluvian* and *flagitious* did not make it into the story: that's ok! Those words can be reattempted the next day, with a new set.

Other Study Techniques

Whack-a-word: Whack-a-Mole is an arcade game in which you have to hit a bunch of mechanical creatures with a mallet before the time runs out. Play whack-a-word by spreading out a huge pile of flash cards on a table, bed, or floor, and then trying to remove words from the pile by defining them before looking at the back of the card. If you get a word wrong, put it aside in a "to review" pile. If you end up with words you don't know anything about, make a stack and try creating a story to help learn the words. Once you've learned those words better, spread them all back out and play whack-a-word one more time. Whack-a-word is also fun with a friend. Take turns defining words and removing them from the spread, working together to clear the space as quickly as possible.

Chat with a study buddy: Another fun technique is to find a study partner and agree to email or text each other every day using a certain number of GRE words in your messages (three seems about right—if you make the task too daunting, it might be too hard to stick with the plan).

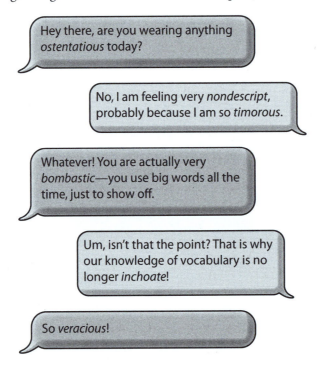

When to Use Roots

Your online syllabus includes a targeted Root List. In this context, the word *root* is the etymological origin of a portion of the word (not a part of a plant). Some portion of the word is "rooted" in another word, usually an ancient Latin or Greek word.

Take judicious advantage of roots. Many words are easily decomposed into roots and can be understood more clearly in terms of them. But some words now have misleading roots or derivations! During the exam itself, you have to be very careful when you resort to root analysis to guess an unknown word's meaning. The GRE often uses words with surprising meanings, or at least, meanings that might be surprising for a test-taker relying solely on roots. For instance, *baleful* does not mean "full of hay bales"—it means "threatening or menacing." Although a *scribe* is a person whose job is to copy by hand, *proscribe* doesn't seem to be about writing—it means prohibit or condemn.

Ironically, even those words that stray furthest from the apparent meaning of their roots can be better learned with knowledge of the roots: if you learn that a word *doesn't* relate very logically to its roots, that surprise can be helpful in itself.

Many words have strange and memorable relationships with their etymological roots. For instance, the word *desultory* means "lacking in method or purpose; disappointing." That's not so interesting, but if you know that the word comes from a Latin word describing circus riders who *jumped from* horse to horse (*de* = from, *sult* = jump), then you might remember the word *desultory* better.

And maybe *proscribe* didn't *seem* to be about writing before, but it is still based off of the same root as a scribe (as in *script, scribble, scripture,* etc.) Why the same root? Because, in ancient times, *to proscribe* was to publish a record of someone's punishment—to condemn or sentence that person publicly. The trick, or rather discipline, is to acknowledge that learning vocabulary through roots is a supplement to your normal vocabulary practice (flashcards? stories? something else?), and not a replacement for it.

Here are a few more favorites (more information like this appears in *500 Essential Words* and *500 Advanced Words GRE® Vocabulary Flash Cards* sets from Manhattan Prep):

Amortize (gradually pay off a debt, or gradually write off an asset) contains the root *mort*, meaning death. **Amortization** is when a financial obligation dies a long, slow death.

Anachronism (something that is not in its correct historical time; a mistake in chronology, such as by assigning a person or event to the wrong time period)—the prefix *ana* means "against," and *chron* means "time." This is one word you can work out entirely with a knowledge of roots: **anachronistic** means "against time."

Legerdemain (sleight-of-hand, trickery, deception) comes from Middle French, meaning "light of hand." The modern French word for hand is *main*, which is related to the root in the English *manual* (relating to hands, as in *manual labor*) and *manumit* (free from slavery, untie the hands).

Malediction (a curse) has the prefix *mal* (meaning "bad"). The root *dict* comes from *dicere* (to say) and also appears in *dictator, dictionary,* and *indict* (connect to a crime), as well as in **malediction**'s antonym, *benediction* (blessing).

Not all words have a cool story or a helpful derivation. For instance, *pulchritude* means "beauty." The reason that seems so weird—"you're so pulchritudinous," really doesn't sound like a compliment—is that the Latin root *pulcher*, meaning "beautiful," doesn't occur in any other English words.

So recognize that roots are just one of many helpful tools. One good way to proceed is to go through the Root List in the Appendix and focus on roots that actually look familiar to you and like something you'd be able to spot in the future; for instance, *circum* (meaning "around") appears in *circumference*, and it's pretty hard to miss the root in *circumnavigate, circumcise, circumambulate,* and *circumlocution*. So you might make a flash card for this and other roots that seem most useful to you.

Specialized Vocabulary in Reading Comprehension Passages

Although knowledge of GRE vocabulary will play a role in your success on Reading Comprehension passages, the GRE will never test you on vocabulary that is unique to the topic of the passage. For example, in a passage about the human brain, the GRE might use the term dendrites—but the GRE would not expect you to know this vocabulary.

When using a term such as "dendrites" that is exclusive to a specialized field, the GRE will define that term within the passage. This is how you determine whether an unknown word in a reading comprehension passage is worth adding to your word list: Does the test itself define the word there in the passage? If the definition is in the passage, then the test-writers do not expect you to know the word, and you do not need to add it to your vocabulary studies.

You will notice this most commonly for words that are particular to specific academic fields, especially technical fields, although this can occur in passages on any topic.

What do you do in the moment, if you see a word in a reading comprehension passage that you do not know? Search inside the same sentence or the following sentence for either an outright definition or context clues that would allow to make your own partial definition. Jot an abbreviation of the word, with your abbreviated definition, on your paper, and move on! Remember, if the test expected you to know the word, the passage would not have given you the definition.

Using Social Networks to Buttress Your Vocabulary Studies

If you have a robust social network, you can use that community as a support group for your studies! Let people know you're studying for the GRE and ask for help with vocabulary: You can make a game out of it. Post a word, and the person who builds the most creative or memorable sentence with that word "wins." That's merely one option: Use anything that will help you remember the vocabulary you are studying.

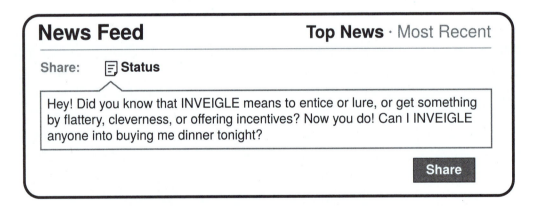

If you post a word and its definition as your status update, it only takes one peculiar comment from a friend (some people have way too much time on their hands) to help you remember the word forever.

Manhattan Prep maintains several social media accounts, and we were pleased to see that one of our followers posted the word *deleterious* (meaning "harmful or damaging") in a status update: "Does anyone actually use that word?"

Another friend wrote back:

> *Deleterious* is used quite a bit in genetics. For example, "Epigenetic silencing of transposable elements may reduce *deleterious* effects on neighboring gene expression in the genome."

The original poster replied, "I looked for examples of this word's use in a sentence. It seems that *deleterious effects* is indeed the way it is most often used."

Now that's how to learn *deleterious*!

Feel free to find, follow, and contribute to any of Manhattan Prep's social networking accounts!

Vocabulary Challenge

> Did you spot these vocabulary words? If not, go back and find them in context! (The word may be in a different form than listed here— "digressing" instead of "digress," for example.) Write your own definitions based on the evidence in the chapter.

1. assiduous (*adj.*), p. 20
2. engender (*v*), p. 20
3. bombastic (*adj.*), p. 24
4. inchoate (*adj.*), p. 24
5. judicious (*adj.*), p. 24
6. buttress (*v*), p. 26

Unit One: **Words and Sentences**

Answers and Explanations

Vocabulary Challenge

1. assiduous (*adj.*): careful, diligent, and persistent in attention or application
2. engender (*v*): to give rise to, create, or cause
3. bombastic (*adj.*): overblown, pompous, inflated, or pretentious
4. inchoate (*adj.*): incipient, still developing or incomplete
5. judicious (*adj.*): demonstrating sound judgement
6. buttress (*v*): to support, strengthen, or shore up

CHAPTER 2
GRE Sentences

In This Chapter...

- Complex Sentences
- Unpacking GRE Sentences
- Principles for Unpacking Sentences
- Link to Real Ideas
- Vocabulary Challenge
- Problem Set
- Answers and Explanations

CHAPTER 2 GRE Sentences

Chapter 1: GRE Vocabulary was all about understanding the meaning of new and difficult words. That said, vocabulary, or challenging word choice within a sentence, is merely the first level of GRE reading. Those complex words get packed into dense and complex sentences that get packed into dense and complex paragraphs that get packed into dense and complex passages. In this chapter, you will learn how to deal with this next level of complexity: the complex sentence.

Here are your Chapter 2 vocabulary words:

>pellucid (A)
>
>daunt (E)
>
>vex (A)
>
>inculcate (A)
>
>opaque (E)
>
>eclectic (E)

Complex Sentences

Consider the following example:

> *Despite assurances to the contrary by governments around the world, the development of space as an arena of warfare is nearly certain, as military success often depends on not ceding the "high ground," of which outer space might be considered the supreme example.*

With the possible exception of the word *ceding*, which roughly means "giving up," most of the words used in this sentence are probably familiar to you. (Also, if you were unsure of the word "ceding," don't accept our assertion that "*ceding* = roughly like giving up." Add *ceding* to your vocabulary list and verify that you understand the specifics of its definition!

Now that you do know what *ceding* means, did this sentence become immediately pellucid? Probably not! Why? Because GRE writers are outstanding at packing a paragraph's worth of information into a single sentence. This isn't great for easy reading, but it is great for testing whether you can quickly and correctly interpret dense (academic) writing.

That only begs the question…what can you do to become more effective at understanding such dauntingly dense writing? The next sections will introduce you to "unpacking" sentences.

Unit One: **Words and Sentences**

Unpacking GRE Sentences

GRE students often feel vexed that the test feels like it's speaking a different language. All the words are English, but arranged in a way that no longer feels like English! They no longer feel like English because, in a sense, they aren't English anymore, at least, not English as it's colloquially spoken.

Let's return to the example sentence:

> *Despite assurances to the contrary by governments around the world, the development of space as an arena of warfare is nearly certain, as military success often depends on not ceding the "high ground," of which outer space might be considered the supreme example.*

Even if you are one of the few who read this sentence and grasped it without issue, exam pressure makes it harder to maintain clarity when the structure of a sentence gets increasingly dense. In fact, the abstract and technical language makes reading sentences such as this one a challenge even outside an exam setting.

How do you make sense of this sentence given how much information is packed into it? Maybe you rephrase it or put it into your own words. Sounds like a good idea in theory, but in practice it often fails to help. Consider the following rephrasing:

Rephrase	Is it Effective?
Despite promises by governments that it isn't true, the development of space as an area of warfare is going to happen, because military success requires not giving up the high ground, and outer space is the ultimate example of high ground.	This is a pure translation: Words have been substituted, but there has been no effort to unpack the dense elements of the original. This translation has not transformed either the verbiage or presentation choices.

Instead of simply swapping out hard vocabulary words and cutting a bit of text here and there, this sentence needs to be more fully unpacked. As you read the two examples of "unpacking" below, consider how much information was contained in the original sentence. It's as if the GRE writers have managed to pack an entire paragraph of information into that single sentence.

Unpacking	Is it Effective?
"High ground" is the military concept of being higher up than your opponent (so easier to win). Outer space is the best of the best "high ground." Therefore space will almost certainly become important to world militaries. Governments around the world say that won't happen—but it will.	This is much more effective! Much of the word choice is the same, but the order of presentation is reversed (last sentence first, first sentence last). This attempt requires more analysis of the intended connections between the statements presented, while at the same time breaking those statements into more manageable chunks; note that one original sentence is now four.
Governments say this isn't true. BUT Space will be a war-place. (Yeah, that's not a word.) WHY? Because being up there would be the highest of "high ground" you could get to.	This is another version of unpacking, and it may be one that resonates more with you. It condenses the entire sentence into two extremely short elements that express the oppositional tension in the sentence: what governments say vs. what will actually happen.

And before you ask, no, you would not write down a complete unpacking on test day. The exercise of putting this down pen-to-paper is crucial during your studies, but you would never have the time to literally write these thoughts down to this extent during the exam. This is a study process to inculcate *mental* habits that you will carry through to test day.

So this begs yet another question…how do you learn to effectively unpack sentences yourself?

Principles for Unpacking Sentences

Hopefully the previous discussion convinced you that paraphrasing by substituting less-abstract words isn't a great way to get past dense sentences. So how do you unpack a sentence?

First, don't just give up on a sentence if it seems too opaque or complex: You do not need to digest the entirety of a long sentence in one bite! Since a dense GRE sentence is really several sentences in disguise, it may be useful to read ahead to later in the sentence to gain context and then come back to the first portion. However you manage it, the earlier you can understand some portion of the sentence, the easier the rest of the sentence will be. Reconsider the sentence from the previous section:

> *Despite assurances to the contrary by governments around the world, the development of space as an arena of warfare is nearly certain, as military success often depends on not ceding the "high ground," of which outer space might be considered the supreme example.*

To push your unpacking skills beyond mere translation, here are five principles that can be applied to your unpacking attempts. You do not need to apply all five for every sentence: Use as many or as few as will do the job!

Five Principles to Unpack sentences

1. **Grab a concrete concept first.**

    I know what outer space is, so I'll start there.

2. **Define something that concept is or does.**

    outer space = high ground

3. **Put only *one* simple thought in a sentence.**

    Military success often depends on having the high ground. Space is the ultimate high ground.

4. **Link each subsequent sentence to the previous one. (In this statement, "subsequent" and "previous" refer to the order of sentences in your unpacking, not necessarily the order presented in the original sentence.)**

    Space is the ultimate high ground, and military success often depends on having the high ground. Because of this, governments will seek to militarize space. They say they won't, but they will.

5. **Simplify or "quote off" details.**

    "arena of warfare" = militarization

And this is how the efficient unpacking from the previous section was created! Done habitually during your studies, this process becomes automatic, and will allow you to work through GRE Verbal problems on the test much more successfully.

Unit One: Words and Sentences

Unpacking the sentence makes the concepts much more accessible than merely paraphrasing or pushing through and hoping you figure it out later. Here's a dense sentence to practice your unpacking skills. Use as many of the five principles mentioned previously as you feel are useful.

Most exobiologists—scientists who search for life on other planets or moons—agree that carbon probably provides the backbone of any extraterrestrial biological molecules, just as it does of terrestrial ones, since carbon is unique among the elements in its ability to form long, stable chains of atoms.

Once you've unpacked the sentence yourself, consider the following options:

Rephrase	Is it Effective?
"Exobiologists" = scientists who search for aliens. They agree that carbon is unique. It can form long, stable chains. Because carbon is unique in this respect, it probably is the building block of any alien biological molecules. In this way, alien biological molecules might be similar to biological molecules on earth.	Yes. Note that the long, single sentence given initially has been broken into multiple smaller sentences (principle 3 of unpacking dense sentences). Exobiologists are now scientists who search for aliens (principle 5), extraterrestrial is now alien, and terrestrial is now "on Earth." (principles 1 and 2). Finally, transitions such as "because" and "in this way" link sentences together in the unpacked version (principle 4).
Scientists (alien hunters) agree this is true, because carbon is unique. ("this" = carbon forms the basis of both alien and earth biological molecules)	This is merely an example of an exceedingly brief unpacking that takes advantage of principle 5 to massively shorten the text you might write. This version is not preferred over the above version, it is merely one other example.

Here is one more example of a possible unpacking of the "exobiologists" sentence, this time arranged in order of principle, from first to fifth. Note that this example is not the same as the previous two. There is no single correct way to unpack a dense sentence. Ultimately, success is determined by your increased understanding of the test writer's intent.

1. **Grab a concrete concept first.**

    The scientists are the main actors in this sentence.

2. **Define something that concept does.**

    The scientists are agreeing.

3. **Put only *one* simple thought in a sentence.**

    The scientists agree that carbon is important.

4. **Link each subsequent sentence to the previous one.**

    <u>They</u> agree on <u>that</u> because carbon makes chains of atoms.

5. **Simplify or "quote off" details.**

    "Exobiologists" are the specific scientists being discussed.

Correspondingly, the unpacking could look like this on your paper:

> The EB scientists agree that carbon is important.
> <u>They</u> agree on <u>that</u> because carbon makes chains of atoms.
> Carbon already uses <u>that</u> trait to make life on Earth.
> It probably does the same thing for life elsewhere.

This unpacking has the same major points, but was created from a different starting point. As long as you begin with something you can understand, you can unpack even the most complex sentences. At the end, no single concept or sentence within your unpacking should be too complex for you to hold in your mind.

Eventually, your pen-on-paper unpacking will become more and more brief, until your test day unpacking (if you unpack on paper at all!) might look like this:

> sci agree this is true
> because
> carbon is unique

Link to Real Ideas

For some of the more abstract concepts, translating the sentence visually or even taking graphical notes can ease the transition to understanding. If even finding the concrete concept is challenging at the start of a sentence, try to grab something and imagine what it might literally look like. Finding that visual representation can make the process much simpler.

In your mind, you might imagine any of the ideas from the exobiologist sentence in the following manner:

Words	Real Ideas
. . . exobiologists—scientists . . . . . . who search for life on other planets or moons . . .	smart folks in white coats who peer through telescopes looking for little green men
. . . carbon probably provides the backbone of extra-terrestrial biological molecules . . .	<u>carbon</u>: charcoal, key element in living things <u>backbone</u>: like a spine to a little molecule
. . . any extraterrestrial biological molecules, just as it does of terrestrial ones . . .	<u>extraterrestrial</u>: little green men (aliens) <u>terrestrial</u>: from Earth; humans, not aliens
. . . its ability to form long, stable chains of atoms.	a literal chain but made up of carbon

Do *not* write the real ideas down (except as an exercise during your studies, as needed). The process should happen quickly in your head so that you find a concrete idea you're comfortable starting with. Moreover, as you read further in a passage, do this less. In fact, if you do it too much along the way, you might introduce too many outside ideas and lose track of what is actually written in the passage. However, making the sentence real can help you make sense of a difficult sentence, so practice this technique.

You can also break down the sentence visually for certain types of sentences, especially science sentences or any sentence describing a multistep process. In these sentences, a T-chart, diagram, or picture can be an effective note-taking method.

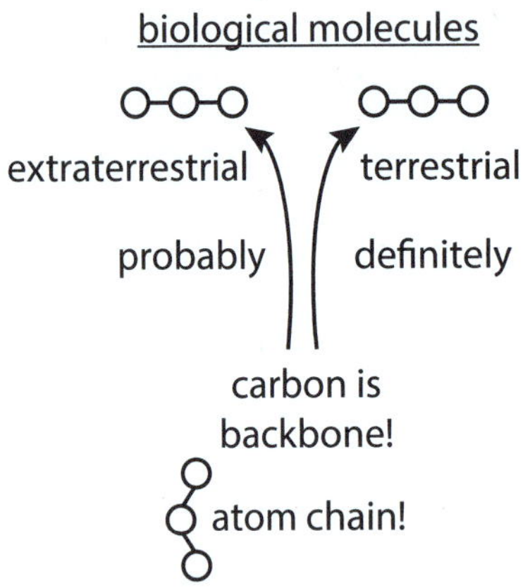

Unit One: **Words and Sentences**

[Diagram: "biological molecules" with two branches — "extraterrestrial" (probably) and "terrestrial" (definitely) — pointing up from "carbon is backbone!" and "atom chain!"]

Practice an eclectic mix of methods so you can choose what will be most effective for each sentence you study.

Vocabulary Challenge

> Did you spot these vocabulary words? If not, go back and find them in context! (The word may be in a different form than listed here—"digressing" instead of "digress," for example.) Write your own definitions based on the evidence in the chapter.

1. pellucid (*adj.*), p. 31
2. daunt (*v*), p. 31
3. vex (*v*), p. 32
4. inculcate (*v*), p. 33
5. opaque (*adj.*), p. 33
6. eclectic (*adj.*), p. 36

Chapter 2: **GRE Sentences**

Problem Set

> In problems 1–6, **unpack** each complex sentence. Find a concrete idea to start, and form a sentence with just a portion of the information in the sentence. Then create a second sentence that adds some additional information to the first. Keep going until you have unpacked all of the detail in the sentence (this might take five or so sentences). Write the sentences down as you work.

Unpacking

These unpacked sentences are examples of the process. Your versions will likely differ. Again, only write down unpacked sentences when absolutely necessary during the GRE, and even when necessary, use as much abbreviation as you can. This exercise is meant to develop your mental muscles so you can take apart complex academic language on test day, without resorting to pen and paper.

1. Various popular works of art have been influenced by syncretic religious traditions such as Candomblé, Santería, and voodoo, but few such works treat these traditions with appropriate intelligence or sensitivity.

2. The rise of Athenian democracy in ancient times can be considered a reaction to class conflict.

3. The simplistic classification of living things as plant, animal, or "other" has been drastically revised by biologists in reaction to the discovery of microorganisms that do not fit previous taxonomic schemes.

4. Neither Chinese nor Japanese verbs, for instance, change form at all to indicate the number or person of the subject; however, personal pronouns in both subject and object roles are regularly omitted in both speech and writing, leaving the meaning to be inferred from contextual clues.

5. Since the success of modern digital surveillance does not obviate the need for intelligence gathered via old-fashioned human interaction, agencies charged with counterterrorism responsibilities must devote significant effort to planting and/or cultivating "assets"—that is, spies—within terrorist organizations that threaten the country.

6. Students learning to fly fixed-wing aircraft are taught to use mnemonic devices, such as the landing checklist GUMPS (gas, undercarriage, mixture, propeller, switches), that remain constant even when not every element of the device is relevant, as in the case of planes with non-retractable landing gear.

Unit One: **Words and Sentences**

Answers and Explanations

Vocabulary Challenge

1. pellucid (*adj.*): transparent; clear, easy to understand
2. daunt (*v*): discourage, dishearten, lessen the courage of
3. vex (*v*): annoy or bother; puzzle or distress
4. inculcate (*v*): to teach, impress, or implant by frequent repetition
5. opaque (*adj.*): not transparent; dark, dull, unclear, or stupid
6. eclectic (*adj.*): various; selecting the best of everything or from many diverse sources

Problem Set

1.

Original Sentence	Unpacked Rephrase
Various popular works of art have been influenced by syncretic religious traditions such as Candomblé, Santeria, and voodoo, but few such works treat these traditions with appropriate intelligence or sensitivity.	There are blended (syncretic) religious traditions: C, S, and V. Some popular art was influenced by / is based on those traditions. But not very much of that art (few such works) really honors those traditions as much as the author thinks they should.

2.

Original Sentence	Unpacked Rephrase
The rise of Athenian democracy in ancient times can be considered a reaction to class conflict.	There was class conflict: People from upper and lower were fighting each other in ancient times? People created the Athenian democracy in response.

3.

Original Sentence	Unpacked Rephrase
The simplistic classification of living things as plant, animal, or "other" has been drastically revised by biologists in reaction to the discovery of microorganisms that do not fit previous taxonomic schemes.	Biologists found some new microorganisms. These MOs don't really fit into any categories (*taxonomic schemes*) that already existed. Biologists used to just call things *plant, animal, or "other,"* but because of these new MOs, that simple classification had to be totally updated.

Chapter 2: GRE Sentences

4.	**Original Sentence**	**Unpacked Rephrase**
	Neither Chinese nor Japanese verbs, for instance, change form at all to indicate the number or person of the subject; however, personal pronouns in both subject and object roles are regularly omitted in both speech and writing, leaving the meaning to be inferred from contextual clues.	C and J verbs don't change form for subject-verb agreement (like they do in English, e.g., she sings vs. they sing). And it seems like they don't even really use pronouns to help. The only way to get at the meaning of a sentence is to use other context clues.

5.	**Original Sentence**	**Unpacked Rephrase**
	Since the success of modern digital surveillance does not obviate the need for intelligence gathered via old-fashioned human interaction, agencies charged with counterterrorism responsibilities must devote significant effort to planting and/or cultivating "assets"—that is, spies—within terrorist organizations that threaten the country.	Even though you can spy with computers and tech now, you still need to have humans out there getting information too (*does not obviate the need for . . .*). So if you're trying to fight terrorists, you still have to spend the time and effort to get your human spies into those terrorist groups.

6.	**Original Sentence**	**Unpacked Rephrase**
	Students learning to fly fixed-wing aircraft are taught to use mnemonic devices, such as the landing checklist GUMPS (gas, undercarriage, mixture, propeller, switches), that remain constant even when not every element of the device is relevant, as in the case of planes with non-retractable landing gear.	When people learn to fly planes, they learn memory tricks. One example is GUMPS. They learn these memory tricks even though some of the pieces aren't always relevant—not sure why they mentioned the specific case of landing gear. So this might mean that students learn GUMPS, even though some of the letters won't always apply? Maybe you don't always care about propeller, for example?

CHAPTER 3

Text Completion and Sentence Equivalence

In This Chapter...

- One-Blank Text Completion
- The Three-Step Process for Text Completions
- Direction Markers
- Drill: Sentence Analysis
- Sentence Equivalence
- Sentence Analysis in Sentence Equivalence
- Answer Choice Analysis
- When to Use (and NOT to Use) Answer Choice Analysis
- Drill: Answer Choice Analysis
- What If I Don't Know the Words?
- Why It Is Important to Learn Words in Context
- Traps in TC and SE

Unit One: **Words and Sentences**

- Text Completion and Sentence Equivalence Recap
- Vocabulary Challenge
- Problem Set (Text Completion)
- Problem Set (Sentence Equivalence)
- Answers and Explanations

CHAPTER 3 Text Completion and Sentence Equivalence

The sentence-deconstruction strategies discussed in Chapter 2: GRE Sentences will be immediately useful on Text Completion and Sentence Equivalence questions. Text Completion questions on the GRE are sentences or paragraphs with one, two, or three blanks for which you must select the appropriate word or words. In this chapter, you will learn methods to answer one-blank Text Completion and the closely related Sentence Equivalence; a discussion of two- and three-blank Text Completion questions can be found in Chapter 7: Multi-Blank Text Completion.

Here are your Chapter 3 vocabulary words:

tortuous (A)
recondite (A)
embellish (E)
paragon (A)
satiate (E)
augment (E)

One-Blank Text Completion

One-blank Text Completion (TC) questions always appear at the very beginning of a GRE Verbal section, and they always consist of a single sentence. The following example shows how one-blank Text Completion questions are laid out:

If the student had been less _____, she would not have been expelled from her grade school.

A	indefatigable
B	persevering
C	delinquent
D	playful
E	indigent

On the real test, you won't see the letters A, B, C, D, and E; each word will just be in its own box.

Unit One: **Words and Sentences**

All one-blank Text Completions have exactly five answer choices, of which exactly one is correct. The answer choices for a given blank will always be the same part of speech. Your task is to find the choice that best fits the meaning of the sentence as a whole. Once you've found the answer that best fits the meaning of the sentence, select it by clicking on the box in which it appears; the test will record this selection by highlighting the entire box. Under standard timing conditions, the whole process would ideally take about 1 minute on average per problem.

On your scratch paper, write down the letters A, B, C, D, and E to keep track of which answers you think are wrong, which ones you think might be right, and which words you don't know (more on this later).

A lot of test-takers regard Text Completion as difficult because of the high-level vocabulary that often appears in the answer choices. However, the GRE's goal in these questions is not primarily to test your lexicon. Rather, the goal of these questions is to test whether you can extract crucial bits of meaning from the written parts of the sentence to inform what should go in the blank.

Therefore, the best approach to Text Completion questions will be to deconstruct the sentence and **predict an answer** before looking at the choices. Many test-takers plug in the choices one by one, rereading the sentence and stopping when it sounds good. The problems with this approach are twofold. First, the sentences are often too tortuous to make quick sense of even if you read words into the blank, leaving you in a position to have to analyze the sentence anyway. Second, the GRE deliberately chooses tempting words for the wrong answers, words that can improperly color your understanding of the sentence or seem superficially to be a good fit for the sentence but that don't actually suit its intended meaning.

The Three-Step Process for Text Completions

You can approach every Text Completion question with the same three-step process:

1. Read only the sentence.
2. Use proof from the sentence to make a prediction.
3. Compare your prediction to each answer choice.

Here's the sentence from earlier in the chapter:

If the student had been less _____, she would not have been expelled from her grade school.

A	indefatigable
B	persevering
C	delinquent
D	playful
E	indigent

1. Read only the sentence.

The answer choices will distract you if you read them before you've made sense of the sentence. The sentence is the truth, but four of the five answer choices are lies. Don't read the lies until you're solid on the truth.

When you first read the sentence, note the structure of the sentence. One-blank Text Completion sentences will often be broken into two parts with a comma or semicolon in the middle. One part of the sentence will have the blank in it, and the best information about what goes in the blank will almost always come from the other part of the sentence. This sentence is separated into two parts by the comma near the middle, and the blank is in the first part.

Chapter 3: **Text Completion and Sentence Equivalence**

2. Use proof from the sentence to make a prediction.

This is the crux of the process for Text Completion. One-blank TC questions always provide proof of the correct answer in the sentence. The proof is what forces the contents of the blank to be perfectly predictable, and Text Completion and Sentence Equivalence questions are designed to test whether you're able use the proof in the sentences to correctly determine the meaning of the blank. After all, the GRE is a standardized test, and as such, every question has to have exactly one objectively right answer or combination of answers. There's no subjectivity to the answers, and you won't need to rely on any specialized outside knowledge to get these questions correct—except, of course, for vocabulary. And while the vocabulary can be challenging, it's worth knowing that in the most difficult of these questions, you're more likely to run into trouble with convoluted sentence structures than with recondite vocabulary.

So how do you find the proof in a sentence? There are two main ways: by unpacking the sentence into several simple sentences (as discussed in Chapter 2: GRE Sentences) or by parsing the sentence into *content clues* and *direction markers*. The sentence above will be used to demonstrate both of these approaches.

Unpacking the sentence

First, take some time to consider how *you* might rewrite the sentence into a few simple sentences. Here's one possible rewrite:

> The student was expelled from her school.
> Therefore, she most likely broke rules.
> She could have *not* been expelled from her school...
> ...but only if she'd been less <u>something</u>.

When you've unpacked the sentence, the next step is to think about what would make the most sense in place of the *something*. If her being expelled from school is a good indication that the student must have broken some rules, then she could have avoided being expelled if she'd been less rule-breaky. Does it matter that "rule-breaky" isn't a real word? Not at all! The goal is not to predict the exact word that will show up in the answer choices, but to come away from the sentence with as clear an idea as possible of the *meaning* of the correct answer.

There are a few things worth explicitly noting in the unpacked version of the sentence above. To start, you may have noticed that the first simple sentence expresses what actually happened in the situation (that is, the concrete truth of the situation) rather than reflecting what the sentence specifically stated. The sentence only says that she would *not* have been expelled *if* something had been different; however, that necessarily implies that she was expelled, and acknowledging this concrete truth is more helpful in understanding the sentence's meaning than is sticking strictly to what the sentence says. When unpacking a sentence, **grab a concrete concept first**.

It's also worth noting that the first simple sentence above came from the second part of the original sentence. In unpacking one-blank Text Completion questions, it will almost always be beneficial to start from the part of the sentence that *doesn't* contain the blank. It's generally true that if the blank is in the first part of the sentence, the proof for the right answer will be in the second part of the sentence (and vice versa). Moreover, the part of the sentence *without* the blank is likely to contain the concrete truth that serves as the best starting point to understanding the meaning of the sentence; the part of the sentence *with* the blank, by contrast, is necessarily incomplete.

Next, the second simple sentence (*Therefore, she most likely broke rules*) is not expressed anywhere in the original sentence. For many, this is the most dangerous part of extracting meaning from the sentences in the GRE.

Unit One: Words and Sentences

Can you know *for sure* from the original sentence that the student broke any rules? No. The student could have been unfairly expelled because the school administrators didn't like her shoes, or she could have been framed by another student for some expulsion-worthy infraction.

On the other hand, *some* information must be added to the sentence to make sense of the first part of the sentence and ultimately to make a prediction for the blank. When adding information to the sentence, **aim for the simplest story possible**. In this case, the truth of the situation is that the student was expelled, and expulsion is generally used as a punishment for wrongdoing. Scenarios such as those outlined above, while technically possible, are less likely to have led to the student's expulsion and will not be the interpretations that determine the meaning of the missing word.

Parse the sentence

You can also parse the sentence into *content clues* and *direction markers*. Content clues are the elements of the story that are relevant to the blank, and direction markers are the words, phrases, and punctuation marks used to relate parts of the sentence to each other. Start by stripping a sentence of all its reversal words—words that indicate an opposite or a negation, such as *not* or *however*. Next, use content clues from the simplified sentence to predict for the blank. Finally, add the reversal words back in one by one, updating your prediction each time. Here's an example of how that process would play out in the sentence above:

Content and direction clues	Prediction and analysis
If **the student** had been ____, **she** would have been **expelled** from her grade school.	**Badly behaved:** The word that goes into the blank is describing the student, meaning that the sentence *must* provide content clues about the student. Because the blank appears in the first half of the sentence, the second part of the sentence is likely to contain information about the student that will serve as the proof for the blank. In this version of the sentence, the only direction marker is *If*, indicating that there will be a causal relationship between the first and second parts of the sentence. Given this relationship and the content clues in the second part of the sentence, whatever goes in the blank must be something that would reasonably cause the student to be expelled: bad behavior.
If the student had been ____, she would **not** have been expelled from her grade school.	**Well behaved:** Add the reversal markers back in one at a time, ideally starting with any reversal markers in the part of the sentence that doesn't contain the blank. In the original sentence, the *not* in the second part of the sentence was a reversal marker. Adding the marker back in is like flipping a switch in the sentence: What goes in the blank must be the opposite of what it was before.
If the student had been **less** ____, she would not have been expelled from her grade school.	**Badly behaved:** Adding the last reversal marker (*less*) back to the sentence effectively nullifies the reversal above, much as two negatives cancel to a positive.

Chapter 3: **Text Completion and Sentence Equivalence**

You might have noticed that this approach has a lot in common with the first approach. While the process of parsing a sentence focuses more explicitly and carefully on direction markers, making the first prediction still requires some unpacking of the sentence. Similarly, while unpacking the sentence doesn't necessarily require you to strip out reversal markers, the process usually begins with stating what *is* the case, even when the sentence itself focuses on what's *not* the case.

Perhaps most importantly, both approaches leave you with a similar prediction for the blank. Write down this prediction as well as letters for answers (A) through (E).

rule-breaky / badly behaved

A
B
C
D
E

3. Compare your prediction to each answer choice.

With a prediction in hand, it's time to head to the answer choices. Here they are again:

| indefatigable |
| persevering |
| delinquent |
| playful |
| indigent |

Compare each answer choice to your prediction to see how well they match. It's usually helpful to think of less familiar words in more common terms:

indefatigable = ?
persevering = never giving up
delinquent = troublesome
playful
indigent = ?

Finally, as you proceed down the answers, mark down one of the following next to your "A B C D E": Good (✓), Bad (✗), Sort Of (∼), or Unknown (?). Your paper might look like this:

rule-breaky / badly behaved

A ?
B ✗
C ✓
D ∼
E ?

The correct answer is in fact (C), since *delinquent* means "troublesome" or even "criminal." But even if you didn't know what *delinquent* means, you might have a shot at getting this problem right through process of elimination, especially if you know the definitions of the other words and trust that the GRE will *always* give you an answer that fits the clues in the sentence.

Unit One: **Words and Sentences**

All told, this process should eventually take an average of 1 minute per question. However, as you're first learning to analyze sentences, the process will likely take considerably longer. That's okay: Analyzing sentences well is the key to success on Text Completion and Sentence Equivalence, and it will get faster (and more accurate) with practice.

Also, you can come up with a plausible and interesting story around some of the wrong answer choices, but the story would be less directly based on the evidence in the sentence. For example, "If the student had been less *playful*, she wouldn't have been expelled" might make sense if the student was constantly playing games during serious lessons. Notice that building a connection between being *playful* and getting expelled requires the addition of extra, unproven story elements (specifically, that the expulsion happened because of the student's behavior during lessons and that playing during lessons is an expellable offense). You might find that this sort of story-building happens automatically in your mind when you consider certain answer choices. This is why it's so important to unpack and interpret the sentence as straightforwardly as possible and to make a prediction before looking at the answers: The GRE has trap answers waiting for those inclined to embellishment. Stick to the story in the sentence, and when possible, recycle words and phrases from the sentence to make your predictions.

> *Strategy Tip:*
>
> **Always predict answers when you practice Text Completion questions.** Proactively practicing sentence analysis is the best way to get faster and more accurate at TC.

Practice the whole three-step process on the following sentence:

Despite his extreme _____, he failed to secure the prestigious university's coveted diploma.

inhibition
depression
lucubration
magnanimity
character

First, read **only** the sentence. Again, it's divided into two parts by a comma and the blank appears in the first part.

Now unpack or parse the sentence to find the proof and make a prediction. What's the concrete truth? The protagonist of this sentence *failed to secure the prestigious university's coveted diploma*. This happened *despite* some truth about the student, so whatever was true about the student *should* have been helpful in securing the diploma. What sort of things are helpful in getting a diploma? The most straightforward story would be *studying* or *intelligence*, and either would make a sensible prediction.

Finally, compare *studying* or *intelligence* with every answer choice:

studying *or* intelligence

A ✗

B ✗

C ?

D ?

E ~

This can be a tough spot to be in. If you don't know the meaning of *lucubration* and *magnanimity*, the choice you make depends on whether any of the words you *do* know is a close match for your prediction (and the sentence as a whole). *Character* kind of works for the sentence, but it's a very general word, and the GRE is likely to give you a word that more specifically fits the story in the sentence. If you don't know the meaning of the words *lucubration* and *magnanimity*, your final consideration is this: Does *lucubration* feel like it could mean studying or intelligence, or does *magnanimity* seem like it might be a better match? You might feel that a word like *lucubration* would denote an action whereas *magnanimity* seems more like a character trait, for instance, and choose accordingly. Or you might have absolutely no idea. In either case, make a choice and move on. As it happens, *lucubration*, meaning intense or laborious study, is a straightforward match for the prediction *studying*, so it's the best choice: Despite his intense studying, he failed. (Of course, it's also helpful to know that *magnanimity* means "generosity.")

Be a little flexible as you make your match. You might not have predicted the exact contours of the right answer, but that's okay. In fact, it was better that you didn't waste time trying to make an extremely precise prediction. And if you have question marks on your scratch paper because you lack some vocabulary knowledge (e.g., *lucubration, magnanimity*), make the most of the words you do know and move on. Spending time staring at words you don't know won't make them suddenly surrender their meaning.

Just decide whether the answer choices you do know keep the sentence's story simple; if those words don't work, choose one of the words whose definition you don't know. The right answer won't always be a word you know, but it must always be a good fit for the sentence.

Unpack or parse the following sentence, and make an explicit prediction for the blank:

In the past decade, the coffee chain has dramatically expanded all across the country, leading one commentator to describe the franchise as _____.

This sentence has two major parts, with the blank in the second part. Read and then unpack the sentence, starting from a concrete truth:

A coffee chain has expanded. It's now all across the country. This has led a commentator to describe it as something.

All you know about the coffee chain is that it's everywhere in the country, and as that concrete fact must have led to the commentator's description, the most straightforward prediction would be something like everywhere or nationwide.

Alternatively, you can parse the sentence into content clues and direction markers:

The first part of the sentence *leads* to the second part (that is, "leading" functions as a causal direction marker). There are no reversal markers to strip out. In terms of content clues, the word in the blank is being used to describe "the franchise," which itself is a reference to the coffee chain mentioned in the first part of the sentence. Look here for descriptions of the coffee chain that will serve as content clues for the blank. The only thing mentioned is that the chain has "expanded all across the country." Keep the prediction simple and straightforward: everywhere or having dramatically expanded.

Having dramatically expanded may seem like an awkward prediction, but recycling words or phrases from the sentence is a good idea. It will ensure that your prediction doesn't stray too far from the proof in the sentence. And in general, your prediction should feel boring, recycling words or ideas already in the sentence. Notice how uninteresting these fill-ins feel:

> In the past decade, the coffee chain has dramatically expanded all across the country, leading one commentator to describe the franchise as everywhere.

> In the past decade, the coffee chain has dramatically expanded all across the country, leading one commentator to describe the franchise as having dramatically expanded.

These would be redundant ways to end the sentence in real life, and as such it's easy to imagine a more colorful description than *everywhere*. For instance, it can be tempting to add a negative or positive spin to your prediction (*a dangerous monopoly, a paragon of capitalism,* etc.). However, the GRE will always go with the boring, redundant answer. It's testing your ability to match evidence in the sentence to a word in the answer choices, not your ability to write an exciting narrative.

If this were a real question and there were answer choices, you'd now be in a position to find a match. In this case, the answer would probably be something like *ubiquitous*, a GRE favorite meaning "being everywhere."

Direction Markers

As mentioned previously in the chapter, direction markers are words, phrases, or punctuation marks that indicate how the parts of a sentence are related to each other. They tend to fall into three general categories: straight-ahead markers, reversal markers, and causal markers.

Consider the different direction markers in each of the versions of the sentence below, and make a prediction for each:

> **Version 1:** In keeping with her reputation for _____, the politician asserted that in a time of crisis it was important to speak honestly.

> **Version 2:** Despite her reputation for _____, the politician asserted that in a time of crisis it was important to speak honestly.

> **Version 3:** Due to her reputation for _____, many expected that in a time of crisis, the politician would speak honestly.

In all versions, the blank describes the politician's reputation and the second part of the sentence sees the politician speaking honestly. However, the direction markers change, leading to opposing predictions:

> **Version 1:** In this version, the marker *in keeping with* is a straight-ahead marker. Since her assertion that honesty is important was **in keeping with** the politician's reputation, she must have a reputation for honesty.

Chapter 3: **Text Completion and Sentence Equivalence**

Version 2: By contrast, this version starts out with *despite*, a reversal marker. If asserting the importance of honesty is something the politician does **despite** her reputation, she must have a reputation for not being honest.

Version 3: This is the most complicated version. **Due to** is a causal marker, meaning that the politician's reputation for something created an expectation that she would speak honestly. Thus, she must have had a reputation for honesty. Notice that while this prediction is the same as the prediction for Version 1, the sentence in this case had an added element: people's expectations. Causal markers tend to function in the same way as straight-ahead markers, but they also invite more complicated sentence structures and require more inferential analysis.

Be redundant. Don't hesitate to recycle the word *honest*. And very importantly, watch for reversals and unpack or parse the sentence carefully around them.

Try another:

For all his studying, his performance on the test was _____.

This one relies on a somewhat uncommon idiom. *For all* means "despite." It's another reversal signal. Studying usually leads to a *good* test performance, so the sentence wants a word that upends the expected result: Despite his studying, his performance was **not** *good*. If you predicted the opposite, make a flashcard for the idiom *for all*. Direction marker idioms are as important to learn as any other vocabulary.

Although he has a reputation for talking too much, others at the party didn't find him especially _____.

Did you say something like *talkative*? Or did you go for *not talkative*? Notice that you have a bit of proof ("a reputation for talking too much" and a signal word that reverses direction: "Although").

But you also have another reversal signal—the *not* in "didn't."

As mentioned earlier, reversing yourself twice (much like turning 180 degrees twice) is like not reversing yourself at all. In your blank, you just want another word for "talking too much."

Although he has a reputation for talking too much, others at the party didn't find him especially talkative.

Here are some common signal words, phrases, and structures, grouped into the three very general categories mentioned above. Pay attention to the reversals, especially when you have more than one of them.

Unit One: **Words and Sentences**

Straight-Ahead	Reversal	Causal
; (semicolon)	Although	As
: (colon)	Anything but	As a result
Also	Belied	Because
And	But	Consequently
Besides	Contrast	Due to
Furthermore	Despite	Hence
Given	Even though	If
In addition	Even with	Since
In fact	For all	So
In light of	However	Therefore
Indeed	Instead	Thus
Just as	In spite of	
Moreover	Nevertheless	
Not only . . . but also . . .	Not	
So . . . as to be . . .	Notwithstanding	
So . . . that . . .	On the contrary	
Such	On the other hand	
X, Y, and Z (items in a list)	Rather than	
	Still	
	Surprise	
	Though	
	Yet	

Chapter 3: **Text Completion and Sentence Equivalence**

Drill: Sentence Analysis

> Analyze each sentence for the proof, and then make a prediction for the blank.

1. The camp established by the aid workers provided a _____ for the refugees, many of whom had traveled for weeks to get there.

2. While others had given only accolades, the iconoclastic critic greeted the book's publication with a lengthy _____.

3. Though many have impugned her conclusions, the studies on which she based her analysis are beyond _____.

4. The ancient poem's value was more _____ than literary; the highly literal work made no attempt at lyricism and ended by warning the reader never to lie.

5. For all the clamor about bipartisanship, in the end, the actual votes _____ to factional loyalties.

6. The notion that digital media should last forever is untenable, considering the warehouses full of computer tape drives and other media that have been _____ by newer technologies.

7. Chad was capricious in his youth, but as an adult he was downright _____.

8. The _____ position he adopted on the issue belied his reputation for equivocation.

Unit One: Words and Sentences

Answers and Explanations

1. This sentence states that *aid workers* are providing something for *refugees*, who have traveled for a long time to get there. In the absence of contradictory information, it's safe to infer that aid workers would be helping the refugees in some way. Therefore, a good prediction would be **refuge** or **sanctuary**.

2. The blank is in the second half of the sentence, so the proof for it is likely in the first part, which starts with the *While*. In terms of content, both parts of the sentence focus on the critical reception of a book. The first part mentions *accolades* received by the book, but the *While* means that the second part will highlight a negative critical response. A good prediction would be something like **condemnation**.

3. The blank—in the second part of the sentence—is describing *the studies* that informed a certain analysis. The first part of the sentence also focuses on this analysis (referenced here as *her conclusions*). It's stated that her conclusions have been *impugned*, a decidedly negative reaction. However, the first part also contains the reversal marker *Though*. So if the first part highlights a negative aspect of her analysis, the second part must be highlighting a positive aspect of it. Be careful. Though the overall impact of the second part of the sentence should be positive say something good about the studies, the blank appears just after a second reversal marker: *beyond*. To convey the fact that the studies are good in some way, the sentence must say that they are *beyond* something bad. A good prediction would be **impugning**. (As a note, though, if it were on the test, this sentence would almost certainly be completed with the expression *beyond* **reproach**).

4. The blank is talking about the poem, stating that it's *more* something *than literary*. Already, you know the poem is *not* very literary, but look to the second part of the sentence for more content clues. Apparently, the poem *made no attempt at lyricism* (further confirmation that it's not literary) and ended with a moral: Never lie. Sticking to the evidence in the sentence, a good fill-in would be **moralistic** or **didactic**.

5. The blank is in the second part of the sentence and is connected to *votes* and *factional loyalties*. Look to the first part of the sentence for a concrete truth. All it says is that there was *clamor about bipartisanship*. That concrete truth is bundled with the reversal marker *For all*. So the second part of the sentence should indicate that the voting was the opposite of *bipartisan*—that is, the votes were partisan. Since *factional loyalties* describe a partisan environment, a good prediction would be **conformed** or **bowed**.

6. The word in the blank will be something that happened to *computer tape drives and other media* as a result of *newer technologies*. The first part of the sentence focuses on the *notion that digital media should last forever*, though it says this notion is *untenable* in light of the second part of the sentence, with *untenable* serving as a de facto reversal marker. Thus, the second part of the sentence should serve to highlight the fact that digital media do not last forever. A good prediction would be **replaced**. GRE-type words that might appear here would be *supplanted* or *superseded*.

7. The blank is describing how Chad was as an adult. The first part of the sentence contains the concrete truth that *Chad was capricious* when he was young. The reversal marker *but* connects the two parts of the sentence, which would ordinarily mean that the word in the blank would have to contradict *capricious*. However, the *downright* subverts this expectation in a subtle way: Rather than an opposite for *capricious*, the *downright* forces the word in the blank to be a more extreme version of *capricious*. Thus, a good prediction might be something like **volatile** or **tempestuous**.

8. The blank describes the person's *position*. The concrete truth in this sentence is that the person in question has a *reputation for equivocation*, meaning that he doesn't generally communicate in a forthright way. Complicating things further is the reversal marker *belied*, which means "contradicted" or "gave a false impression of." So a good prediction would go in the opposite direction of *equivocation*—something like **clearly communicated** or **firm**.

54

Chapter 3: **Text Completion and Sentence Equivalence**

Sentence Equivalence

Sentence Equivalence (SE) questions on the GRE are very similar to one-blank Text Completion questions. Here's what ETS says about this question type:

> *Like Text Completion questions, Sentence Equivalence questions test the ability to reach a conclusion about how a passage should be completed on the basis of partial information, but to a greater extent they focus on the meaning of the completed whole. Sentence Equivalence questions consist of a single sentence with just one blank, and they ask you to find two choices that both lead to a complete, coherent sentence and that produce sentences that mean the same thing.*

Essentially, the only difference between Sentence Equivalence and Text Completion is that rather than picking the single best answer for the blank, you will have to pick *two* answers that give the sentence an equivalent meaning. Consider the following example:

The judge dismissed Steffen's lawsuit, ruling that since Steffen had been the first to _____ the contract, the company he was suing was no longer obligated to uphold the provisions of the original agreement.

- [A] forswear
- [B] transmute
- [C] breach
- [D] abrogate
- [E] vituperate
- [F] slake

Throughout the exam (in math, too), the GRE uses square checkboxes, not circles, to indicate questions that can have more than one correct answer; in this case, you'll choose two answers. Sentence Equivalence problems will always have six answer choices, so use the answer letters A through F to keep track of your work on your scratch paper.

To get credit for a Sentence Equivalence question, you must select **both** correct answers. There is no partial credit. In the previous question, the correct answer is *breach* and *abrogate*, which both mean "fail to do what is required by."

Although the idea of two correct answers is an interesting test-making twist, it doesn't necessarily make the questions any harder for you. In fact, it opens up the strategic tool of Answer Choice Analysis, which will be explained in this chapter.

All of the skills you have already learned for Text Completion still apply here. You will still unpack or parse the sentence and come up with a prediction for the blank, and you'll still look to add as little as possible to the story.

There are two main methods of attack for a Sentence Equivalence question, both of which will be reviewed in the pages that follow:

1. Sentence Analysis
2. Answer Choice Analysis

Unit One: **Words and Sentences**

Sentence Analysis in Sentence Equivalence

Like Text Completion questions, Sentence Equivalence questions ask you to fill in a blank based on the information contained in the text around it.

The sentences are not anything like sentences pulled from a newspaper, with a few words blanked out. In such a real-life case, you might not be able to fill in the missing word, since a lot of the necessary context would be contained in other sentences, not in the sentence in question.

On the GRE, all of that necessary context has to be provided in the one sentence you're reading. In fact, as discussed with regards to Text Completion, the GRE has to go further: The test makers have to write sentences containing definitive proof for the words that have to fit in the blank. If that weren't the case, the problem would not have two objectively correct answers and four objectively incorrect answers.

The basic process for Sentence Equivalence is the same as it is for Text Completion. As a reminder, here are the three steps:

1. Read only the sentence.

Don't let yourself get distracted by trap answer choices.

2. Use proof from the sentence to make a prediction.

The same sentence-deconstruction tools work, and just as for Text Completion, you should write down your prediction and aim to recycle text from the sentence whenever possible.

3. Compare your prediction to each answer choice.

If you're approaching Sentence Equivalence using sentence analysis, this is the only step in the process that differs from the one-blank Text Completion process. In Sentence Equivalence, you need to find exactly *two* good matches for your prediction, not just one. However, it's important to note that both words might not feel like an equally apt fit. Often only one of the correct answer choices will fit your prediction perfectly, while the other correct answer will be correct by association: It'll be the closest synonym for the first correct answer.

Here's an example problem with some admittedly tough vocabulary:

The village's water supply had been _____ by toxic industrial byproducts that had seeped into groundwater.

A adumbrated

B contaminated

C abashed

D adulterated

E truncated

F abridged

The blank is about something that happened to the water supply. What do you know about that supply? You know that *toxic* substances seeped into it—that's a very strong and very negative word. There is no reversal marker to send the meaning in the opposite of the expected direction. If you had to pick a single word as proof for the blank, *toxic* would be that word.

So your fill-in could be *made toxic* or something similar, like *contaminated*.

Finally, look for two matches among the answer. The correct answers are *contaminated* and *adulterated*. *Contaminated* is a perfect fit for the sentence and is in line with the prediction above. *Adulterated* is the best match for *contaminated* among the answer choices, though it's more often used for a new substance that cheapens or degrades what it's added to. Note that among the incorrect answers, *truncated* and *abridged* both mean roughly the same thing ("shortened"), *adumbrated* means "outlined or sketched lightly," and *abashed* means "made to feel shame."

Try another hard one:

Unlike the more genial researchers, who often went out together after work, the _____ Dr. Spicer believed that socializing was nothing more than a distraction, and thus made few friends at the lab.

A sedulous
B baneful
C standoffish
D partisan
E glacial
F assiduous

The blank is describing Dr. Spicer. A key reversal marker is the word *Unlike*, which sets up a comparison between *the more genial researchers* and *the _____ Dr. Spicer*.

Since the two are *unlike*, the blank should be something that means "*not* genial," in contrast to the *genial* folks. You could use *not genial* itself as your prediction, or you could put down *unfriendly*, as using more common words can make your prediction more immediately comprehensible and thus easier to use effectively.

The answers are *standoffish* and *glacial*. Both words can mean "emotionally cold and distant." (*Glacial* can also mean "slow, physically cold, or pertaining to glaciers.") Both are a good enough match to *not genial* or *unfriendly* to be the winners.

Rounding out the vocabulary lesson, *sedulous* and *assiduous* mean "hardworking or persistent," *baneful* means "harmful," and *partisan* means "biased, in favor of only one's own side or party."

Unit One: **Words and Sentences**

Answer Choice Analysis

When ETS introduced the Sentence Equivalence format, most people's natural response was, "So we pick a pair of synonyms, right?" ETS officials insist that the two correct answers don't have to be precise synonyms:

> *Do not simply look among the answer choices for two words that mean the same thing. This can be misleading for two reasons. First, the answer choices may contain pairs of words that mean the same thing but do not fit coherently into the sentence, and thus do not constitute a correct answer. Second, the pair of words that do constitute the correct answer may not mean exactly the same thing, since all that matters is that the resultant sentences mean the same thing.*

Hmm. When the two correct answers are inserted into the sentence, do the resulting sentences mean the same thing? Sounds like those words would have to be pretty close, right?

What seems to be going on is that the GRE is being overly respectful of the English language. To quote the famous science-fiction writer, Theodore Sturgeon, "There are no synonyms." In other words, subtleties of meaning technically separate any two words you find listed in any individual entry in a thesaurus. *Deluge* and *flood* don't mean the exact same thing (a *deluge* is, by definition, a severe flood). The GRE wants to acknowledge that the two words you pick will likely differ in terms of some nuance.

However, unless you are trying to write some very stylish and precise prose, the difference between *deluge* and *flood* doesn't really matter. And for Sentence Equivalence on the GRE, that difference definitely won't matter. In fact, in almost every real Sentence Equivalence problem we've seen, the two correct answers are pretty close to being 100 percent synonymous. (We can only think of one official counterexample, a question whose correct answer is *susceptibility* and *characteristic*.)

Consider this example:

> Many people at the dinner party were inordinately interested in questioning the _____ new guest, who refused to reveal his profession or even where he used to live.
>
> A acerbic
> B mysterious
> C insightful
> D trenchant
> E intrepid
> F inscrutable

Look for the proof. The blank describes the new guest, who *refused to reveal* things about himself. If there were a word meaning "not self-revealing," you'd pick it. The word needs to be something like *secretive* or *mysterious*.

As it turns out, *mysterious* and *inscrutable* are the correct answers. *Inscrutable* means "not able to be scrutinized" and often indicates hiding emotions. It's not exactly the same thing as *mysterious*, but there's more overlap between their meanings than between *mysterious* and any other answer.

Most correct answer pairs are at least as closely related as these two. Think of the correct answers as **near-synonyms**. There is a second approach to Sentence Equivalence questions that takes advantage of this property of the answers: Answer Choice Analysis.

So far, you've used **Sentence Analysis** to answer questions, focusing first on the meaning of the given sentence and analyzing it closely to come up with your own prediction. **Answer Choice Analysis**, by contrast, involves ignoring the sentence completely and instead going straight to the answer choices, *sorting them into pairs of near-synonyms.* The right answer must be one of these pairs. And given that there are only six answer choices, there just can't be that many reasonable pairs.

While Sentence Analysis should still be the default approach to Sentence Equivalence, there can be circumstances in which the sentence doesn't yield its proof as readily as you might like. Answer Choice Analysis can work better in these cases (and if your vocabulary is strong, it can even work well as a primary approach).

On the surface, going straight to the answers might seem like a bad idea. Mathematically, your chance of randomly guessing the correct answer pair is 1 in 15. That's less than 7 percent. Those odds are so low that it seems like a waste of time to bother looking at the answers when you aren't following the sentence in the first place. But good Answer Choice Analysis can raise those chances *dramatically*. It can get you from 1 in 15 to 1 in 3 or 1 in 2. It even sometimes gets you to 1 in 1; that is, it gets you all the way to the right answer.

How? The correct answer will be two words that (mostly) mean the same thing. If you know what the six words mean, you can group them into near-synonym pairs. And given that there are six answer choices, at most you'll find three pairs.

Let's look at some examples. Many sets of Sentence Equivalence answer choices are "two by two"—that is, among the six choices there are two different pairs of synonyms, plus two "loose," unrelated words.

Typical two by two:

horrible
nice
pleasant
impoverished
terrible
dying

Horrible and *terrible* are a pair of synonyms. *Pleasant* and *nice* are a different pair of synonyms. *Impoverished* and *dying* are unrelated.

This leaves only two viable answers to consider: the two different pairs of synonyms. At this point, you have a 50 percent chance of guessing correctly. Notice also that the two pairs are antonyms of each other. While this doesn't always happen, it does happen very often, a sign to be meticulous with any reversal markers in the sentence itself.

Here is a weaker variant of a two by two:

wicked
healthful
evil
qualified
gifted
well-practiced

Wicked and *evil* are a pair. *Gifted* and *well-practiced* are sort of a pair—that is, *gifted* implies an ability that comes from within, whereas *well-practiced* implies an ability that comes from (obviously) practice. However, both are different paths to the same goal (being talented or skilled). They're a weak pair.

In the case that a set of choices provides a closely related pair and a less closely related pair, *the more closely related pair is more likely to be the answer*. However, make sure that the pair has some support in the sentence before you choose it.

Unit One: **Words and Sentences**

Occasionally, three words will seem to match up (a *triplet*). In such cases, usually two are really synonyms and the third is off in terms of spin, strength, or usage. For instance, in the case of *excoriate*, *admonish*, and *castigate*, the real pair is *excoriate* and *castigate*—both mean "to criticize or scold very harshly," and *admonish* means "to scold mildly." Note that if all three triplets really were synonyms, they would necessarily all be wrong, since there can only be two correct answers. However, this doesn't happen often. Indeed, it more often happens that the two true synonyms in a triplet end up being the right answer, with the third word included as a trap answer for test-takers who understood the sentence but are unaware of the nuance difference among the three words.

Here's a set of answers with another false triplet:

   determined
   talkative
   hapless
   unsuccessful
   unlucky
   resolute

Determined and *resolute* are a pair. *Hapless*, *unsuccessful*, and *unlucky* seem to be a triplet. (*Talkative* is not related to the others.)

Hapless really does mean *unlucky* (*hap* is actually a rarely used Old English word for "luck" or "lot"). But a person can be *unsuccessful* without being *unlucky*. *Hapless* and *unlucky* are the true pair.

It is also possible to have just one pair, or three.

Only one pair:

   pale
   flexible
   hidden
   celebrated
   equitable
   fair

Equitable and *fair* are a pair. The other four words are unrelated. Answer Choice Analysis gets you all the way to the right answer!

Three pairs:

   candid
   latent
   ingenuous
   inimical
   dormant
   hostile

Candid and *ingenuous* are a pair. *Latent* and *dormant* are a pair. *Inimical* and *hostile* are a pair. Answer Choice Analysis gets you down to three choices.

Even in this last case, this is still a huge jump in your random-guessing chances, from about 7 percent to about 33 percent.

When to Use (and NOT to Use) Answer Choice Analysis

When you use Answer Choice Analysis as your main tool for Sentence Equivalence questions, you proceed to the choices first, before even reading the sentence. For instance:

Blah blah blah blah blah blah blah blah blah blah blah blah blah _____, blah blah blah blah blah blah blah blah blah.

- [A] toadies
- [B] aesthetes
- [C] tyros
- [D] lackeys
- [E] anchorites
- [F] novices

As you examine the answers, attempt to make pairs: *toadies* and *lackeys* are subordinates who follow without question. *Tyros* and *novices* are both beginners. *Aesthetes* love or study beauty, and *anchorites* are recluses, especially religious hermits, and thus those two words are not related.

Therefore, the answer must be *toadies/lackeys* or *tyros/novices*. The only question you need to ask at this point is, "Does the sentence call for a *suck-up* or a *beginner*?" Here is the complete problem:

It may be true that everyone likes flattery, but a good manager is not unduly persuaded by it, and thus not taken in by _____, who use wheedling and fawning to get ahead.

- [A] toadies
- [B] aesthetes
- [C] tyros
- [D] lackeys
- [E] anchorites
- [F] novices

There is a lot of proof (such as *flattery* and *wheedling and fawning*) that the question is calling for *toadies* and *lackeys*.

Answer Choice Analysis is at its most effective when you know all of the words in the choices.

However, most test-takers don't have strong enough vocabularies to be able to complete Answer Choice Analysis consistently, especially when the words get really tough.

Moreover, most of the time this approach does *not* get you all the way to the right answer. You'll either need to lightly deconstruct the sentence or, if the sentence proves too inscrutable, to guess one of the pairs. That's unsatisfying.

So in general, start a Sentence Equivalence question by quickly scanning the answer choices. If the words are all familiar, Answer Choice Analysis is a viable option; keep it in mind as a backup plan, and then proceed to the sentence. For most, Sentence Analysis ought to be the first line of attack.

Unit One: **Words and Sentences**

But when should you break out this backup plan? When you read and reread the sentence, but you're not getting anything out of it. Maybe the topic or the structure is really confusing. Or under the pressure of time and the exam, you just can't get a handle on the original text. Or maybe you've understood a lot of the sentence, but you're still struggling to come up with a prediction for the blank. In this case, you might be starting to hit a state of *semantic satiation*. Have you ever repeated some word over and over, until it loses meaning and sounds like nonsense? That's semantic satiation.

Under exam pressure, even the glimmers of this state can lead to a downward spiral. As meaning slips from your grasp, you reread the sentence even more frantically, berating yourself for not getting it, falling even further into semantic satiation, distraction, and panic…

Stop it. Break out of the spiral. If you're familiar with the words in the answer choices, it's time to invoke Answer Choice Analysis. You'll make good progress toward the goal. If you come back to the sentence, you'll be refreshed and ready to take in its meaning. Moreover, it'll be an easier prospect to deal with the sentence at that point, as rather than coming up with the meaning of the sentence from scratch, you'll just have to decide between two or three meanings (depending on how many answer pairs you find). If you still can't decide, make a good guess and move on.

In fact, as you progress through the exam, you might proactively change it up for yourself. Go ahead and decide to attack the next Sentence Equivalence question with Answer Choice Analysis from the outset. That strategic decision will reassure you. It will remind you that you're in charge of the exam, not the other way around. However, that will only work if you've practiced Answer Choice Analysis before test day, so as you study Sentence Equivalence, make sure that you proactively alternate between Sentence Analysis and Answer Choice Analysis so that you hone both skills.

Chapter 3: **Text Completion and Sentence Equivalence**

Drill: Answer Choice Analysis

> For each set of choices, match up the pairs. Most, but not all, sets of choices consist of two pairs of near-synonyms and two other unrelated words. A few will have one or three sets of near-synonyms.

1. verbose
   turbid
   diffident
   prolix
   self-effacing
   pious

2. amicable
   pithy
   scholarly
   arcane
   succinct
   esoteric

3. distend
   traduce
   alienate
   flatter
   slander
   complement

4. auxiliary
   cardinal
   principal
   ordinal
   collateral
   prefatory

5. hawkish
   cogent
   turgid
   eloquent
   bombastic
   intelligible

Unit One: **Words and Sentences**

6. pellucid
   transparent
   rustic
   sedulous
   assiduous
   earthy

7. eclecticism
   aberrance
   deviation
   idiosyncrasy
   adulation
   eccentricity

8. bevy
   modicum
   paucity
   excess
   surfeit
   bunch

9. disclosure
   epitome
   scruple
   apothegm
   contumely
   maxim

10. pique
    slake
    quench
    succor
    fructify
    stimulate

Chapter 3: **Text Completion and Sentence Equivalence**

Answers and Explanations

1. Two pairs: **Verbose** and **prolix** are a pair, each meaning "talkative." **Diffident** (lacking confidence) and **self-effacing** (putting oneself down) are a pair; they are not perfect synonyms, but they are close enough for Sentence Equivalence questions on the GRE. *Pious* and *turbid* have no relationship.

2. Two pairs: **Pithy** and **succinct** both mean "short and to the point." **Arcane** and **esoteric** both mean "obscure or specialized, known to only a few" (about information). *Amicable* and *scholarly* are not related.

3. One pair: **Traduce** and **slander** are a pair, meaning "tell malicious lies about." *Complement* and *flatter* are a TRAP—*complement* (to complete, to make up a whole with) is *not* the same word as *compliment* (to say something nice about). *Distend* and *alienate* are also unrelated. If these were the answer choices in a real question, *traduce* and *slander* would be the correct answer.

4. Two pairs: **Auxiliary** and **collateral** mean "secondary, off to the side." **Cardinal** and **principal** (first, main) are actually synonyms with each other *and* antonyms with *auxiliary* and *collateral*. *Ordinal* and *prefatory* are not related, though watch out for an association trap: *Cardinal* and *ordinal* are both used to designate kinds of numbers and so may initially seem as though they form a pair.

5. Two pairs: **Turgid** and **bombastic** are a pair. *Bombastic* means "pompous, overinflated" and is used to describe speech. While *turgid* can simply mean "swollen," when it is applied to speech, it has the same meaning of "overinflated, showing off." **Eloquent** and **cogent** are a weak pair—*eloquent* means "beautiful and articulate" (about speech), and *cogent* means "compellingly persuasive." *Intelligible* and *hawkish* are not related.

6. Three pairs: **Pellucid** and **transparent** are a pair (see-through), as are **rustic** and **earthy** (primitive, of the earth, undeveloped) and **assiduous** and **sedulous** (hardworking).

7. Two pairs: **Aberrance** and **deviation** are a pair (being different from the normal). *Eclecticism, idiosyncrasy,* and *eccentricity* may all seem similar. However, **idiosyncrasy** and **eccentricity** (harmless personal oddness) are a true pair. *Eclecticism* (having mixed, wide-ranging tastes) is unrelated to *adulation* (excessive admiration).

8. Two or three pairs: **Bevy** and **bunch** are a pair, as are **surfeit** and **excess**. **Modicum** and **paucity** are questionable as a pair because they differ in spin—*modicum* means "a little," and *paucity* means "not enough." It's the subtle but key difference between *having a little* and *having little*.

9. One pair: **Apothegm** and **maxim** are a pair (proverb; pithy statement). *Disclosure, epitome, scruple,* and *contumely* are unrelated.

10. Two pairs: **Pique** and **stimulate** are a pair. **Slake** and **quench** (satisfy, especially of thirst) are a pair. *Succor* (provide comfort or relief) might seem related to the second pair, but one *succors* a person, and one *slakes* or *quenches* a desire. *Fructify* (make productive) is unrelated.

Unit One: Words and Sentences

What If I Don't Know the Words?

It almost seems as though Sentence Equivalence on the GRE was designed to prevent lucky guesses. On a standard choose-one multiple-choice question with choices (A) through (E), a test taker has a 1 in 5 chance of randomly guessing the correct answer. On a Sentence Equivalence, however, there are six answers total and you must choose two. A random guess here has only a 1 in 15 chance of being correct.

If you know *one* of the correct choices and randomly guess on the other, your chance of getting the question correct is 1 in 5. Thus, it is very important that you *assiduously augment* your vocabulary.

That said, even a little Answer Choice Analysis can help you make a good guess, increasing your odds of success. Many Sentence Equivalence questions match the two-by-two format. That is, the answer choices contain two pairs of synonyms or near-synonyms and two other loose words.

So if you can find a single pair of synonyms in the choices, there is about a 50 percent chance that that pair is correct (it is only *about* 50 percent, since not all sets of choices follow a two-by-two format). Here is an example:

- [A] agog
- [B] akimbo
- [C] obeisant
- [D] dyspeptic
- [E] kowtowing
- [F] crotchety

If you were able to pick out that *dyspeptic* and *crotchety* were a pair—or that *obeisant* and *kowtowing* were—then test that pair in the sentence and pick it if it seems to be a good match. (As will be the case in most questions, the two remaining words, *agog* and *akimbo*, have no relationship.)

If the pair that you are able to find is not a fit for the sentence, cross off both words. You now have a 1/6 chance of guessing correctly.

If you cannot find a synonym pair, you are unlikely to get the question correct. Accept that fact and don't waste time. Your strategy here is simply to make a guess and move on. Save time for questions that you will be able to answer later.

Although the GRE allows you to move around within a section and come back to questions you previously left blank or wish to reconsider, keep in mind that **if you don't know the words, you probably won't do any better by attempting the question twice**. You'll only waste time and lower your chance of getting other questions correct. (One caveat: Every now and then, a word you didn't know when you attempted an earlier question will come up in a passage later in the section. Keep your eyes open!)

To be clear, though, if you don't know the words, **do not leave the question blank**. There's no penalty for choosing the wrong answer on the GRE, and there's no advantage whatsoever to leaving a question blank—if you do, you're *guaranteed* to get it wrong. Make your best guess on the question and move on. Don't waste time deliberating over it, and don't mark it for review. That extra time will be better spent on Reading Comprehension or other vocabulary questions that you are able to answer more effectively.

Why It Is Important to Learn Words in Context

ETS tells you not only to check that the two answers you select for a question create sentences that mean the same thing, but also to make sure that each one "produces a sentence that is logically, grammatically, and stylistically coherent."

Hmm. Asking test-takers to check that the completed sentences are grammatically coherent implies that some of the choices will create sentences that are not. Here's an example:

Education advocates argued that the free school lunch program was vital to creating a school environment _____ to learning.

[A] conducive
[B] inimical
[C] substantial
[D] appropriate
[E] beneficial
[F] hostile

"Education advocates" are certainly in favor of learning; your fill-in might be something like *helpful*.

Looking at the choices, *conducive*, *appropriate*, and *beneficial* all seem to be matches.

However, if you place each word into the sentence, one choice creates an incorrect idiom. *Conducive to* and *beneficial to* work, but *appropriate to* is not a correct idiom—instead, you would say "appropriate *for* learning." The Idioms list in your online syllabus contains several examples of these idiomatic expressions.

Thus, it is important not only to memorize dictionary definitions of words, but also to be able to use those words in context, in a grammatically correct way.

Here's another example:

He's a _____ fellow, always grandstanding and deploying his formidable lexicon for oratorical effect.

[A] declamatory
[B] grandiloquent
[C] didactic
[D] florid
[E] titanic
[F] cabalistic

The blank describes what kind of *fellow* he is, and the content clue is *grandstanding and deploying his formidable lexicon for oratorical effect*. That is, he speaks in a pompous way, as though showing off his vocabulary for an audience.

Unit One: Words and Sentences

The word *florid* seems appropriate—it means "flowery" and often applies to words, as in *florid poetry*. But wait! *Florid* applies to writing, speech, decor, etc., not to the people who produce those things. (Actually, you can apply *florid* to people, but in that context it means "flushed, ruddy," as in having rosy cheeks, which is not appropriate here.)

The answer is **declamatory** and **grandiloquent**, both of which describe pompous orators (that is, people who make speeches) or the speech of such people.

Memorizing that *florid* means "flowery" is better than nothing, but it doesn't really tell you what kinds of things can be described by that word or how to use it metaphorically. Once again, it is important to learn words in context.

There are several ways to do this. Manhattan Prep's *GRE® Vocabulary Flash Cards* provide example sentences for all 1,000 words. Many online dictionaries provide quotes from literature in which the word being defined is used in context. In some cases, it is fruitful to simply Google a word to see how different writers are using it.

Whatever your process, your goal is to be able to do two things for any given word: first, to define it in a concise and straightforward way and, second, to be able to use it in a sentence in a descriptive way (such that someone reading the sentence would understand what it meant from the context).

You want to be comfortable when seeing a word used in any legitimate way. For instance, you would understand if the word *darkness* were used metaphorically (*While she at first resisted going on antidepressants, she ultimately decided that she would do anything that might lift the darkness*) or if the word *enthusiastic* were used sarcastically (*As enthusiastic as I am about unnecessary surgery, I will have to decline your offer to appear on an extreme makeover reality show*).

To perform with excellence on the GRE, you want to know your new words inside and out. You want to be *flexible* in how you use and interpret those words. The online resources associated with this book provide more guidance for formidably fortifying your lexicon.

Traps in TC and SE

Here is a list of common trap answer types and other twists the GRE can use to make Text Completion and Sentence Equivalence questions easier to miss. As you practice, keep your eye out for these traps and make an explicit note of any that you fall into. By paying specific attention to which traps you're vulnerable to as you study, you'll be better prepared to dodge those same traps on test day. Also, bear in mind that this list is not comprehensive; be on the lookout for other traps along the way.

- **Double reversal markers,** which create **opposite traps**
- **Story traps,** which tempt you to add unproven elements to the story of the sentence
- **Unfamiliar style/content,** which can confuse you and cause you to abandon your process
- **Familiar content,** which can lead to picking answers based on what you know to be generally true rather than what's actually written in the sentence
- **Idiom traps,** which are answer choices that form part of a common phrase with a word near the blank and therefore artificially feel like a good fit
- **Red herring clues,** which, while in the sentence, are not related by content to the blank
- **Blanks in tough spots,** which require careful unpacking or parsing of the sentence

- **Theme traps,** where wrong answer choices are thematically related to elements of the sentence but not logical fits for the blank
- **Spin traps,** in which a wrong answer has a nearly apt dictionary definition but the wrong connotation (positive or negative)
- **Close but not close enough traps,** where wrong answers have the right spin but are incorrect in degree, detail, or fit
- **Vocab traps,** where the GRE takes advantage of visual similarities between words to trick you into thinking one word has a similar meaning to another

Text Completion and Sentence Equivalence Recap

This is the three-step process for Text Completion and Sentence Equivalence:

1. Read only the sentence.
2. Use proof from the sentence to make a prediction for the blank.
3. Compare your prediction to each answer choice.

For Sentence Equivalence, if a quick glance at the answer reveals only familiar words, you have the additional option of using Answer Choice Analysis:

1. Group the answer choices into pairs of near-synonyms. Eliminate any answers that don't form a pair.
2. Consider which pair's meaning best fits the sentence.

Practice both of these approaches as you study TC and SE, with a special focus on predicting answers.

Vocabulary Challenge

> Did you spot these vocabulary words? If not, go back and find them in context! (The word may be in a different form than listed here— "digressing" instead of "digress," for example.) Write your own definitions based on the evidence in the chapter.

1. tortuous (*adj.*), p. 44
2. recondite (*adj.*), p. 45
3. embellish (*v*), p. 48
4. paragon (*n*), p. 50
5. satiate (*v*), p. 62
6. augment (*adj.*), p. 66

Unit One: **Words and Sentences**

Problem Set (Text Completion)

As you do these questions, look for the proof before going to the answer choices, write down your own prediction in your scratch work, write out the letters A B C D E, and use process of elimination. Try to identify the traps mentioned in this chapter. Also, make a list of vocabulary words to look up later.

If your current vocabulary is extremely limited, here's another idea: Go through the following questions looking at the answer choices only, without reading the sentences. Make flash cards for all of the words you can't precisely define (look words up on Google, dictionary.com, m-w.com, thefreedictionary.com, etc.). Learn all of the words, and *then* come back later to try these questions.

1. Although it appeared to be _____ after its stagnation and eventual cancellation in 1989, *Doctor Who* returned to the BBC in 2005, becoming the longest-running science-fiction show in history.

A	lackluster
B	ascendant
C	unflagging
D	defunct
E	sated

2. _____ against China's record on environmental protection has become a ubiquitous pastime at energy summits, especially among those already inclined to invective on such topics.

A	Inveigling
B	Speculating
C	Needling
D	Ranting
E	Lauding

3. In 1345, the brothers of Queen Blanche of Namur, Louis and Robert, were appointed _____ to her spouse, conveying upon them the protection of King Magnus Eriksson in exchange for their homage and fealty.

A	protégés
B	vassals
C	vanguards
D	precursors
E	partisans

Chapter 3: **Text Completion and Sentence Equivalence**

4. Social critic Neil Postman identified what he saw as a sort of intellectual _____ when he wrote, "What Orwell feared were those who would ban books. What Huxley feared was that there would be no reason to ban a book, for there would be no one who wanted to read one."

A	pondering
B	mulishness
C	degeneration
D	cerebration
D	banishment

5. The doctor's presentation went into great detail about the supposed _____ of the treatment, but failed to discuss any way of obviating damage to auxiliary structures.

A	diagnosis
B	mien
C	prognosis
D	costs
E	benefits

6. It takes only a smattering of dry shrub for an errant spark to touch off a full-blown _____.

A	wasteland
B	renewal
C	scintilla
D	emergency
E	conflagration

7. While it would be a relief if the announcement were _____, many shareholders have doubts, based on the prevarications that have marked the CEO's long tenure at the company.

A	libelous
B	credible
C	nullified
D	unverified
E	forestalled

8. In determining sentencing, the judge will take into account whether the defendant acted on _____ motives or, as the prosecution alleges, acted primarily to protect himself and his profits.

A	altruistic
B	hidden
C	pathological
D	lucrative
E	violent

Unit One: Words and Sentences

9. During years of mismanagement by the Socialist Party, Burma drifted into economic _____ and isolation, a far cry from the power and influence exerted by the country at the peak of the Toungoo Dynasty in the 16th century.

A	monotony
B	opulence
C	nonchalance
D	feebleness
E	recriminations

10. As the new government revealed itself to be far more authoritarian than the people ever could have guessed, and curfews and roadblocks threatened the _____ of citizens, the public houses began to fill with whispers of a possible coup d'état.

A	insolence
B	epitome
C	belligerence
D	recidivism
E	autonomy

11. He is the most hubristic individual his colleagues have ever met, never missing an opportunity to _____ his own accomplishments.

A	flout
B	augment
C	dictate
D	downplay
E	vaun

12. The negotiator's _____ was so incomprehensible to the Royal delegation, accustomed to speaking only in formal Queen's English, that the parties struggled to complete the negotiation.

A	fortitude
B	patois
C	equanimity
D	diffidence
E	consternation

13. Traditional upper-class _____ such as fox hunting and cricket have largely given way to more egalitarian amusements over the course of the last century.

A	stereotypes
B	diversions
C	vocations
D	canards
E	professions

14. Professor Honeycutt was known as a probing questioner of her students; she always wanted to get to the _____ of any intellectual matter.

A	emotions
B	academics
C	pith
D	periphery
E	examination

15. After Bismarck's cunning leadership helped the Prussians overcome years of infighting, they were able to turn the aggression outward, becoming known across Europe for their _____.

A	ennui
B	extravagance
C	opulence
D	covetousness
E	truculence

16. The idea, espoused by such heavyweights as Peter Singer, that each sentient being deserves fair treatment on par with human beings clashes with the ecological insight that _____ some members of a species is occasionally necessary to prevent the devastating effects of overpopulation.

A	protecting
B	culling
C	murdering
D	reintroducing
E	depleting

17. After renouncing the advantages of his noble birth, he wandered from village to village as a _____; along with the other members of his religious order, he maintained that this reliance on alms was the life best suited to one who wished to see both the miserliness and the generosity of humanity.

A	abettor
B	mendicant
C	rube
D	anachronism
E	malefactor

Unit One: Words and Sentences

18. A crotchet of many grammarians is that the serial comma is _____ addendum to a perfectly clear sentence structure; obviously, they're wrong, as the serial comma is critical to understanding the sentence's meaning, cadence, and grammatical delineations.

A	an unnecessary
B	a proper
C	a misunderstood
D	a dogmatic
E	an inspired

19. In contrast to American social conventions regarding neighborly relations, in which families and individuals often interact on a familiar basis, residential _____ does not necessarily imply intimacy (or even amity) among the English.

A	commodiousness
B	amiability
C	reciprocity
D	proximity
E	cordiality

20. It is quite dangerous to _____ unnecessarily through the city these days, when explosions shake the buildings to their foundations without letup; it is best to conduct only essential errands, and to do so with haste.

A	bop
B	saunter
C	circumambulate
D	sidle
E	reconnoiter

Chapter 3: Text Completion and Sentence Equivalence

Problem Set (Sentence Equivalence)

In this set, try to practice both approaches to Sentence Equivalence: Sentence Analysis and Answer Choice Analysis. Write out A B C D E F on your scratch paper, and remember to choose two answers that are near-synonyms. As in the Text Completion set, make sure to add unfamiliar words to your vocab list after you attempt the questions, and try to identify any traps.

> **Directions**
>
> For the questions in this set, select the two answer choices that, when used to complete the sentence, fit the meaning of the sentence as a whole and produce completed sentences that are alike in meaning.

1. The children's story—seemingly a simple tale of animals gathering for a picnic in the forest—took a _____ turn at the end, admonishing readers to always be honest.

    A magnanimous
    B beneficent
    C didactic
    D garrulous
    E moralistic
    F futile

2. Floodwaters had already breached the library's walls, but hopeful volunteers in hip boots worked tirelessly to _____ the damage.

    A mitigate
    B exacerbate
    C abase
    D bolster
    E forestall
    F flummox

3. The candidate campaigned on a platform of willingness to cooperate with the members of other political parties, yet many commentators were nevertheless surprised that she indeed turned out to be less _____ than her predecessor.

    A irate
    B divisive
    C impulsive
    D wily
    E infuriated
    F combative

Unit One: **Words and Sentences**

4. When Sven got angry, whether it was during an argument with his family or just with a coworker, it proved almost impossible to _____ him and thereby return him to his normal demeanor.

    - [A] condemn
    - [B] pacify
    - [C] judge
    - [D] incense
    - [E] mollify
    - [F] influence

5. The graduate student's experiment yielded results as surprising as they were promising; her next step was to pursue additional data that would _____ her findings.

    - [A] undergird
    - [B] buttress
    - [C] gainsay
    - [D] undermine
    - [E] eschew
    - [F] lecture

6. There is no fundamental difference between a person who quietly _____ a bigoted viewpoint to a friend and one who spews chauvinist vitriol on television.

    - [A] eschews
    - [B] espouses
    - [C] professes
    - [D] denies
    - [E] reneges
    - [F] substantiates

7. A 1957 lawsuit against the U.S. Department of Agriculture regarding aerial pesticide spraying was the _____ for Rachel Carson to begin the writing of her environmentalist manifesto *Silent Spring*, though she had become concerned about and started researching the practice years earlier.

    - [A] stimulus
    - [B] conspiracy
    - [C] atrocity
    - [D] impetus
    - [E] catastrophe
    - [F] climate

Chapter 3: **Text Completion and Sentence Equivalence**

8. A commentator with a more _____ worldview would not find it so easy to divide up the nation into good guys and bad guys.

    A belligerent
    B subtle
    C philosophical
    D aberrant
    E peaceful
    F nuanced

9. James Joyce's *Finnegan's Wake*, written in a stream-of-consciousness style full of convoluted puns and obscure allusions, has a deserved reputation for linguistic _____.

    A elaborateness
    B opacity
    C meaninglessness
    D informality
    E uniqueness
    F inscrutability

10. The financial situation in many European nations is _____ enough that even a small incident could lead to catastrophe.

    A drab
    B unstable
    C illegitimate
    D unsafe
    E precarious
    F churlish

11. While the argument for global warming may not be _____ by the record low temperatures reported this year, this data does not undermine the overall trend of steadily higher global temperatures.

    A bolstered
    B fortified
    C subverted
    D defined
    E supplanted
    F undercut

Unit One: **Words and Sentences**

12. The debate coach expected some gravitas from her team, arguing that pithy quips and gibes, while sometimes effective, had no place in a _____ argument.

    A polite
    B shallow
    C competitive
    D serious
    E cantankerous
    F sober

13. Last year it was discovered that *South Park* writers _____ part of its *Inception* spoof from a similar *College Humor* sketch.

    A amalgamated
    B filched
    C indulged
    D combined
    E poached
    F assumed

14. Some critics view Abstract Expressionism, which is characterized by geometric shapes and swaths of color, as a _____ of realist painting.

    A rejection
    B manifestation
    C renunciation
    D memento
    E commemoration
    F vindication

15. The first spy of the nascent United States, Nathan Hale, was captured by the British when he attempted to _____ British-controlled New York City to track enemy troop movements.

    A thwart
    B penetrate
    C infiltrate
    D permeate
    E research
    F conquer

16. Romantic comedies of the 1950s were characterized more by _____ than by the straightforward vulgarity that characterizes dialogue in today's rom-coms.

    A conversation
    B blatancy
    C insinuation
    D illusion
    E innuendo
    F rapport

17. Inflation isn't dead, only _____; as the economy turns around, the purchasing power of the dollar is likely to fall again.

    A paralyzed
    B dormant
    C immobile
    D itinerant
    E problematic
    F quiescent

18. Some boxers talk about trying to access their more _____ selves in order to counter the fact that civilized people generally don't punch each other in the face.

    A seething
    B barbaric
    C irate
    D insidious
    E nefarious
    F primitive

19. Many people assume that creative work is less _____ than manual labor, but they underestimate the difficulty of being entirely self-motivated (as well as writing one's own paychecks).

    A inventive
    B collaborative
    C serious
    D arduous
    E taxing
    F grave

Unit One: **Words and Sentences**

20. The education debate is only getting more _____ as politicians demonize teachers unions and every special interest group jumps into the fray.

    A vehement
    B overt
    C heated
    D problematic
    E tired
    F unavoidable

21. While many individual religions insist on the primacy of their particular deity, syncretism advocates the _____ of multiple religious beliefs, attempting to reconcile even opposing principles and practices.

    A exclusion
    B marriage
    C commingling
    D division
    E transgression
    F schism

22. The ambassador was invested with _____ power by her government and hence did not hesitate to draft and finalize the agreement unilaterally, without first consulting even the president.

    A tertiary
    B consummate
    C enigmatic
    D tyrannical
    E complete
    F dictatorial

23. Sometimes it seems that today's politicians will exploit any opportunity to _____ their views to the world, no matter how sordid or partisan.

    A declaim
    B invoke
    C disparage
    D parrot
    E adduce
    F trumpet

24. The many scattered chapters of the organization decided that a mandatory national _____ would be the best way to bring leadership together and reconcile what had become a haphazard and often chaotic set of bylaws and regulations.

    [A] introduction
    [B] acclamation
    [C] intervention
    [D] colloquium
    [E] symposium
    [F] mediation

25. Though it seems implausible that one could be a great writer without some experience of life, many famous authors have led a(n) _____ existence.

    [A] idiosyncratic
    [B] cloistered
    [C] hermetic
    [D] enigmatic
    [E] sheltered
    [F] cryptic

26. Though she wasn't particularly well-known as a humanitarian, her deep sense of responsibility for those who were suffering was real, and was belied by an outward appearance of _____ .

    [A] concern
    [B] sagacity
    [C] mirth
    [D] felicity
    [E] nonchalance
    [F] indifference

27. Excessive patriotism is ineluctably _____, as the elevation of one country to the rank of preeminent on Earth necessarily requires some amount of demonization of other people.

    [A] minatory
    [B] xenophobic
    [C] unethical
    [D] bigoted
    [E] nationalistic
    [F] truculent

Unit One: Words and Sentences

28. One possible explanation for the mandatory debauchery of most bachelor parties is that if the husband-to-be is able to practice _____ in those circumstances, he must be ready for the self-restraint attendant to marriage.

    - [A] forbearance
    - [B] gentility
    - [C] fiat
    - [D] tenacity
    - [E] temperance
    - [F] autonomy

29. Jon Stewart's "Rally to Restore Sanity" was purportedly organized to prove that it was possible to discuss politics humorously but civilly, without _____ those on the other side of the fence.

    - [A] bespeaking
    - [B] eulogizing
    - [C] lampooning
    - [D] vilifying
    - [E] caricaturing
    - [F] maligning

30. Though occasionally used in practice, very few forms of corporal punishment have been _____ by the military, due less to the prescriptions of the Geneva Conventions than to the overwhelmingly negative popular response to reports of abuse.

    - [A] upbraided
    - [B] sanctioned
    - [C] endorsed
    - [D] considered
    - [E] rejected
    - [F] rebuked

31. The budget debate progressed well for the first few months, in spite of all the ardent and sometimes bitter squabbling, but slowly descended into a _____ of competing interests and claims.

    - [A] quagmire
    - [B] covenant
    - [C] feud
    - [D] morass
    - [E] quarrel
    - [F] accord

Chapter 3: Text Completion and Sentence Equivalence

32. The difference between similes and metaphors is subtle, but for the poet who takes his or her work seriously, it is absolutely _____.

    [A] frivolous
    [B] superfluous
    [C] dispensable
    [D] crucial
    [E] trifling
    [F] requisite

33. It is _____ reasoning to ascribe to Keynesian economics a recommendation that the limit on how much debt the government can incur should be perpetually raised, when Keynes states clearly that deficit spending must be done responsibly.

    [A] indigenous
    [B] corrupt
    [C] venial
    [D] fallacious
    [E] specious
    [F] axiomatic

34. In many ways, teenage rebellion can be seen as the effect of a communication gap between an older generation's calcified language and the protean _____ of the new generation.

    [A] argot
    [B] defiance
    [C] prolixity
    [D] insubordination
    [E] verbosity
    [F] jargon

35. His cantankerous reputation was cemented by years of _____ at every conceivable opportunity.

    [A] imputing
    [B] grousing
    [C] assaulting
    [D] carping
    [E] convulsing
    [F] imbibing

Unit One: Words and Sentences

36. The police were called when people in the neighborhood witnessed a small _____ in progress outside of a bar.

    - [A] fracas
    - [B] discourse
    - [C] altercation
    - [D] battle
    - [E] colloquy
    - [F] mutiny

37. Given her sheltered upbringing and the limited breadth of experience imposed on her by economic circumstance, her work reflected a surprisingly _____ sensibility.

    - [A] shallow
    - [B] eclectic
    - [C] profound
    - [D] multifarious
    - [E] callow
    - [F] facile

38. Many people expect documentary filmmakers to be dispassionate and objective, but Michael Moore has a reputation for never missing a chance to _____ against those with whom he disagrees.

    - [A] rail
    - [B] advertise
    - [C] fulminate
    - [D] censure
    - [E] strain
    - [F] aspirate

39. The movie critic was best remembered for the way she used the language of food to describe films, for example, how she praised Iñarritu's action sequences by comparing them to _____ empanada.

    - [A] an insipid
    - [B] a spectacular
    - [C] a brilliant
    - [D] a piquant
    - [E] a zesty
    - [F] an astonishing

Chapter 3: **Text Completion and Sentence Equivalence**

40. Every few years, someone manages to survive a skydive with a parachute that doesn't open, often with only a few broken bones, some _____ , and a gash or two.

    [A] torpor
    [B] trauma
    [C] bruises
    [D] finesse
    [E] lesions
    [F] contusions

41. As official _____ to this country, she was called upon to answer questions about the Japanese government's position on various issues.

    [A] envoy
    [B] tyro
    [C] emissary
    [D] neophyte
    [E] ascetic
    [F] libertine

42. While the group's street protests had had an aggressive, uncompromising tenor, once admitted to the halls of power to begin formal lobbying, its leaders wisely chose to _____ the stridency of their rhetoric.

    [A] metamorphose
    [B] gild
    [C] wane
    [D] palliate
    [E] succor
    [F] damp

43. The women's rights movement has been mostly _____ in the Middle East, but it is likely that activists will be newly galvanized by the political upheavals currently sweeping the region.

    [A] dogged
    [B] stagnant
    [C] interminable
    [D] lissome
    [E] abeyant
    [F] tenacious

Unit One: Words and Sentences

44. Debate rages on between proponents and detractors of corporal punishment and the death penalty, though even the most ardent supporter agrees that punishments must be _____ and the justice system evenhanded and thorough.

    - [A] meet
    - [B] clement
    - [C] delimited
    - [D] apposite
    - [E] tantamount
    - [F] merciful

45. Peer-reviewed journals are a sacred cow of most scientific rationalists, but studies have shown that the premise of impartiality is _____, as results are always colored by the personal proclivities and suppositions of the experimenters.

    - [A] inane
    - [B] prejudicial
    - [C] fatuous
    - [D] chimerical
    - [E] unachievable
    - [F] vexing

46. The description of the restaurant as a garden of _____ delights is fair enough, as Chef Marcel conjures up a menu of texture and taste that calls into question one's preconceived notions of what constitutes a meal.

    - [A] salubrious
    - [B] epicurean
    - [C] carnal
    - [D] voluptuous
    - [E] terrestrial
    - [F] gustatory

47. Most of the book drones on for chapter after chapter, each one providing yet another example of her thesis, the _____ of which can be found in précis form in the tome's first few pages, and which is recapitulated from that point on.

    - [A] gist
    - [B] adage
    - [C] pith
    - [D] stub
    - [E] nimbus
    - [F] aphorism

Chapter 3: **Text Completion and Sentence Equivalence**

48. In order to ascertain the efficacy of the new exam vis-à-vis the old one, it will be necessary not only to collect, but also to _____ detailed score reports of test-takers from both groups, as only by studying the differences and similarities in results can proper inferences be drawn.

    A aggregate
    B deduce
    C collate
    D juxtapose
    E agglomerate
    F glean

49. In World War I, trenches were dug so that the soldiers could avoid the near constant _____ from the other side of the line of battle, but not even a trench could protect a battalion from grenades or aerial bombardment.

    A volleys
    B provocations
    C fervency
    D imprecations
    E goading
    F salvos

50. Cary Grant's reputation as a _____ ladies man extended beyond the silver screen to his real life, where he was known to never let a woman pull out her own chair, in keeping with the custom of gentlemen at that time.

    A consummate
    B genteel
    C debonair
    D waggish
    E courtly
    F cosmopolitan

51. Focusing primarily on self-awareness, empathy, and honest self-expression, the communication process known as "nonviolent communication" states that the attempt to find parity in a relationship is a fallacious principle, as any notion of fairness is entirely _____.

    A subjective
    B introverted
    C pragmatic
    D utilitarian
    E illicit
    F personal

Unit One: **Words and Sentences**

52. Education has become a kind of albatross in American politics, in that a speech with any hint of _____ is actually more pernicious to a politician's reputation than one with numerous signs of ignorance, or even outright stupidity.

    A bromide
    B erudition
    C patrimony
    D condescension
    E cerebrality
    F bloviation

53. Laurent Cantet's *Time Out* tells the true story of a man so obsessed with retaining the _____ of plenitude after he is discharged from his employment that he doesn't even tell his wife and his kids about his termination.

    A corollaries
    B paradigms
    C semblance
    D prepossessions
    E veneer
    F consequences

54. What people fail to remember about Don Juan is that his astronomical number of amatory adventures were due more to his _____ approach to seduction than to any surfeit of charisma or skillfulness.

    A sumptuous
    B lurid
    C covert
    D indiscriminate
    E blanket
    F hedonistic

55. Even the most far-reaching campaign finance reform proposals will fail to _____ the influence of money, which doesn't just buy speedboats and golf weekends in the Bahamas, but directly relates to a politician's capacity to run for office.

    A quash
    B graft
    C pander
    D check
    E importune
    F indemnify

88

Chapter 3: Text Completion and Sentence Equivalence

56. In their landmark study of Victorian literature's relationship to feminism, Gilbert and Gubar _____ the many ways in which 19th-century women writers created characters that fit into archetypes of "angel" and "monster."

    A delineate
    B interpolate
    C debunk
    D limn
    E explode
    F castigate

57. While it's inarguably prejudiced to imply that there is some kind of innate _____ in certain countries, it's more reasonable to say that certain cultures are more willing to prioritize relaxation and a sense of moderation between work and play.

    A obtundity
    B enfeeblement
    C enervation
    D indolence
    E seemliness
    F lethargy

58. Autodidacts may argue that the enforced lucubration of a standard education is _____ , but while some people are able to learn without outside guidance and strictures, most people learn better when accountable to others.

    A slack
    B prudent
    C lax
    D extraneous
    E unnecessary
    F sagacious

59. The best of Sigur Ros's music evokes _____ landscape, as if the music had transported one to some twilit avenue in a long since abandoned city.

    A a dusky
    B an urban
    C a crepuscular
    D a precipitous
    E an avuncular
    F a civic

Unit One: **Words and Sentences**

60. Some historians argue that at least in so far as the broad strokes are concerned, cataclysmic events such as the Great Depression are _____ , due to what some have termed "the inertia of history."

   | A | ineluctable
   | B | incontrovertible
   | C | interminable
   | D | inviolate
   | E | inexorable
   | F | ineffable

Chapter 3: **Text Completion and Sentence Equivalence**

Answers and Explanations

Vocabulary Challenge

1. tortuous (*adj.*): winding; containing numerous twists, turns, or bends

2. recondite (*adj.*): related to or something abstruse or little understood

3. embellish (*v*): to enhance by adding details, often fanciful or invented

4. paragon (*n*): a model of excellence or virtue

5. satiate (*v*): to satisfy fully; or, to satisfy overmuch or to excess

6. augment (*adj.*): to enlarge, make greater, more intense, or more numerous

Solutions: Problem Set (Text Completion)

1. defunct: The blank in the sentence is describing the show *Doctor Who*, and the immediate proof offered is that the show stagnated and was canceled in 1989, so a good prediction would be dead or over.

A *lackluster* (dull) show might be canceled, but it doesn't make sense that *Doctor Who* appeared to be dull *after* it was canceled. A canceled show is unlikely to appear in a positive light, such as *ascendant* (upwardly moving) or *unflagging* (not tiring; steady and unrelenting). *Sated* (fully satisfied, maybe too much) wouldn't be used to describe a television show.

2. Ranting: The blank will be filled by an action ("pastime") undertaken "against China's record on environmental protection." The second part of the sentence, which is connected to the first by the straight-ahead marker "especially," describes the people participating in the mystery pastime: "those already inclined to invective." "Invective" means "harsh criticism," so the word that goes in the blank must be something to do with criticism.

Inveigling (winning over by flattery) doesn't fit, but a similar word *inveighing* (speaking with hostility) would have fit. This is a vocab trap. *Speculating* (guessing at) is too neutral, and *lauding* (praising) is too positive. *Needling* (teasing or provoking) is close, but would likely be done to someone or to some group—not "against China's record." Plus, *ranting* is a better match with "invective."

3. vassals: The queen's brothers "were appointed something to her spouse," the king. The word for the blank will be a noun; in such cases, part of the sentence will usually give a definition for that noun. The second part of the sentence states that the brothers received "the protection of King Magnus Eriksson in exchange for their homage (publicly expressed respect) and fealty (loyalty)." Look for an answer that reflects this exchange.

Protégés are like apprentices; *vanguards* are leaders of movement in a certain direction, including militarily; *precursors* are forerunners, people who come before others; and *partisans* are dedicated (and perhaps biased) supporters. Several of these are roles that a King or Queen might appoint, but they don't match the exchange of protection for loyalty. *Vassal* (someone who earns something, but has obligations to a leader) fits the exchange aptly.

4. degeneration: The blank appears in the first part of the sentence and is connected to something "intellectual." The first part of the sentence offers no hints as to what word would work, so the proof must be in Postman's quote. Look there for content clues that relate to something intellectual. Only the talk about books is salient to intellectual concerns, and more specifically, a society in which no one wants to read books anymore is suggestive of an intellectual weakening or decline.

Pondering (thoughtful consideration) and *cerebration* (thinking about something) are near-synonyms to each other and are too positive in tone, and thus the opposite of what the blank requires. They're also theme traps. *Mulishness* (unreasonable stubbornness) is theoretically a reason someone wouldn't want to read a book, but stubbornness isn't alluded to specifically in the sentence. *Banishment* (condemnation to exile) is unrelated to the actual proof in the sentence.

5. benefits: Take care unpacking the sentence. The main reversal marker here is "but," meaning the two parts of the sentence contradict each other. However, the second part of the sentence also contains more subtle vocabulary reversal markers: "failed" and "obviate." Start concrete: The treatment causes "damage to auxiliary structures." If the doctor had discussed some way of "obviating damage" (that is, preventing damage), it would have been a good thing, but the doctor "failed to discuss" that—which is a bad thing. Since the "but" makes the two parts of the sentence opposites, the doctor must have gone "into great detail about supposed good things about the treatment."

Diagnosis (determination of disease) and *prognosis* (forecast of medical outcome; chances of recovery) both relate to the medical theme, but neither fits in the blank, as they aren't specifically positive things. *Mien* (appearance, bearing) is unrelated. *Costs* is the opposite of the blank, as the blank should discuss the positive aspects of the treatment.

6. conflagration: The blank is presented as a "full-blown" outcome of the ill-advised combination of "dry shrub" and "an errant spark." The most sensible prediction would be fire, particularly a big fire or a wildfire.

A *wasteland* might be what's left of the landscape after the *conflagration* sweeps through it, but it's not something that would be "touched off" directly by a spark. Similarly, a *renewal* of the landscape might follow in the years after the fire, but it won't be the immediate consequence of an errant spark. A *scintilla* is itself a spark, though it's almost exclusively used in a figurative way (for instance, *a scintilla of inspiration*)—not a good fit for the blank. *Emergency* is probably the toughest to eliminate. A situation in which a giant fire erupts is almost by definition an emergency. However, it's not a perfect fit. As discussed above, the content clues more strongly suggest a fire, and in one-blank Text Completions, the GRE is almost certain to give you a word that's apt to the content clues. If you didn't know the meaning of *conflagration* (a large and destructive fire), it could be especially hard to pass *emergency* up—and indeed, one of the hardest things you'll have to do in TC is pick a word you don't really know instead of a word you *do* know but that doesn't quite fit.

7. credible: The blank describes an "announcement," and it's something that would be "a relief" to shareholders. Whatever goes into the blank must be something good. The rest of the sentence provides opportunities to predict something more specific. It mentions that shareholders have "doubts" about the announcement and that those doubts are based on "prevarications" (lies) that have been common under the CEO's management. Therefore, a good prediction for the blank would be truthful.

Libelous (which deals with printed lies) is the opposite of what the blank demands. *Nullified* (invalidated or voided) and *forestalled* (prevented or delayed) don't fit the truth/lying theme in the sentence, and *unverified* (unconfirmed) would likely only add to the shareholders' doubts.

8. altruistic: The missing word describes the motives that a defendant acted on, and it's part of a larger *whether… or…* structure, which generally functions as a reversal marker. The prosecution claims that the defendant acted "to protect himself and his profits," and the judge is choosing between this explanation *or* a contrary explanation. The word in the blank should offer that contrary explanation, so a good prediction would be not self-interested.

You can stretch *hidden* into an answer for the blank, especially since "hidden motives" makes sense in the context of a courtroom. But this doesn't contradict the prosecution's characterization of the defendant's motives, at least not nearly as directly as *altruistic* (unselfish, giving). *Pathological* (related to physical or mental disease) introduces a theme of illness that's not mentioned in the sentence. *Lucrative* (producing large profit) has proof in the sentence ("his profits"), but it's the opposite of the word needed. *Violent* is a theme trap relating to a trial, but there is no evidence of violent action.

9. feebleness: You know that Burma was being mismanaged, so look for the word in the blank to be something bad. "A far cry" serves as a reversal marker, revealing that the missing word and "isolation" are contrasted with "power and influence." Just as isolation and influence are (somewhat) counterpoints, you can expect the blank to be a counterpoint to power: something like not power or weakness.

Monotony (lack of variety, tedious repetition) is negative, but no proof in the sentence supports this meaning. *Opulence* (wealth, abundance) is opposite of the desired meaning. Both *nonchalance* (casual lack of concern) and *recriminations* (counteraccusations) don't make sense following *economic*.

10. autonomy: What would an authoritarian government threaten with "curfews and roadblocks"? Most likely, something like free movement.

Belligerence (aggressiveness) might describe these citizens' behavior, but it does not describe something that is "threatened" that they might lose. Likewise, *insolence* (rude and disrespectful behavior) does not work in the blank. The remaining choices, *epitome* (a perfect example of something) and *recidivism* (tendency to relapse to previous behavior, often criminal), are not indicated by clues in the sentence.

11. vaunt: "Hubristic" means "arrogant"—a hubristic person would never decline an opportunity for bragging about his accomplishments.

Flout (blatantly disregard) is closer to the opposite of the prediction, but its similarity to *flaunt* makes this a potential vocabulary trap. *Augment* (make or become greater in size) is not quite right, as a hubristic would be inclined to brag about their accomplishments more, but may not necessarily have more or better accomplishments. *Dictate* can be stretched to sort of fit, but it's usually used in a more technical context. *Downplay* accomplishments is directly opposite of what a hubristic person would do. *Vaunt*, meaning to boast or praise, fits perfectly.

12. patois: Since the negotiators find the negotiator "incomprehensible," there must be something in the negotiator's speech that is confusing them. The proof in the sentence pertains to the dialect that the delegation employed: "formal Queen's English." Therefore, the word in the blank should meet this comparison head-on, making dialect a good prediction.

The Royal visitors would not find any of the other characteristics—*fortitude* (courage, resilience), *equanimity* (composure, mental calmness), *diffidence* (hesitance or resistance to speak), *consternation* (amazement or dismay that leads to confusion)—"incomprehensible," nor do any of these relate to the clue about styles of speech. *Patois* (the dialect of a region's common people) fits the evidence well.

13. diversions: The blank describes how the upper class sees things "such as fox hunting and cricket." There's also another piece of proof later in the comparison to "more egalitarian amusements." The blank must mean something like amusements.

Vocations and *professions* both contradict the idea of these activities as "amusements." Fox hunting and cricket are not examples of *canards*, which are unfounded rumors or stories, or of *stereotypes*. *Stereotypes* is, however, a theme trap; while fox hunting and cricket may be seen as stereotypical activities of the upper class, they are not themselves *stereotypes*.

14. pith: A "probing questioner" probably wants to get to the bottom of things. The semi-colon and "always" serve as straight-ahead direction markers. Professor Honeycutt is looking for the <u>central point</u> of a matter.

Emotions certainly might be revealed under probing questioning, but they also might not, depending on the questions. *Periphery* (the outside edges) is the opposite of where a probing questioner hopes to arrive. *Examination* and *academics* are traps that go with the scholastic theme, but they aren't supported by the sentence. *Pith* (the essence of something) is exactly what a probing questioner would likely be looking for—at the very least, it is more likely that Professor Honeycutt is seeking *pith* generally than *emotions* specifically.

15. truculence: The blank is a word describing how Europe viewed the Prussians after they "were able to turn the aggression outward." As such, <u>aggression</u> makes sense as a prediction for the blank.

Ennui (listlessness arising from boredom) is nearly the opposite of aggression. *Covetousness* (envious desire to possess something) could work if you imagine that the purpose of the Prussians' aggression is to acquire the lands and property around them, but there is no such evidence. An answer for which you have to make extra context assumptions is a story trap. *Extravagance* and *opulence* (both mean lavishness) are too close in meaning to each other to be correct, and they have nothing to do with "aggression." *Truculence*, which is similar to belligerence, fits nicely.

16. culling: The discussion is about doing something to "some members of a species…to prevent the devastating effects of overpopulation." The word should oppose "overpopulation," so something like <u>removing</u> or <u>getting rid of</u> would work in the blank. Such a grim prospect would definitely "clash" with the idea outlined in the first part of the sentence.

Protecting and *reintroducing* are both theme traps (due to their association with species) and opposite traps—they do not clash with the idea of fair treatment of sentient beings. *Depleting* can apply to a resource, but not to individual "members." *Murdering* and *culling* are both types of killing, but *culling* is the better option since it is a technical term for killing individual members to avoid overpopulation. (Bonus: If you understand this sentence, you've got a handle on one of the key debates among environmentalists.)

17. mendicant: The character "renounced the advantages of his noble birth," with "renouncing" serving as a reversal marker. This part of the sentence reveals that the blank should oppose those advantages. In the second part of the sentence, "this reliance" indicates a direct callback to something mentioned earlier in the sentence. Because it appears as part of the phrase "this reliance on alms" (which is to say a reliance on charity), there's sufficient proof to predict a word like <u>beggar</u> for the blank. A *mendicant* is indeed a beggar; even better, it often carries a religious connotation, a particularly good fit for something undertaken by a "religious order."

The other choices all introduce meanings that the rest of the sentence doesn't suggest. Both *abettor* (a person who supports an action, typically wrongdoing) and *malefactor* (evildoer) introduce the unsupported idea that the character was immoral in some way. *Rube* (unsophisticated or naïve person) only works if certain extra assumptions are made, and there are no clues suggesting an *anachronism* (person or object out of its proper time).

18. an unnecessary: The blank is connected to "the serial comma" and its relationship to a "sentence structure." The sentence does start with a minor clue ("crotchet"); however, you'd be forgiven if that word is totally unfamiliar to you. Luckily, there are more clues to be found in the second part of the sentence, which starts by indicating a reversal ("obviously, they're wrong") and goes on to describe the serial comma as "critical." The blank should therefore be something like <u>not critical</u>.

Among the incorrect answers, *a proper* and *an inspired* are both too positive for the blank. *A misunderstood* doesn't fully oppose the "critical" role the author assigns to serial commas. *A dogmatic* (marked by absolute adherence to rules or principles) likewise has no basis in the proof. (By the way, did you look up "crotchet"? Remember to add any unfamiliar words you encounter to your vocabulary list.)

19. proximity: The reversal marker "In contrast to" at the beginning of the sentence indicates that the two parts of the sentence will contradict. The main contrast drawn is between neighborly individuals interacting "on a familiar basis" in America and the fact that there's no guarantee of "intimacy (or even amity)" in England. This contrast only works if the description in the last part of the sentence is also about "neighborly relations," and since "residential" immediately precedes the blank, the word in the blank must be something like closeness to properly mirror "neighborly relations." *Proximity* is the only answer that comes close. (Pun 100% intended.)

The other answer choices all deal with comfort or friendliness, and their association with "neighborly" and "amity" makes them theme traps: *commodiousness* (spaciousness), *amiability* (friendliness), *reciprocity* (relationship with mutual exchange of favors or benefits), and *cordiality* (amity). Amiability and cordiality in particular are the opposite of the correct fill-in, since the passage states that amity is "not necessarily implied," meaning it is potentially not present at all.

20. saunter: The blank describes something dangerous to do "through the city," and it's later contrasted with "only essential errands" and "with haste." It certainly sounds dangerous to conduct non-essential errands…but a more likely prediction is to move without haste.

All five of the answer choices describe movements or related activities, but *saunter*, to stroll without haste, offers the best fit for the clues. Both *bop* (move or travel energetically) and *sidle* (walk timidly or sideways) carry a strange spin and don't effectively contrast "haste." *Circumambulate* means "walk all the way around," which would entail avoiding the city rather than going "through" it. *Reconnoiter* (make a military observation of a place) carries a militaristic spin that makes it a good theme trap but doesn't fit the evidence about doing this action "unnecessarily," or the comparison to errands.

Solutions: Problem Set (Sentence Equivalence)

1. didactic; moralistic: The children's story was "seemingly" simple—which means it was not actually simple. Instead, the story took some kind of "turn"—meaning that it changed in some way—and admonished "readers to always be honest." That is, it took a turn by talking about morals or prescribing correct behavior. A good prediction would be moralistic, and *didactic*, which means intended to teach, is a near enough synonym to work.

Magnanimous (generous) and *beneficent* (good, or doing good) are an incorrect pair. *Garrulous* (overly talkative, wordy) and *futile* (ineffective, useless) have no relationship to each other or the sentence.

2. mitigate; forestall: That "floodwaters had already breached the library's walls" sounds very bad—the water is already inside. The direction marker "but" tells you that the sentence is going to change direction, and indeed, the volunteers are "hopeful." So you're looking for something good in the blank—although it doesn't seem like they're going to cure the problem entirely. A good fill-in would be something like limit.

Exacerbate (make more severe, aggravate), *abase* (reduce in prestige, humiliate), *bolster* (support, boost), and *flummox* (confuse) do not contain any pairs. *Exacerbate* would also constitute an opposite trap, since the goal is to improve the flooding problem. *Mitigate* (to make less severe) and *forestall* (to prevent) are not precise synonyms, but they both fit the blank and create equivalent narratives of the volunteers' work.

Unit One: **Words and Sentences**

3. divisive; combative: The first part of the sentence gives you the concrete truth that the candidate is interested in cooperation, but the second part of the sentence is full of direction markers: "yet," "nevertheless," "surprised," "indeed," and "less." A case with this many markers can be difficult to untangle, but luckily the "indeed" alone offers a lot of help. As part of the phrase "she indeed turned out to be," "indeed" confirms that what was expected actually happened: The candidate *did* cooperate with others. Still, watch out for the direction marker "less" just before the blank. If the candidate is indeed cooperative, the thing she would be *less of* is uncooperative.

Irate and *infuriated,* both of which mean angry, are an incorrect pair and together represent a story trap—an angry person is probably less willing to cooperate, but the fit isn't as direct as *divisive* and *combative,* both of which directly imply a difficulty working with others. *Impulsive* (moved or swayed by emotional or involuntary urges) and *wily* (crafty or cunning) have no relationship.

4. pacify; mollify: This sentence provides the clues that when Sven "got angry," returning him "to his normal demeanor" was "almost impossible." His normal demeanor must be something like *not angry*, so you're looking for something like the verb calm in the blank.

Condemn (censure; sentence), *judge* (form an opinion about), *incense* (infuriate), and *influence* (determine or guide) do not contain any strong pairs. Even if you do consider *condemn* and *judge* a close enough pair, there's no reason to believe that judging Sven would "return him to his normal demeanor."

5. undergird; buttress: The blank is a verb that denoting the effect that additional data will have on the student's findings. Those results "were promising" (but "surprising," indicating some uncertainty about the apparent conclusion). The semicolon is a straight-ahead direction marker. Thus, her next step would likely be to verify or corroborate the findings.

Gainsay (deny or prove false) and *undermine* (weaken or subvert secretly) are an opposite trap. *Eschew* (shun, avoid, or abstain from) and *lecture* (speak at length) are unrelated to each other or to the sentence (though *lecture* is a theme trap). *Undergird* and *buttress* both mean something like "to support," so they fit the sentence nicely.

6. espouses; professes: This sentence originally posits that there is "no fundamental difference" between two things, but the overall point is that the two things might appear different on the surface. The "between . . . and . . ." structure contrasts the first person who speaks quietly to a friend, and the second person who "spews" on television. They're both focused on different ways of communicating the same thing, so a good prediction would be communicates.

Denies and *reneges* (renounces or denies) are an incorrect pair. *Eschews* is also pretty close to that pair. *Substantiates* (to support or verify) goes beyond simple communication and also fails to fit the context (in that *substantiation* is something more apt to the courtroom than to a quiet conversation between friends).

7. stimulus; impetus: Prior to 1957, Rachel Carson was already concerned about "aerial pesticide spraying" and had begun researching it, but the lawsuit caused her "to begin the writing" of her book. A good fill-in would therefore be cause.

Atrocity (extremely wicked or cruel act) and *catastrophe* (disaster) have similar spins, but they don't match the prediction and are not really a pair—an *atrocity* usually has to be perpetrated by another person, but a *catastrophe* generally isn't. *Climate* (the general weather conditions in an area over a long period) and *conspiracy* (a secret plan by two or more people to do something unlawful) have no relationship, though *climate* represents a theme trap.

Chapter 3: **Text Completion and Sentence Equivalence**

8. subtle; nuanced: The blank pertains to a "worldview," and the concrete truth in this sentence is that the commentator's worldview makes it "easy" to split people into good and bad categories. This is a very simplistic take on the world. Someone with a more complex worldview would be unlikely to break things down so simplistically.

Belligerent (aggressive), *philosophical* (devoted to the study of knowledge), *aberrant* (atypical), and *peaceful* (tranquil) have no relationship.

9. opacity; inscrutability: Joyce's book is described as "stream-of-consciousness," with "convoluted puns and obscure allusions." The adjectives "convoluted" and "obscure" are the most important parts of this sentence. They tell you that the novel is likely hard to understand. The final bit of proof—that the novel's reputation is "deserved"—tells you that the blank will agree with the preceding characterization. A good prediction would be difficulty or incomprehensibility.

The novel is not necessarily *meaningless*, its meaning is simply hard to decipher. Similarly the novel is not necessarily *unique*—even if this style is unusual, there may be others like it. The novel may well be *elaborate* (complex and intricate) or *informal* (relaxed in style), but neither word has a strong pair. *Opacity* (not transparent) and *inscrutability* (difficult to understand) match each other well when applied to a novel, and both fit the prediction.

10. unstable; precarious: The situation in Europe is described as something enough that even a small incident might lead to a catastrophe. This means that everything is on the brink of disaster. You could fill in the blank with something like shaky.

Drab (dull, colorless, or cheerless), *illegitimate* (not authorized by the law), *unsafe* (not safe; dangerous), and *churlish* (uncivil, boorish, or vulgar) all have the correct negative tone, but none have strong pairs.

11. bolstered; fortified: All you need to notice is the contrast between "warming" and "record low temperatures," as well as the signal word "While." Record low temperatures would not directly help an argument about global warming, so a good fill-in would be helped.

Subverted (undermined, in terms of power or authority), and *undercut* (weakened) form a pair, but they constitute an opposite trap. *Defined* (described exactly) and *supplanted* (replaced, substituted for) have no close relationship to each other.

12. serious; sober: The debate coach values "gravitas" (seriousness) and argues that "quips" (witty remarks) and "gibes" (taunts) don't belong in a certain kind of argument. *Serious* and *sober* is the only pair that works.

Polite could work, but it has no pair and it doesn't follow as well from "gravitas." *Shallow*, *competitive*, and *cantankerous* (disagreeable or difficult to deal with) have no relationship, though *competitive* constitutes a theme trap due to its connection to debate.

13. filched; poached: The most important word here is the adjective "similar." If both *South Park* and *College Humor* created a similar spoof, then one of them may have derived the sketch from the other. The fact that something was "discovered" about the *South Park* writers implies that they're the ones responsible, and that there may have been some wrongdoing. Copied would be a good prediction.

Amalgamated and *combined* are an incorrect pair. *Indulged* (allowed oneself to enjoy) and *assumed* (supposed without proof) have no relationship. *Assumed* can mean "took or began to have (power or responsibility)" or even "took on or adopted (an appearance, manner, or identity)," but you wouldn't use *assume* in the context of taking any other kind of item, such as a comedy spoof. This is a close but not close enough trap. *Filched*

Unit One: **Words and Sentences**

and *poached* both mean "stolen," which is a bit more severe than the prediction of copied but nonetheless fits the sentence effectively.

14. rejection; renunciation: Abstract Expressionism is described as "characterized by geometric shapes and swaths of color." Clearly, this is very different from "realist painting." A good fill-in would thus be something like *repudiation*, which means a rejection or a refusal to deal with something.

Memento (an object serving as a reminder) and *commemoration* (a service or celebration serving to remember a person or event) are an incorrect (and imperfect) pair. *Manifestation* (the action or fact of showing an abstract idea; symptom or sign) and *vindication* (exoneration, acquittal) have no relationship, and they indicate a similarity between Abstract Expressionism and realist painting, rather than a contrast.

15. penetrate; infiltrate: You are told that Nathan Hale was a spy working for the United States and that he was captured by the British. That means he must have been involved in some kind of espionage in "British-controlled" New York. A good fill-in would be sneak into or possibly observe.

Thwart (prevent someone from accomplishing something) and *conquer* (take control of by military force) are vaguely related, but are not quite a pair. *Conquer* is also a theme trap. *Permeate* (spread throughout; pervade) and *research* have no relationship to each other, though they're both individually close but not close enough traps. *Research* in particular is something Hale may have been doing, but *penetrate* and *infiltrate* both mean something like "to force into something." Their similarity makes them the correct pair.

16. insinuation; innuendo: The phrase "more by … than …" implies a contrast between the two elements. The second element here is "straightforward vulgarity," so look for a word that means non-straightforward language or non-vulgar language. *Insinuation* and *innuendo* both match the prediction.

Conversation (an informal verbal exchange) and *rapport* (a harmonious relationship) are not quite a pair. *Blatancy* (obviousness) and *illusion* (something that looks or seems different from what it is) are almost opposites.

17. dormant; quiescent: The blank is there to describe "inflation" in a way that contrasts the notion that inflation is entirely "dead." You're told that in the future, "the purchasing power of the dollar is likely to fall," a literal description of inflation. So while inflation isn't dead, the sentence avers that it may come back at any time. A good fill-in would be something like dormant (there aren't a lot of simple words that get across this meaning).

Paralyzed (unable to move or act) and *immobile* do form a pair, but they also represent a close but not close enough trap: While they both indicate a sort of inactivity, they don't capture the idea that inflation could return "as the economy turns around." *Itinerant* (traveling from place to place) and *problematic* (presenting a difficulty) have no relationship. *Dormant* and *quiescent* both correctly imply inflation is in a state of rest but might someday awaken.

18. barbaric; primitive: It's a concrete truth that boxers "punch each other in the face," which according to the sentence isn't "civilized." If they need to "counter" this civilized tendency, then they must access a part of themselves that is not civilized.

Seething and *irate* are an incorrect pair, both meaning "angry," but they are a story trap—if you convince yourself that angry people find it easier to punch each other in the face, these could kind of work. But compared to the correct answers, they're not as perfect a counterpoint to "civilized." *Insidious* (seductive but harmful; treacherous, deceitful) and *nefarious* (wicked or criminal) are likewise an incorrect story-trap pair.

19. arduous; taxing: The concrete truth in this sentence is that people "underestimate the difficulty of being entirely self-motivated," and the reversal marker "but" means that this concrete truth is contradicted in the first part of the sentence. People must assume that creative work is relatively easy, but given the reversal marker "less" just before the blank, a good fill-in would be difficult.

Serious and *grave* are an incorrect (albeit tempting) pair. The proof in the sentence is not about the seriousness of creative work but rather about its difficulty. *Inventive* and *collaborative* are words that you might associate with creativity, but they are not a pair and again do not fit the contrast related to difficulty.

20. vehement; heated: The concrete truth is that "politicians demonize teachers unions" and others are jumping "into the fray." Both "demonize" and "fray" characterize the debate as intense and antagonistic, both of which could serve as good predictions (though the correct answers are closer in meaning to the former.)

Overt (done openly) and *unavoidable* (impossible to ignore) are not quite a pair and aren't supported by the sentence. *Problematic* and *tired* have no relationship, so even if *problematic* might work for the sentence, it can't be chosen. *Vehement* and *heated*, both meaning something like "passionate and forceful" do form a strong pair in addition to fitting the sentence.

21. marriage; commingling: This sentence begins with the marker "While" before describing religions that "insist on the primacy of their particular deity." "Syncretism" on the other hand relates to "multiple religious beliefs," and attempts to "reconcile even opposing principles and practices." Because of that concrete truth about syncretism and the reversal marker at the opening, there's good reason to believe that syncretism is in favor of multiple religious beliefs. The prediction should be something like reconciliation or mixing.

Division and *schism*, which often refers to a division within something like a religious organization, are an opposite trap. *Exclusion* (deliberate act of omission) and *transgression* (act that violates a rule or duty) have no relationship. *Schism* and *transgression* are also individual theme traps due to their religious connotations.

22. consummate; complete: The blank is about the ambassador's power. You have a straight-ahead marker ("hence") and an important clue is that, due to this power, she is performing some of her functions "unilaterally." A good prediction would be something like unilateral or total.

Tyrannical and *dictatorial* are a pair that goes too far, introducing a negative spin (exercising total power in a cruel or unjust way) that isn't supported by any proof in the sentence. *Tertiary* (third-ranking) and *enigmatic* (mysterious) have no relationship.

23. declaim; trumpet: The blank focuses on what politicians do with "their views to the world." There is not much direct evidence about what this action might be, but a reasonable prediction might be announce or spread. The fact that their views are later characterized as "sordid" and "partisan"—the kinds of views one would think *shouldn't* be broadcast to the world—but connected to the rest of the sentence with the reversal marker "no matter" is further confirmation that indeed the politicians are somehow putting these ideas out into the world.

Invoke (reference something in support of an argument) and *adduce* (reference something as evidence) are an incorrect pair. *Disparage* (belittle or discredit) and *parrot* (repeat mindlessly) have no relationship. *Declaim* and *trumpet* both aptly mean something like "to speak confidently and proudly."

24. colloquium; symposium: The concrete truth in this sentence is that the organization, which has "many scattered chapters," has somehow acquired a "haphazard and often chaotic set of bylaws and regulations." Thus, it wants to "bring leadership together" in order to reconcile all these rules. A good prediction would be meeting or conference.

Unit One: Words and Sentences

Intervention and *mediation* are a close but incorrect pair—while both might help, they don't reflect the proof ("bring leadership together") as well as *colloquium* and *symposium*. *Introduction* and *acclamation* (loud demonstration of approval or welcome) have no relationship.

25. cloistered; sheltered: The marker "Though" tells you that the first part of the sentence is going to be contradicted by the second part. Be careful as you unpack the rest of the first part, though, as it's replete with reversal markers. The situation that seems implausible is becoming a great writer without life experience, but the second part of the sentence must contradict this, so the "many famous authors" in question should in fact have a lack of life experience. It may be difficult to put this concept into one word, but "a not-full-of-experience existence" is a perfectly fine made-up prediction.

Enigmatic and *cryptic* (having hidden meaning; mysterious) are an incorrect pair. *Idiosyncratic* (unique to an individual; eccentric, quirky) and *hermetic* (completely sealed) have no relationship. Careful with *hermetic*, though. It's both a vocabulary trap due to its similarity to *hermitic* (which might have worked for the blank) and a close but not close enough trap due to its inappropriateness to the context (it's usually used for containers). *Cloistered* (kept away from the outside world) and *sheltered* (kept *safe* from the outside world) both correctly imply that these authors would not have had many worldly experiences.

26. nonchalance; indifference: In this sentence, the key is the word "belied," which functions as a kind of reversal marker. *Belie* means "to misrepresent or disguise," suggesting that whatever goes in the blank should contrast the underlying concrete truth: She feels a "deep sense of responsibility." A good fill-in for the blank would be not caring.

Mirth and *felicity* are a trap pair, both meaning something like "happiness" and thus contradicting "suffering." However, the blank must relate to the subject of the sentence ("her deep sense of responsibility"), as that is what's "belied" by her outward appearance. *Concern* and *sagacity* (keen judgment) have no relationship, and *concern* is the opposite of the prediction.

27. xenophobic; bigoted: The blank here is defined by the second half of the sentence. The "patriotism" that the blank describes is defined as "the elevation of one country to the rank of preeminent on Earth," a process that the author claims requires the "demonization of other people." The word "ineluctably," meaning "inescapably," serves as a straight-ahead marker, so the blank should reflect this demonization. A good fill-in would be prejudiced.

Minatory and *truculent* are not quite a pair (the former means "threatening," while the latter means "aggressively defiant"), and even if you take them as a pair they don't quite fit, as the sentence does not describe particular actions taken against "other people," more so the opinions of those people. *Unethical* and *nationalistic* both arguably fit the sentence, but neither has a pair word as strong as the pair *xenophobic* and *bigoted*, both of which specifically relate to prejudiced opinions against groups of people.

28. forbearance; temperance: It's important to know the word "debauchery" (meaning "excessive indulgence in sensual pleasures") to solve this question. The sentence describes a husband-to-be who will *not* be engaging in debauchery at the bachelor party, as debauchery is implicitly contradictory to "self-restraint." So you need a word that describes someone who exhibits some amount of restraint.

Fiat (authoritative decree) and *autonomy* (the right to self-government; independence) are not quite a pair and would be incorrect anyway. *Gentility* (the state of belonging to polite society; refinement of manner) and *tenacity* (the quality of being persistent or stubborn) have no relationship.

29. vilifying; maligning: The rally here is described as discussing politics "civilly, without" doing the thing in the blank. Since "without" functions as a reversal marker and the blank is connected to "those on the other side of the fence," a good recycled prediction for the blank would be being uncivil to.

Lampooning and *caricaturing* make an incorrect pair, both meaning "mocking or ridiculing," The sentence mentions that the rally was "humorous." This means that *lampooning* and *caricaturing*, both of which imply a kind of humorous teasing, would be welcome at the rally, so not a great fit for the blank. They're also not particularly uncivil. *Bespeaking* (suggesting; ordering or reserving something in advance) and *eulogizing* (to praise highly, especially at a memorial service) have no relationship, and the latter is the opposite of what you want here.

30. sanctioned; endorsed: The blank focuses on how the military has handled "corporal punishment," a phrase meaning punishment involving physical force. The first part of the sentence tells you that such punishments are "occasionally used in practice," but the reversal marker "though" indicates that the blank will somehow contradict this. The second half of this sentence contains the concrete truth that "reports of abuse" (a reference to corporal punishment) receive an "overwhelmingly negative popular response." This means that despite using them on occasion, the military would be unlikely to condone or formally adopt these forms of abuse.

Upbraided and *rebuked* (both meaning criticized or scolded) form an incorrect pair—if the military has criticized "few" forms of corporal punishment, it might well *approve* of such punishment, a bad fit for the meaning of the sentence. These choices also constitute a theme trap due to their relationship with "punishment." *Rejected*, similarly, implies that the military may actually be using many of these punishments. It's possible that few such punishments have been *considered* by the military, but this has no clear pair, while *sanctioned* and *endorsed* both mean something like "approved of publicly."

31. quagmire; morass: The first part of the sentence, which describes how the budget debate "progressed well" is very important: If you miss that, you might be tempted to choose the wrong words here. The part of the sentence with the blank, which starts with the reversal marker "but" and contains the negative content clues "descended" and "competing interests and claims," is describing a worsening situation. The negativity of that situation wouldn't be a good contrast for the *also* negative picture of "bitter squabbling" in the part of the sentence that immediately precedes the part with the blank. Instead, the part of the sentence with the blank must be contrasting the positivity of the first part of the sentence, meaning that the blank should be something contrary to "progressed well." A good prediction would be mess or muddle.

Feud and *quarrel* are an incorrect pair. While they correctly get across the negative spin you want for the blank, they don't address the idea of progressing badly. They constitute a theme trap for their similarity to "squabbling." *Covenant* and *accord* are an incorrect pair, both indicating an agreement. They are part of a red herring trap in that they both contrast the middle part of the sentence, a part that, as outlined above, has no bearing on what goes in the blank despite its proximity to the blank. *Quagmire* and *morass* both correctly mean something like "a complex and difficult situation."

32. crucial; requisite: This is a tough question, because the sentence gives you only "subtle" as a content clue. The blank should oppose it, but the opposite of "subtle" would be something like obvious, and there's no match for *obvious* among the answers. This is a good time to try Answer Choice Analysis.

Among the answers, there are three pairs:

- *frivolous* and *trifling* (having little value or importance)
- *superfluous* and *dispensable* (unnecessary)
- *crucial* and *requisite* (necessary)

Unit One: Words and Sentences

Consider each pair's meaning in the context of the sentence. Which offers the best contrast to the subtleness of "the difference between similes and metaphors"? Add in the fact that the blank describes how this difference is perceived by "the poet who takes his or her work seriously," and the choice becomes clearer. A serious poet would consider the difference between these two poetic devices important, even if its subtleness can make the difference hard to distinguish. Only **crucial** and **requisite** work. *Frivolous* and *trifling* both contrast "seriously," and *superfluous* and *dispensable* have no connection to any of the content clues in the sentence.

33. fallacious; specious: This sentence leans heavily on content clues, so it's important that you understand all of it. You are given two statements about economics. Start with the more concrete one: "Keynes states clearly that deficit spending must be done responsibly." Then come back to the first part of the sentence. If Keynesian economics is ascribed a belief that the limit on government debt "should be perpetually raised," a belief that contrasts what Keynes actually states, then it must be the product of faulty reasoning.

Indigenous (native to or naturally occurring in a region), *corrupt*, *venial* (forgivable or pardonable), and *axiomatic* (self-evident or unquestionable) have no relationship. In addition, *axiomatic* is the opposite of what is needed for the blank.

34. argot; jargon: This sentence is describing rebellion as the effect of a "communication gap." On one side of the communication gap is "an older generation's calcified language"; on the other side is "the protean something of the new generation." Given that the gap is laid out in the descriptors here ("older generation's" vs. "of the new generation" and "calcified" vs. "protean"), the blank should probably just be language.

Defiance and *insubordination* are an incorrect pair, both meaning something like "disobedience." *Prolixity* and *verbosity* are another incorrect pair. They constitute a theme trap, as both words mean "wordiness," which might superficially feel like a good fit for a sentence about communication.

35. grousing; carping: "Cantankerous" means "bad-tempered and argumentative." Because there is no reversal marker here, you simply need a word that means those things. A good fill-in for the blank would be arguing or complaining.

Imputing (attributing or blaming), *assaulting* (physically attacking), *convulsing* (suffering violent involuntary contraction of the muscles), and *imbibing* (drinking) have no relationship. *Grousing* and *carping* on the other hand are very close both to each other, and to our prediction of complaining.

36. fracas; altercation: In this sentence, you need to figure out what kind of thing would result in the police being called—likely, some kind of crime or fight. Only the latter has matches in the answer choices.

Discourse and *colloquy* are an incorrect pair, both meaning "conversation." *Battle* may be close to what you want, but it implies a certain level of (often military) organization among the two opposing sides that's inappropriate to the bar setting and would rarely be remedied by calling the police. *Mutiny* (open rebellion against authorities) is not related to the others.

37. eclectic; multifarious: In this sentence, the word "surprisingly" acts as a reversal marker, so the part of the sentence with the blank contrasts the part before the comma. The woman had a "sheltered upbringing" and a "limited breadth of experience," so the blank should be the opposite of that. A good fill-in would be varied or worldly.

Shallow and *facile* are an incorrect pair, in that both can mean "superficial." *Profound* has the right spin, but it isn't such a good counterpoint to "limited breadth" (it would be a better counterpoint to "limited depth"). *Callow* (immature or inexperienced) has no relationship with the other choices, and it incorrectly agrees with "limited breadth of experience." *Eclectic* (derived from a wide range of sources) and *multifarious* (of many types) both fit the prediction of varied.

38. rail; fulminate: The word "but" is a signal to reverse course here, taking you in the opposite direction of the "dispassionate" and "objective" nature initially used to define documentary filmmakers. A good fill-in would be speak out.

Advertise (draw attention to publicly in order to promote sales), *censure* (express strong disapproval of), *strain* (make a strenuous effort), and *aspirate* (pronounce a sound in the exhalation of breath) have no relationship to each other. Note that *censure* forms a false triple with *rail* and *fulminate*; it is incorrect largely because it's unidiomatic to say "censure against" something. "Rail against" and "fulminate against" both work, and both imply speaking out or protesting.

39. a piquant; a zesty: There are two important portions of this sentence to focus on. First, the word "praised" implies that the critic's review will be positive. Second, the way she's described as using "the language of food to describe films" implies that, if possible, the correct answers should also use the language of food. So you want two words that are positive and that are also preferably in food-language.

A spectacular, a *brilliant*, and *an astonishing* form a sort of triple, at least inasmuch as they're all very positive words. However, there's no need to figure out which one doesn't fit with the other two: The two food words (*piquant* and *zesty*) reflect more of the proof in the sentence and therefore are better choices. *Insipid* (bland, tasteless, or flavorless) is a food word, but its negative spin makes it an opposite trap.

40. bruises; contusions: In this sentence, a short list of possible injuries after a skydiving accident is described. Two of the items are "broken bones" and "a gash," which means your blank should be a physical injury different from those two. A good fill-in would be bruises.

Torpor (a state of physical inactivity; apathy, lethargy) and *finesse* (skillful or adroit handling) are not physical injuries, so they don't fit with the other two items on the list provided. *Trauma* (physical injury; shock following a disturbing event or injury) and *lesions* (wounds, ulcers, tumors, etc.) are both things that someone might experience after a skydiving accident, but neither has a synonym pair.

41. envoy; emissary: The person in question is serving as "official" something for Japan to another country, and is "called upon to answer questions about the Japanese government's position." This role sounds like an ambassador.

Tyro and *neophyte* are an incorrect pair, both meaning "beginner." *Ascetic* (self-denying; austere) and *libertine* (one who is debauched or without moral restraint) are not synonyms, though both have something to do with self-control, in opposite ways.

42. palliate; damp: The blank is about both the leadership and the "stridency of their rhetoric"—you need the relationship between those two things. "While" is a reversal marker. In the first part of the sentence, the protests are "aggressive" and "uncompromising." Thus, in the second part, they should be softer and more in favor of compromising. "Stridency" means harshness and is on the same side as "aggressive" and "uncompromising," so the group must have chosen to reduce the stridency.

Wane means "decrease" and is an attractive trap answer. However, *wane* is an intransitive verb—that is, something (such as the moon) *wanes* on its own; you can't *wane* an object. Therefore, the word's usage does not fit in this sentence. *Metamorphose* (change) could work, but it doesn't indicate the direction of the change (increase or decrease), which the blank needs to do in order to show that the leaders "wisely" chose to do something. *Gild* (cover in gold; give a deceitfully pleasing appearance to) and *succor* (aid, assist, or relieve) have no relationship to each other or to the sentence.

Unit One: **Words and Sentences**

43. stagnant; abeyant: The key bit of proof that you're looking for here is that "activists will be newly galvanized." Because of the reversal signal "but," you need a blank that means the opposite of "galvanized." A good fill-in word would be dormant (implying that the movement is quiet but could rise again).

Dogged (stubbornly determined) and *tenacious* form an opposite-trap pair. *Interminable* (endless) and *lissome* (flexible or easily bent) have no relationship. *Stagnant* and *abeyant* both mean something like "temporarily stopped."

44. meet; apposite: The first half of this sentence sets up the topic, but the important information is in the second half. There, you're introduced to the hypothetical "most ardent supporter" of corporal punishment who agrees with detractors on at least one thing, for which "evenhanded and thorough" is a content clue. A good prediction for the blank would be fair. *Meet* (in this case meaning suitable) and *apposite* (appropriate) mostly fit that prediction, but you'll probably have to use some process of elimination before fully signing off on them.

Clement and *merciful* both add a positive spin that wouldn't be adopted by "the most ardent supporter" of corporal punishment and the death penalty. *Delimited* (having limits established; bounded) and *tantamount* (equivalent; virtually the same as) are not related. *Tantamount* may remind you of the idea of the punishment fitting the crime, but the sentence would need to establish *what* the punishments are tantamount to.

45. chimerical; unachievable: The portion of this sentence after the blank tells you that "results are always colored by...personal proclivities and suppositions." Meanwhile, the blank is describing "the premise of impartiality." Since being "colored by personal proclivities" directly clashes with "impartiality," the fact that results are "always" colored by these things would make impartiality impossible.

Inane and *fatuous* are an incorrect pair, both meaning "silly." While the "premise of impartiality" may not be accurate, that doesn't make it silly—this pair is a spin trap. *Prejudicial* (detrimental) and *vexing* (irksome; irritating) have no relationship.

46. epicurean; gustatory: Everything in this sentence relates to food, whether it's the "texture and taste" or the "notion of what constitutes a meal." The type of "delights" referred to in the blank must relate to food. A good fill-in would be culinary.

Carnal (relating to physical, especially sexual, activities) and *voluptuous* (characterized by luxury or sensual pleasure) are an incorrect pair, relating to sensuality rather than specifically food. *Salubrious* (promoting health or well-being) and *terrestrial* (of, on, or relating to the Earth) have no relationship.

47. gist; pith: The verb "drone" has a very specific meaning, implying that someone is going on at length in a dull or boring way. The implication is that the point could be made more efficiently. This sentence then tells you that a "précis" (summary) containing the thesis can be found in "the tome's first few pages." A good prediction would be something like succinct summary or essence.

Adage (a traditional expression of a common observation) and *aphorism* (a pithy expression of a common truth) form a good pair, but the pair is not appropriate to the context (that is, you can't meaningfully talk about the *adage* or *aphorism* of a thesis). *Stub* (a short part left after a larger part was broken off) and *nimbus* (a circle of light) have no relationship.

48. collate; juxtapose: The final portion of this sentence describes "studying the differences and similarities" between two different things. "Vis-à-vis" likewise means "in relation to." Clearly you'll be doing some form of comparison between the old and new exam, so a good fill-in word would be compare.

Aggregate, *agglomerate*, and *glean* are an incorrect triple, all meaning "gather." While gathering the data together is required in order to make a comparison, the sentence already said "not only to collect." All of these words are just fancy versions of "collect," which you don't need to repeat—the blank calls for something beyond simple collection. *Deduce*, which means "to arrive at a conclusion logically," doesn't match any other choice. In addition, it doesn't quite fit the context: you can reason logically *about* the score reports, but you wouldn't reason the score reports themselves. *Juxtapose* (place next to each other to compare) and *collate* (to place in order or compare) are not quite synonyms but both correctly result in comparing the score reports.

49. volleys; salvos: Most of what you need to know in this sentence comes from the few words before the blank: "trenches were dug so that soldiers could avoid" something. What would you avoid in a trench? Perhaps <u>bullets</u>? This is backed up by the second part of the sentence, which compares the trenches' successful protection against the blank with their unsuccessful protection against "aerial bombardment." A prediction borrowed from the passage could be <u>non-aerial bombardment</u>.

Provocations and *goading* are an incorrect pair—the sentence is not discussing being taunted or provoked by the enemy. *Fervency* (fervor; strong feeling of excitement) and *imprecations* (offensive words or phrases said in anger) have no relationship. *Volleys* and *salvos* both correctly represent a series of military gunfire.

50. genteel; courtly: The blank concerns "Cary Grant's reputation," a reputation that was earned both on screen and in real life. What else is mentioned about his reputation? A specific example is given (that he "never let a woman pull out her own chair"), and it's mentioned that his actions were in keeping with the "custom of gentlemen." A good prediction would be <u>gentlemanly</u>.

Debonair and *cosmopolitan* are an incorrect pair. These words mean "sophisticated," but they don't necessarily imply good manners or gentlemanly conduct. *Consummate* (complete or perfect) and *waggish* (humorous in a playful way) are words that could make sense in describing a "ladies man," but they have no relationship. *Genteel* and *courtly* fittingly both mean "polite."

51. subjective; personal: The blank pertains to "any notion of fairness" in a relationship. In the section just before the blank, the sentence states concretely that the attempt to find "parity," or fairness, is "fallacious," or logically incorrect. How could fairness be illogical? Given the focus on "self" behind the communication process in question, a good fill-in would be <u>subjective</u> or <u>unachievable</u> (these are fairly disparate predictions, but luckily, only the former has matches among the answers).

Pragmatic and *utilitarian* are a near-pair meaning "practical." This is almost the opposite of the evidence, as something "fallacious" likely wouldn't be very practical. *Introverted* (introspective) and *illicit* (unlawful) are not related.

52. erudition; cerebrality: The blank pertains to "a speech," and the sentence contrasts the speech that the blank describes with speeches that feature "ignorance" and "stupidity." Further, the first part of the sentence presents education as a liability (from the figurative interpretation of "albatross"). A good fill-in would be something the opposite of ignorance or stupidity, perhaps <u>knowledge</u>.

Bromide (commonplace or trite saying) and *bloviation* (talking at length in a pompous or boastful way) both have some relationship to speech, but they aren't really a pair, and neither relates to "education" or "ignorance." *Condescension* (patronizing attitude; disdain) is similar to *bloviation*, but neither reflects the anti-education message in the sentence or contrasts properly with "ignorance." *Patrimony* (inheritance from a father or other male ancestor) is unrelated to everything else. *Erudition* (learnedness) and *cerebrality* (intelligence) both appropriately oppose ignorance.

Unit One: Words and Sentences

53. semblance; veneer: In this sentence, you're told about a man who has been fired and doesn't tell his wife and kids. This somehow relates to "plenitude," which means "abundance" or "completeness." If you get fired and don't tell your family, it could be because you want to seem like you're still okay. A good fill-in word would be <u>appearance</u>.

Corollaries and *consequences* are an incorrect pair. *Paradigms* (things serving as an example or model) and *prepossessions* (attitudes or beliefs formed beforehand) have no relationship.

54. indiscriminate; blanket: The sentence tells you that Don Juan had "an astronomical number of amatory adventures," but that it was not because he had a "surfeit of charisma or skillfulness." If Don Juan didn't have any particular skills when it came to seduction, what else could account for that astronomical number? Perhaps if Don Juan wasn't very choosy. A good fill-in for the blank would be <u>not choosy</u>.

Sumptuous and *hedonistic* are an incorrect pair, meaning "luxurious" and "devoted to luxury or pleasure," respectively. While they both describe someone like Don Juan (and so are a theme trap), they don't explain how he had so many lovers. *Lurid* (gruesome, shocking) and *covert* (not openly done; veiled) have no relationship.

55. quash; check: The sentence indicates that "Even" major campaign finance reform will "fail" to do something to "the influence of money." This money "directly relates" to a politician being able to become a politician, so the influence of money must be pretty strong. Thus, the reform proposals will fail to <u>eliminate</u> or <u>strongly reduce</u> the influence.

Graft (join or unite), *pander* (cater to the lowest or most base desires), *importune* (harass with constant demands; annoy, irritate), and *indemnify* (protect against loss or damage) have no relationship. On the GRE, the choices for a given blank will always be of the same form of speech; here, they are verbs. Don't confuse the verb *graft* with the noun *graft*, which means "acquisition of money (or other valuable) in dishonest or questionable ways" and represents a theme trap here. Indeed, the GRE loves to use alternative definitions of common words, so don't be too hasty to write off *check* in this problem! Here *quash* (to put an end to) and *check* (to slow the progress of) both fit the evidence.

56. delineate; limn: There are no signals to reverse course in this sentence, so you simply need a word that fits the description of a book that explores the "many ways in which 19th-century women writers . . ." In other words, you can just fill in the blank with <u>explore</u> or <u>present</u>.

Debunk and *explode* are an incorrect pair, both meaning "disprove" in this context. *Interpolate* (insert between parts, pieces, or things) and *castigate* (criticize or punish severely) have no relationship. *Castigate* almost fits into a triple with the incorrect pair, but it's more of a criticism than an attempt to disprove something. Both *castigate* and the pair *debunk* and *explode* represent story traps. Gilbert and Gubar *might* have focused on disproving things in their study, but there's no evidence to directly support that expectation. This makes *delineate* and *limn*, both of which are fairly neutral and can mean "to describe in detail," a safer pair to choose.

57. indolence; lethargy: With the reversal marker "While," this sentence creates a contrast between a positive and negative view of the same fact. The positive view is the one that's more concretely established: Certain cultures prioritize "relaxation" and "moderation between work and play." The negative or "prejudiced" view of this same quality would be something like <u>laziness</u>.

Enfeeblement and *enervation* are an incorrect pair, meaning "weakening" or "weakness." Though they are close to what you want, they imply a taking away of energy, which is not the same as being innately lazy or inactive. *Obtundity* (lessening of intensity; dulling or deadening) and *seemliness* (conforming to standards of proper conduct) have no relationship.

58. extraneous; unnecessary: The blank describes the opinion autodidacts hold regarding "standard education," and the reversal marker "but" reveals that this opinion will be contrary to the concrete truth revealed later. That truth is that "most people learn better when accountable to others," implying that autodidacts believe the opposite of this. They must have a negative opinion of standard education—perhaps that it is <u>unhelpful</u> or even <u>misguided</u>. Note that this prediction can be made by unpacking the sentence *without* understanding the word "autodidacts" or even if understanding its definition (people who teach themselves things) is useful.

Slack and *lax* are an incorrect pair meaning "loose." *Prudent* and *sagacious* are an incorrect (and opposite of our prediction) pair meaning "wise, having good judgement."

59. a dusky; a crepuscular: The only piece of real proof in this sentence comes in the second half, a "twilit avenue in a long since abandoned city." So you want a word that relates to "twilit" or "abandoned city," such as <u>darkish</u> or <u>desolate</u>.

Urban and *civic* are something of a pair here. Though they both reflect the sentence's reference to a "city," they fail to correctly account for the descriptor "abandoned," as *urban* is associated with the active character of a city and *civic* is associated with a city's functioning. *Precipitous* (extremely steep) and *avuncular* (relating to an uncle; kind to younger people) have no relationship. *Dusky* (dimly lit) and *crepuscular* (relating to twilight) are not exact synonyms, but both aptly fit the evidence of a twilit environment.

60. ineluctable; inexorable: The key phrase here is "the inertia of history." Inertia is resistance to change, so this phrase must mean that history is difficult to change. So your blank here should be something like <u>difficult to change</u> or <u>unavoidable</u>.

This question gives six words all with the prefix "in-" but not all six have similar meanings. *Incontrovertible* (not able to be denied or disputed), *interminable* (endless), *inviolate* (untouched or unspoiled), and *ineffable* (not able to be expressed in words) have no relationship. But *ineluctable* and *inexorable* both match the prediction of <u>unavoidable</u>.

UNIT TWO

Paragraphs and Passages

This unit provides you with a comprehensive approach to the study of the final building blocks of GRE Verbal problems: paragraphs and passages. Included are tools for analysis of relationships across long bodies of text. Finally, this unit introduces longer, multiple-blank Text Completions and the various Reading Comprehension types.

In This Unit...

- Chapter 4: GRE Paragraphs
- Chapter 5: Short Passages in Reading Comprehension
- Chapter 6: Argument-Based Reading Comprehension
- Chapter 7: Multi-Blank Text Completion
- Chapter 8: Reading Comprehension Problem Set
- Chapter 9: Issue Essay

CHAPTER 4
GRE Paragraphs

In This Chapter...

- Making Connections
- Signals and Pronouns
- Components of Paragraphs
- The Main Idea (and Archetypes)
- The Big Picture
- Don't Just Read, Do Something!
- A Note-Taking Exercise (Sample Notes)
- Common Notations
- Vocabulary Challenge
- Problem Set
- Answers and Explanations

CHAPTER 4 GRE Paragraphs

Previous chapters address the challenges of GRE Vocabulary and GRE Sentences. In this chapter, you will learn how to evaluate the relationships between sentences within a paragraph. (For the purposes of this book, a paragraph is any text that consists of two or more sentences.)

Here are your Chapter 4 vocabulary words:

>   exhaustive (E)
>   qualified (E)
>   abreast (A)
>   facilitate (E)
>   disparate (A)
>   precipitate (A)

Making Connections

Hopefully, the discussion of Sentences in Chapter 2: GRE Sentences convinced you of the value of unpacking sentences in GRE Verbal problems. The next layer of GRE complexity requires you to string those sentences together to make sense of the underlying meaning and purpose of each paragraph or passage.

Revisit the following example from Chapter 1:

> *The Biblical portrayal of flagitious times preceding the great deluge stands in stark contrast to the ancient Greek representation of the antediluvian past as a Golden Age from which humanity has slowly descended into godless chaos. Such observations can easily give rise to the notion that stories about the past are less faithful attempts at reconstruction than allegories, expressing both our cultural fears and hopes.*

How was the vocabulary? If you didn't know some of the words, look them up, make flash cards, and read the paragraph again.

Did simply knowing the words make it substantially easier to read? Probably not! Why? Because the sentence structure itself is dense, and you need to deal with that, too.

Unit Two: Paragraphs and Passages

Start by unpacking just the first sentence. Try it on your own before reading the rephrase below.

Sentence	Rephrase
The Biblical portrayal of flagitious times preceding the great deluge stands in stark contrast to the ancient Greek representation of the antediluvian past as a Golden Age from which humanity has slowly descended into godless chaos.	According to the Bible, the time before the great flood (deluge) was shameful and bad (flagitious). The Greeks also talked about the time before the great flood (antediluvian past), but said it was actually *good* before, but had gotten bad after. Wow, the Bible and the Greeks had exactly opposite views.

How did it go? Hopefully unpacking is feeling a little more efficient now that you've been practicing.

So what now? You'll continue through a paragraph, unpacking each sentence as you go. However, in order to understand the meaning or purpose of the paragraph as a whole, you'll also need to make connections between the sentences you're unpacking.

Take, for example, a pure unpacking of the second sentence without any attempt to connect it to the first.

Sentence	Rephrase
Such observations can easily give rise to the notion that stories about the past are less faithful attempts at reconstruction than allegories, expressing both our cultural fears and hopes.	There are observations. Something about how stories might be more symbolic (allegories) than actually trying to "reconstruct" a factual history. Because they're symbolic, these stories are more about the hopes and fears of the people writing them.

This sentence is a little bit more clear now (maybe), but without any connections to earlier sentences, it's difficult to build a complete story of the paragraph.

You need connections to get the larger story. Consider the following unpacking of the second sentence, built by connecting back to the first.

Paragraph	Rephrase + Connections
The Biblical portrayal of flagitious times preceding the great deluge stands in stark contrast to the ancient Greek representation of the antediluvian past as a Golden Age from which humanity has slowly descended into godless chaos.	According to the Bible, the time before the great flood (deluge) was shameful and bad (flagitious).
	The Greeks also talked about the time before the great flood (antediluvian past), but said it was actually *good* before, but had gotten bad after.
	Wow, the Bible and the Greeks had exactly opposite views.
Such observations can easily give rise to the notion that stories about the past are less faithful attempts at reconstruction than allegories, expressing both our cultural fears and hopes.	Everything in the first sentence (such observations) leads people to think that (gives rise to the notion that) . . .
	. . . stories might be more symbolic than just trying to "reconstruct" a factual history. How else could you explain the two drastically different stories about the exact same time period?
	And if they're symbolic, they represent the hopes and fears of the people writing them.

Now the bigger story is becoming more clear; connections allow you to find deeper meaning during your initial read of a paragraph. For that reason, making connections as you read sentences is the subject of the rest of this chapter.

Signals and Pronouns

As paragraphs get longer or more complex, conventions of good writing thankfully encourage the use of specific types of words and phrases as signposts, directly connecting one part of a sentence or paragraph to another. You already saw many of these direction markers in Chapter 3: TC and SE, but if you have not reviewed that chapter recently, now would be a good time to look back.

Signal Words and Phrases

Signal words and phrases (direction markers) indicate relationships between different parts of text. Take, for example, this sentence from Chapter 3: TC and SE.

> *Despite her reputation for _____, the politician asserted that in a time of crisis it was important to speak honestly.*

The word *despite* is a signpost of contrast. The information before the comma is going to be in opposition to the information after the comma.

As you learn to recognize these signal words, you'll note additional subtleties in their meaning (see the differences among *in contrast*, *despite*, and *however* in the table below). The following are a number of such words and phrases alongside their relationship implications.

Signal	Relationship
As for; Regarding; In reference to	Focus attention
Furthermore; Moreover; In addition; As well as; Also; Likewise; Too	Add to previous point
On one hand/on the other hand; While; Rather; Instead; In contrast; Alternatively	Provide contrast
Granted; It is true that; Certainly; Admittedly; Despite; Although	Provide conceding contrast (author unwillingly agrees)
But; However; Even so; All the same; Still; That said; Nevertheless; Nonetheless; Yet; Otherwise; Despite	Provide emphatic contrast (author asserts own position)
In any event; In any case	Dismiss previous point
Likewise; In the same way	Point out similarity
First, Second, etc.; To begin with; Next; Finally; Again	Structure the discussion
For example; In particular; For instance	Give example
In general; To a great extent; Broadly speaking	Generalize
In conclusion; In brief; Overall; Except for; Besides	Sum up, perhaps with exception
Therefore; Thus; As a result; So; Accordingly; Hence	Indicate logical result
Because; Since; As; Resulting from	Indicate logical cause
In other words; That is; Namely; So to speak	Restate for clarity
Apparently; At least; Can, Could, May, Might, Should; Possibly; Likely	Hedge or soften position
After all; Must, Have to; Always, Never, etc.	Strengthen position
Actually; In fact; Indeed; Yet; Surprisingly	Introduce surprise
Fortunately; Unfortunately; Luckily; So-called	Reveal author's attitude

Feel free to use this as a starter list for your studies; choose a few phrases and search for them in anything you read throughout the day. You can also practice using those same phrases in your own writing. While this list is long, it is not exhaustive; as you practice more GRE problems, add new signal phrases and words to your list as you encounter them.

Pronouns

Pronouns are used to refer to something indirectly; they take the place of nouns. In that sentence, *they* pointed back to *pronouns*.

Some pronouns are more obviously seen as "pronouns"—he, she, it, or they—and they point back to a specific noun or term earlier in the sentence or paragraph. Take, for example, the exobiologist sentence from earlier in the book: *carbon probably provides the backbone of any extraterrestrial biological molecules, just as it does of terrestrial ones.* The word *it* in that sentence refers to *carbon*.

But there are also pronouns that aren't so obvious! Did you notice the word *ones* at the end of the exobiologist sentence? *Ones* refers back to *biological molecules*: *carbon probably provides the backbone of any extraterrestrial biological molecules, just as it does of terrestrial [biological molecules].*

The main examples of these less obvious pronouns are *one*, *such*, *this*, *that*, *these*, and *those*. Although you might not think of these unique pronouns when you think about pronouns, the GRE does use them quite frequently! Add these pronouns to your list of signal words and phrases to practice. The faster you notice the signposts, the faster you make connections on test day.

And while many pronouns point back to a specific word or simple noun earlier in the text, they are also used to refer back to abstract ideas or even complete sentences. You encountered this scenario in the paragraph about the flood in the previous section: The *such* in *such observations* at the start of the second sentence referred back to the content of the *entire* previous sentence.

When you see *any* pronouns, either the more or the less familiar to you, pause and verify that you know exactly what it is referring to. The author is linking back to a previous idea.

Can you spot the pronoun(s) in the following paragraph? What do they refer back to?

> Most anemones, sea creatures that belong to the group Cnidarians, reproduce asexually through budding, longitudinal fission, or basal laceration. This trait is essentially a form of cloning that theoretically enables them to live forever absent predators and disease.

The more familiar pronoun *them* in the middle of the second sentence refers back to the *anemones*, but did you spot the subtle pronoun *this* at the start of the second sentence? The phrase *this trait* refers to the fact that *most anemones…reproduce asexually*. The second sentence is expanding upon that initial concept. The list of different types of asexual reproduction is meant to distract you from determining what the word *this* is actually referring to.

When you're unsure what a pronoun is pointing to, unpack the sentence to see what could be substituted for the pronoun. In the above example, the second sentence makes sense if you substitute the broader concept for the word *this*: the trait that most anemones have of reproducing asexually is essentially a form of cloning…

Components of Paragraphs

Before going any further, it is important to take a step back and look at the real goal for the GRE Verbal section: Can you identify the central message the author means to convey? In order to know what words fill in the blanks for TC and SE, you need to understand what the whole sentence is trying to say. Similarly, in order to answer any questions about a Reading Comprehension passage, you need to understand what the whole passage is trying to say.

You're already improving your vocabulary and applying the skills of unpacking sentences and identifying connections. Next is to bring it all together under one cohesive story. In other words, you're trying to understand **the author's main idea or primary purpose** behind writing any of the text you encounter on the test.

Unit Two: Paragraphs and Passages

Sometimes an understanding of that main idea might follow naturally from the steps you've taken so far. But on tougher passages, it can help to more formally understand what each sentence in a paragraph is *doing* to create that overarching idea.

Imagine parts of speech when working to understand the grammar of a sentence. Within a sentence, verbs tell you the action, nouns tell you who or what is doing the action, and adjectives and adverbs provide additional description. You don't always need to know the parts of speech in order to make sense of the sentence, but knowing how the parts fit together can help when sentences become particularly confusing.

In the same way, paragraphs and their storylines are created through the intentional use of the following specific components:

1. Conclusion
2. Premises
3. Point and Counterpoint
4. Background
5. Implications

Most paragraphs contain only a few of these components, but some might contain them all. They can come in any order, not necessarily the order above.

As the GRE adds more paragraphs to passages, these components can and will spread beyond the bounds of a single paragraph. For now, though, focus on learning to identify these component pieces within individual paragraphs.

The Conclusion

Some paragraphs contain a clear position from the author: They are convinced of something, and they also want to convince you. These paragraphs contain a very active, opinionated author's point of view.

Not all GRE paragraphs will contain conclusions, but if they do, that conclusion will form the basis of the main idea and primary purpose.

When reading a GRE paragraph, strive to maintain an understanding of the point of view presented from each sentence. Is this sentence the author's own point of view, or some other point of view? If a sentence contains a strongly stated, active point of view from the author (e.g., the author argues, rejects, justifies, challenges, proposes, etc.), then you are probably reading a conclusion. Your next step would then be to identify any premises.

Premises

The premises in a paragraph are the assertions and opinions that support a conclusion. If there is a conclusion, there is at least one premise for that conclusion. They may be facts, opinions, or claims. If they are opinions or claims, they will not be the overall claim the author is making; rather, they will be some intermediate claim the author is using to support the overall claim (conclusion).

Points and Counterpoints

Counterpoints undermine or go against a stated position. Occasionally, a paragraph will present both sides of an issue, with evidence to support both. The author might themselves take one side, or merely present opposing sides. Regardless of whether the author takes a side, when you find competing positions, you have point and counterpoint components.

Background

The background is information presented without opinion or information that doesn't specifically work for or against a conclusion. The context and the basic facts about the topic are given in the background.

In some paragraphs, the author may simply wish to inform the reader of facts, rather than convince the reader of a debatable position. In these cases, the entire paragraph could be called background. These types of paragraphs are common in passages that you'll encounter later in the book in Chapter 6: Argument-Based RC.

Differentiating background from premise or counterpoint can be tricky! If a paragraph contains a conclusion, it is crucial to distinguish whether a given piece of information is working for or against the conclusion or whether the information is purely background.

Implications

Implications, if present, are the predicted consequences of other information or positions. In other words, the author has given you information, opinions, or both, and now wishes to enumerate potential results of that information. Implications are not always present, but when they are, they tend to be important.

As you continue your GRE Verbal studies, consider how the components of paragraphs impact your understanding of Verbal problems. This understanding can impact your ability to solve Reading Comprehension problems of all varieties, and can also play a role in your ability to solve the multi-blank Text Completion questions, as some of those problems contain multiple sentences.

As a final summation, here is a list of questions to ask as you read:

1. Is this the main belief or claim? If so, this is the conclusion.
2. Is this supporting evidence for the conclusion? If so, this is a premise.
3. Is this opposing evidence for the conclusion? If so, this is a counterpoint.
4. Is this neutral information that gives context to the conclusion? If so, this is background.
5. Is this a consequence of another fact or opinion? If so, this is an implication.

The Main Idea (and Archetypes)

As mentioned in the last section, your goal as you read on the GRE is to get into the head of the author and understand their big picture story: You need to understand the author's purpose for writing the text and the main idea that the text conveys.

In many ways, you can think of main idea and primary purpose as getting at the same idea. However, there is a subtle but important difference: The main idea is the *what* of the paragraph, while the primary purpose is the *why* of the paragraph. For example, the main idea might be "Elephant trunks are signs of an evolutionary adaptation," while the primary purpose might be "explain how elephants evolved trunks." The main idea is a declaration: This fact is true. The primary purpose is an action: Explain why this fact is true.

The Main Idea

The main idea is the *what* of the paragraph. What central concept does the author wish to convey? This main idea is sometimes directly stated in the paragraph; if there is a sentence in which the author asserts their own point of view, that sentence forms at least part of the main idea.

If the paragraph does not contain a point of view statement from the author, then an analysis of the paragraph components discussed in the previous section will reveal the main idea. Perhaps the author merely presents competing positions on an issue, but does not state an opinion of their own. In that case, the main idea is the existence of that debate. Or perhaps the author presents facts laying the background of an existing situation, and then poses questions regarding the future outcomes for that situation. In that case, the main idea is that this situation may lead to these various outcomes.

Notice that both of the examples in the previous paragraph arose directly from a recognition of the components in the paragraph: point and counterpoint, and background plus implications, respectively. While these components have many possible combinations, there are some that the GRE uses more often than others.

Passage Archetypes

Just as there are patterns in wrong answers (think back to Chapter 3: TC and SE), there are patterns in the passages themselves! Think of a film or TV genre that has predictable elements, like a superhero movie where you know the hero and villain will have a final showdown or a cooking show where you know something is going to go horribly wrong for one contestant right before the commercial break. Those patterns actually make the stories easier to understand and more fun to watch! If you pay attention, you might be able to achieve the same effect with GRE passages.

Many GRE passages follow one of the "archetypes" described below—a predictable pattern of information. These archetypes can occur within one paragraph, or across multiple paragraphs. Note that the archetypes have nothing to do with the topic of the passage, but everything to do with the structure of the passage. Whatever topic you see (say, the Japanese textile industry in the 19th century . . .) will almost certainly be something you've never seen before. But if you're familiar with the GRE's favorite structures, you'll still have something to hold onto to better understand the passage.

We can understand the archetypes through their use of the elements of paragraphs discussed previously—Conclusion, Background, Premises, Points and Counterpoints, and Implications. The main idea gives the archetype its structure, and it defines the relationship between the other elements.

1. **Explanation of a concept**

    - **Main idea:** ___ is a concept/theory/subject that exists, and ___ is how it works/why people believe it.
    - **Background:** an introduction to the concept itself—maybe a historical theory, a scientific process, or artistic
    - **Premises:** facts that help to explain the concept
    - **Implications:** not always present, but might be a summary of why the concept is impactful or worthy of discussion

2. **Competing theories on a subject**
   - **Main idea:** One person or group thinks ____ about ____, but another person or group thinks ____.
   - **Background:** an introduction to the subject itself
   - **Premises:** the reasons why each side believes what it does about the subject
   - **Point and Counterpoint:** There are two opposing sides to the issue.
   - **Implications:** not always present, but might be the author's prediction of which side will "win" the debate, or what will happen next in the conflict

3. **A critic's opinion of a work**
   - **Main idea:** ____ is a subject people have opinions on, and one particular critic thinks ____ about it.
   - **Background:** an introduction to the subject itself
   - **Premises:** the reasons why the critic thinks what they do about the subject
   - **Implications:** not always present, but might be a summary of how people responded to the critic's opinion

4. **The author's opinion of a work**
   - **Conclusion:** ____ is a subject people have opinions on, and the author thinks ____ about it.
   - **Background:** an introduction to the subject itself
   - **Premises:** the reasons the author thinks what they do about the subject
   - **Implications:** not always present, but might be an outcome the author wishes to see based on their opinion

5. **A change in perception over time**
   - **Main idea:** People used to think ____. But then ____ happened, and now people think ____.
   - **Background:** the previous prevailing opinion
   - **Premises:** the reasons why opinions on the subject might be changing
   - **Implications:** This type of story typically has implications: What's the outcome of the change that occurred?

This should be qualified by a few caveats: This list of archetypes is not exhaustive—nor are these archetypes officially defined anywhere by the GRE. Not every passage is going to follow one of these archetypes, and not every example of an archetype will have every element of that archetype—just like not every superhero movie will have every type of scene you expect to see in a superhero movie. Some harder passages might combine multiple archetypes into one: For example, a paragraph might contain a change in perception over time and then supply the author's opinion of that (archetypes 5 and 4) or a critic's opinion of another critic's opinion (archetypes 3 and 2).

But despite all those caveats, if you look through official GRE reading comprehension passages, you'll start to see the threads of these archetypes repeating themselves. That familiarity will help you better orient yourself to new passages, especially those that are particularly difficult.

The Big Picture

Let's expand on the discussion of the sample short paragraph at the beginning of the chapter and see how the previous section's discussion applies.

> *The Biblical portrayal of flagitious times preceding the great deluge stands in stark contrast to the ancient Greek representation of the antediluvian past as a Golden Age from which humanity has slowly descended into godless chaos. Such observations can easily give rise to the notion that stories about the past are less faithful attempts at reconstruction than allegories, expressing both our cultural fears and hopes.*

If needed, take a moment to revisit the sentence-by-sentence translation in the initial section of this chapter. Then, consider the purpose behind the paragraph author's choice of words to begin the second sentence: "such observations can . . . ." What does this word choice imply about the relationship between the first and second sentences?

The author intends to link the second sentence to the first: The first sentence contains facts while the second sentence states the implications the author would draw from those facts. As such, the first sentence would be characterized as background, and the second sentence would be characterized as implications. A possible main idea for this paragraph would be "the contrast in portrayals of the ancient past suggest that cultural characteristics influence these portrayals more than literal history," while the author's purpose would be to "derive implications of what stories of the ancient past reveal about the cultures that produced them."

Apply the discussion to another example, drawn from the Chapter 1: GRE Vocabulary. Read the paragraph, make your own characterizations of what components exist, and see if you can paraphrase the main idea.

> *Architectural cognoscenti such as Koolhaas recognized Hadid's talents early and encouraged their development. By 1977, only a few years after their initial encounter, she had perfected her heteromorphic style, inspired equally by such disparate styles as Malevich's sparse constructivism and the flowing calligraphy of her native Arabic.*

As always, take any time needed to review potential vocabulary issues: Who are *cognoscenti*? What is *heteromorphic*?

Once done with that task, consider the various transition choices: *such as*, *by 1977*. In this instance, the author of the passage indicates that Koolhaas is merely an example of the general sentiment regarding Hadid's talents. In this paragraph, *by 1977* indicates a continuation of the earlier sentence, expanding on the remarkable nature of Hadid's talents. And finally, *such disparate styles as* serves a similar purpose to the *such as* in the first sentence. Malevich's sparse constructivism and flowing calligraphy are only two examples of a larger statement regarding Hadid's inspirations. Since each sentence gives examples to illustrate facts regarding Hadid, both sentences are technically background. But in this particular example, although both sentences are background (merely stating factual elements regarding Hadid), you have an example of a potential for point of view analysis.

Point of View Analysis: A Supplement to Component Analysis

In the first sentence, the author references *cognoscenti such as Koolhaas* to establish an external point of view—how did the architectural community at large view Hadid? But in the second sentence, notice that there is no attribution to other groups or people; there are no cognoscenti telling the reader that Hadid had *perfected her heteromorphic style*. This is a clue to the author's view of Hadid. This point of view analysis can be particularly helpful when attempting Reading Comprehension questions of almost all varieties; if you can identify when the author begins speaking for themselves in a paragraph, you can become much more efficient when addressing the answer choices. For this example, a possible main idea could be that the author shares the architectural community's admiration for Hadid.

(As an aside, if you are not abreast of Zaha Hadid's work, take a few moments to look her up in the search engine of your choice: You will not be disappointed!)

Don't Just Read, Do Something!

If you are struggling with a paragraph, instead of passively reading, take notes. You can build your comprehension more quickly and effectively—*especially* when the paragraph is unfriendly—by using more than one learning method. Writing as you read activates a second learning process that facilitates comprehension. Now, what you write during the GRE must be different from other kinds of notes you have taken (e.g., during a college lecture). In college, you take notes in order to study from them later. In contrast, **you take notes during the GRE to precipitate comprehension right then and there**.

Identifying and writing down key elements of the paragraph will force you to read *actively* as opposed to passively. If you proactively write the translation as you read (in a massively-abbreviated fashion—more on this in a moment), your comprehension of unfriendly paragraphs will improve dramatically.

Of course, it is not possible to translate, pencil to paper, every sentence, paragraph, and passage on the GRE in the time given. And in fact, the Text Completion and Sentence Equivalence questions must be answered too quickly to allow note-taking: If you find yourself needing to take notes on one of these questions during the test, guess and move on!

But even if you could not, or would not, make notes for a particular paragraph, practicing a note-taking strategy during untimed review will improve your comprehension skills on the test, for all question types. Therefore, practice a writing strategy for every paragraph during untimed review, even if you would not write anything for a particular paragraph during the actual test. And when you *would* take notes on the test—for example, on a dense Reading Comprehension problem set—that process will be natural, smooth, and fast.

How would you take notes on these example paragraphs from the earlier pages?

> *The Biblical portrayal of flagitious times preceding the great deluge stands in stark contrast to the ancient Greek representation of the antediluvian past as a Golden Age from which humanity has slowly descended into godless chaos. Such observations can easily give rise to the notion that stories about the past are less faithful attempts at reconstruction than allegories, expressing both our cultural fears and hopes.*

Unit Two: Paragraphs and Passages

Architectural cognoscenti such as Koolhaas recognized Hadid's talents early and encouraged their development. By 1977, only a few years after their initial encounter, she had perfected her heteromorphic style, inspired equally by such disparate styles as Malevich's sparse constructivism and the flowing calligraphy of her native Arabic.

When you've made your notes on these two paragraphs, continue to the next section to see some sample notes. And after the sample notes for these paragraphs, you will see a few suggestions for common notations to save time when you find yourself taking notes during the test.

A Note-Taking Exercise (Sample Notes)

The Sentence	Possible Notes
The Biblical portrayal of flagitious times preceding the great deluge stands in stark contrast to the ancient Greek representation of the antediluvian past as a Golden Age from which humanity has slowly descended into godless chaos. Such observations can easily give rise to the notion that stories about the past are less faithful attempts at reconstruction than allegories, expressing both our cultural fears and hopes.	**B vs AG** (The Biblical portrayal is opposite that of the ancient Greeks.) **story → not lit. but alleg.** (This observation leads to the notion that the stories are not literal, but allegorical.)
Architectural cognoscenti such as Koolhaas recognized Hadid's talents early and encouraged their development. By 1977, only a few years after their initial encounter, she had perfected her heteromorphic style, inspired equally by such disparate styles as Malevich's sparse constructivism and the flowing calligraphy of her native Arabic.	**K = arch: H talent** (Koolhass is an example of architects who recognized Hadid's talents.) **(auth) H perf'd style** (This is the author speaking to the reader. Hadid perfected her style, and the author seems to really like Hadid's style.)

Common Notations

To create your translation on paper as quickly as possible, consider some following notation suggestions:

- Abbreviate long terms, particularly proper nouns.
- Use arrows (e.g., →) to indicate cause-effect relationships or changes over time.
- If a passage contains speakers, writers, points of view, arguments, and so on, keep them organized by using a colon to indicate who is providing a particular opinion. For example, if a passage says that historians believe that economic interests led to the outbreak of war, you might write: **H: econ int → war**.
- If you write down examples, mark them with parentheses or "Ex." For example: **Ex: Insects = inflexible (wasp)**.
- Create images. This may mean sketching a quick diagram of a planet with three moons in orbit or it may mean adding smiley and frowny faces to indicate the author's opinion.

You will have your own note-taking style. Regardless of the notations you use, practice them and keep them *consistent*. You do not want to use up precious focus during the GRE figuring out how to indicate that the passage presents a problem and a solution when you could have shorthand already in place for this common structure!

Vocabulary Challenge

> Did you spot these vocabulary words? If not, go back and find them in context! (The word may be in a different form than listed here—"digressing" instead of "digress," for example.) Write your own definitions based on the evidence in the chapter.

1. exhaustive (*adj.*), p. 116
2. qualified (*adj.*), p. 121
3. abreast (*adj.*), p. 123
4. facilitate (*v*), p. 123
5. disparate (*adj.*), p. 122
6. precipitate (*v*), p. 123

Unit Two: **Paragraphs and Passages**

Problem Set

1. Read the following passage and jot down any notes within 2.5–3 minutes (this is a bit more time than you'll want to spend on the actual exam). After answering the questions below the passage, compare your notes to the sample in the answer key. How well did your notes succeed in pushing you to read actively? How well did they capture the main idea of the passage without getting bloated with details?

Passage A: Arousal and Attraction

In 1974, psychologists Dutton and Aron discovered that subjects who had just crossed a precarious wire-suspension bridge reacted to an attractive interviewer differently than subjects who had instead crossed a low, solid bridge. Specifically, in response to a questionnaire that secretly measured sexual arousal, subjects from the wire-suspension bridge revealed significantly more sexual imagery than the others; moreover, a far greater fraction of wire-suspension subjects than of solid-bridge subjects contacted the interviewer afterward. Dutton and Aron explained their results in terms of misattribution. In their view, subjects crossing the wobbly bridge experienced physiological fear reactions, such as increased heart rate. Such reactions with ambiguous or suppressed causes are easily reinterpreted, in the presence of a potential partner, as sexual attraction. However, Foster and others later found that an unattractive interviewer is actually perceived as much less attractive by subjects physiologically aroused by fearful situations. Thus, the arousal is reinterpreted either as attraction or as repulsion, but in either case, the true cause is masked.

2. What is the main idea of this passage? Justify your choice.

3. Identify the other components of the passage, if present: conclusion, premises, point and counterpoint, background, and implications. Again, justify your assignments.

4. Read the following passage and take notes in 1.5 minutes. After answering the questions below the passage, compare your notes to the sample in the answer key and provide critiques.

Passage B: Animal Treatment

In the early nineteenth century, educated Britons came to accept the then-novel notion that animals must be treated humanely, as evidenced by the outlawing of certain forms of domestic animal abuse, as well as the founding of the Society for the Prevention of Cruelty to Animals in 1824. This trend may be regarded as part of a broader embrace of compassionate ideals, such as abolitionism and alleviation of poverty. For instance, in 1785 the Society for the Relief of Persons Imprisoned for Small Sums persuaded Parliament to restrict that archaic punishment, and similar societies focused on various issues of humane treatment emerged around this time. However, a deeper explanation should be traced to socioeconomic conditions related to ongoing industrialization. Those protesting cruelty to animals were city dwellers who viewed animals as pets rather than as livestock, despite the ubiquity of horse transport. In fact, nature was no longer considered menacing, since society's victory over wilderness was conspicuous. Animals were to some extent romanticized as emblems of a bucolic, pre-industrial age.

5. What is the main idea of this passage? Justify your choice.

6. Identify the other components of the passage, if present: conclusion, premises, point and counterpoint, background, and implications. Again, justify your assignments.

Chapter 4: GRE Paragraphs

Answers and Explanations

Vocabulary Challenge

1. exhaustive (*adj.*): comprehensive, thorough; exhausting a topic or subject, accounting for all possibilities
2. qualified (*adj.*): modified, limited, conditional on something else
3. abreast (*adj.*): side-by-side; keeping up with, staying aware of, or remaining equal in progress with
4. facilitate (*v*): make easier, help the progress of
5. disparate (*adj.*): distinct, different
6. precipitate (*v*): cause to happen suddenly; fling, plunge, or hurl down

Problem Set

1. Read the following passage and jot down any notes within 2.5–3 minutes (this is a bit more time than you'll want to spend on the actual exam). After answering the questions below the passage, compare your notes to the sample in the answer key. How well did your notes succeed in pushing you to read actively? How well did they capture the main idea of the passage without getting bloated with details?

    <u>Arousal and Attraction</u>—Sample Notes
    Psychs D+A:
    Wire bridge: aroused → attr
    Expl: misattrib physiol fear AS attractn
    BUT actually: attr OR repuls masks the cause ← main idea

2. What is the main idea of this passage? Justify your choice.

    The author draws a collective conclusion about the results of two separate sets of studies: that people experiencing a fearful situation are likely to unconsciously redirect that feeling of fear into a feeling of attraction toward another person and that this could manifest as either increased or decreased attraction to that person. Everything in the passage leads up to this final conclusion.

3. Identify the other components of the passage, if present: conclusion, premises, point and counterpoint, background, and implications. Again, justify your assignments.

    The paragraph is all background and support (premises), leading up to the conclusion at the end.

4. Read the following passage and take notes in 1.5 minutes. After answering the questions below the passage, compare your notes to the sample in the answer key and provide critiques.

    <u>Animal Treatment</u>—Sample Notes
    19th c: Educ B's: animal cruelty = bad
    Why: Part of broader embrace of compassn. Ex's
    Deeper Why: Industzn → city dwellers ← main idea
    Nature romantic

Unit Two: Paragraphs and Passages

5. What is the main idea of this passage? Justify your choice.

The author of this passage uses the direction marker "however" to indicate a relationship between the first few sentences and the last few sentences. The change in direction indicated by "however" combined with the opinionated "should" language in the same sentence indicates that this is the author's conclusion. A main idea statement for this passage could be the following: The push for humane animal treatment in nineteenth-century Britain was because of the socioeconomic conditions related to industrialization.

6. Identify the other components of the passage, if present: conclusion, premises, point and counterpoint, background, and implications. Again, justify your assignments.

The paragraph begins with background (all the text before the conclusion sentence), then states the conclusion (the deeper reason). That conclusion is followed by the premises (support for the deeper reason).

CHAPTER 5
Short Passages in Reading Comprehension

In This Chapter . . .

- Two Types of Passages
- Scanning Ahead
- Strategy for General Questions
- Strategy for Specific Questions
- Common Wrong Answer Categories
- Summary of Strategies for Answer Choice Eliminations
- Comprehensive Strategies for All Reading Comprehension
- Vocabulary Challenge
- A Short Introduction to the Problem Set
- Problem Set
- Answers and Explanations

CHAPTER 5   Short Passages in Reading Comprehension

While the skill of reading comprehension is something that you've been practicing throughout this book, what the GRE specifically calls *Reading Comprehension* (RC) is the family of questions that are based on specific passages. Those passages will be either content-based or argument-based. In this chapter, you will learn the initial strategies for content-based passages, and practice them on short passages—on the GRE, short passages are generally one paragraph.

Here are your Chapter 5 vocabulary words:

> perspicacious (A)
> harrowing (A)
> indeterminate (E)
> prudent (E)
> dubious (E)
> wanton (A)

Two Types of Passages

While *The Official Guide to the GRE® General Test* labels all Verbal questions that are neither TC nor SE as *Reading Comprehension*, there are actually two different types of passages used for RC.

Content-based passages (CBP) look like text you'd pull from a college textbook or some other reference material, and they typically discuss science, arts, history, or other academic topics. So far in this book, all of the practice paragraphs that you've been interpreting have been content-based.

Alternatively, **argument-based passages (ABP)** read more like short persuasive arguments that are based on real-world concepts, but often include fictional cities, companies, and other such details.

But the differences don't just stop at the topics you'll be reading about in each passage type. CBPs are longer and often multi-paragraph; even the single paragraph CBPs are quite lengthy. Difficult vocabulary is common, the text is dense (as you've seen already), and you will be tested on your ability to determine the meaning of words in context. ABPs, on the other hand, are typically short paragraphs consisting of only a couple of sentences. Vocabulary and jargon are less frequent, and you're more concerned with making sense of how the sentences work to build a cohesive argument or claim.

Perhaps the most profound difference, though, is in the questions that you'll be asked about each type of passage. For CBPs, questions test whether you understood the passage by asking you to extract information from what you read. You'll see anywhere from one to five questions (although five-question passages are very rare) based on a single content-based passage, and topics include stating the main idea or correctly identifying details that were mentioned. The rest of this chapter will focus on the strategies for content-based questions.

ABPs, however, are always accompanied by a single question that tests your understanding of not only what you read but also the underlying types of arguments that can be made. These questions will expect you to bring in new, outside information in order to strengthen, weaken, or evaluate the argument in some specific way. The next chapter, Chapter 6: Argument-Based RC, will focus on the strategies to apply for argument-based questions.

The table below is a summary of the primary differences between the two types of passages and their questions. Anytime you encounter a passage on test day, your first goal is to determine its type.

Content-Based Passages (CBPs)	Argument-Based Passages (ABPs)
One or more lengthy paragraphs	Single (shorter) paragraph
Passages discuss science, social science, and business: content typical of textbooks and reference material.	Passages make persuasive arguments; the information included might be fictional.
One to five questions per passage	One question per passage
Questions typically ask you to pull information from the passage.	Questions typically ask you to add information to the passage.

Scanning Ahead

Because passages can have multiple questions, the test clearly identifies which question numbers accompany that passage in a banner at the top of the screen; for example, it might say *Questions 9 to 12 are based on the following passage*. This is true even when there is only a single question.

Before you begin reading, it is helpful to use the questions as a sort of pre-scan. By clicking through any accompanying questions to see what you will be asked to do, you can better direct your focus once you begin reading. This is not suggesting that you read the question and answer choices thoroughly, just that you skim the question stems and possibly jot down a few words for each. This is meant to supplement your understanding of the passage, *not* to take up so much time that you sacrifice your ability to fully read and unpack the text.

As you scan, you will encounter one of two types of questions: those asking for general (big picture) understanding and those asking for information about something specific. The following two sections will go through the process for handling each.

> *Strategy Tip:*
>
> For all passages, scan the questions, but not the answer choices, before reading the passage.

Additionally, make note of how many questions are associated with the passage. How long you have on the entire segment, both reading the passage and answering the questions, is dictated by how many questions there are. With an average time of approximately two minutes per question, you can spend approximately half of the total time to read. The Introduction of this book and a later section of this chapter list a more detailed breakdown of timing. For now, consider budgeting approximately one minute per question to read, but not more than four minutes. For example, if you see that the passage has three questions, you have about three minutes to read. The following table has approximate timing benchmarks for reading comprehension based on the number of questions for a passage:

# of Questions	Time Spent Reading	Time Spent in Answer Choices	Total Time
1	1 minute 30 seconds	45 seconds	2 minutes, 15 seconds
2	2 minutes	45 seconds	3 minutes, 30 seconds
3	3 minutes	45 seconds	5 minutes, 15 seconds
4 (very rare)	3 minutes	45 seconds	6 minutes

Passages will likely have only one to three questions (or, rarely, four).

Strategy for General Questions

The following is a step-by-step breakdown of the process for RC questions. After absorbing the components of the process, read on to see how this process applies to general questions.

1. **Scan the question(s).**
    - Whether there is only one question or several, this step is always valuable.
    - Jot notes from the question (but *not* the answer choices) to aid your reading.
2. **Read and deconstruct the passage.**
    - Always seek out the main idea.
    - Use the Chapter 4: Components of Paragraphs concepts to aid your analysis.
3. **Address each question in turn, predicting an answer if you can.**
    - Always anchor your prediction to the text.
4. **Eliminate and select.**
    - Keep track of your eliminations on your scratch paper as you go.
    - If you have a prediction, does an answer choice match it?
    - If you do not like any of the choices, focus on eliminating wrong answers.
    - Guess if needed. As best you can, match the tone of the answer choice to the tone of the text.

Unit Two: **Paragraphs and Passages**

Recognizing and Answering General Questions

General questions follow the forms listed in the following table (the bold is for emphasis here and will not appear in actual questions):

Type of General Question	Common Phrasing
Main Idea	Which of the following best expresses **the main idea** of the passage?
Primary Purpose	The author's **primary purpose** is . . .
	The passage is **primarily concerned with** which of the following?

Your understanding of the paragraph from your initial read-through provides the key to answering general questions. The good news is that you're already reading for the main idea, assuming you're following the advice from Chapter 4. Because the answer will come from that initial read, the expectation is that you can answer most general questions in around 30 seconds.

Don't reread the passage. Instead, first predict the answer in your own words (step 3). This is the same as Text Completion and Sentence Equivalence: Predicting an answer can help you avoid trap answers and keep you engaged with your own interpretation of the text. It is also the same as TC and SE in that the goal isn't to predict the *exact* phrasing of the answer choice. Just predicting the general shape or theme will help you spot it more perspicaciously.

Once you have a prediction, dive right into the answer choices and start eliminating. Arming yourself with an effective interpretation of the paragraph will allow you to eliminate two or three choices quickly.

If you find yourself stuck with several answers left, you can apply a scoring system: On general questions, an answer choice that incorporates elements from more parts of the paragraph or passage is a better candidate, as it likely covers a greater overview of the whole passage.

If you're still unsure of your final answer after making some eliminations, be careful about going back and forth between answer choices. It is better to just pick something rather than spending the time that was budgeted for other questions. If you think a fresh look will help you decide, click the Mark for Review button and come back to it later if you have time.

> *Strategy Tip:*
>
> For general questions, articulate a prediction in your own words, and eliminate answers that do not match.

Strategy for Specific Questions

The step-by-step process for specific questions does not differ significantly from the process outlined in the previous section. However, your process for predicting an answer and eliminating wrong choices may have more nuance.

Recognizing and Answering Specific Questions

Specific questions follow the forms listed in the following table (the bold is for emphasis here and will not appear in actual questions):

Type of Specific Question	Common Phrasing
Specific Detail	In the example discussed in the passage, **what is true** about poppy seeds in bread dough, once the dough has been thoroughly mixed? The passage **states** . . .
Inference	It can be **inferred** from the passage that . . . The author **suggests** . . .
Select a Sentence	**Select the sentence** that, according to the author, would best explain the early nineteenth-century trends toward more humane treatment of animals.
Specific Purpose	The author references the work of Von Neumann primarily **in order to** . . .
Word in Context	In the context in which it appears, "abstruse" (line 27) **most nearly means** . . .

Specific questions deal with details and inferences from specific elements within a paragraph, but in a variety of ways.

Two of the examples in the table (specific detail and inference) ask either what is true or what can be inferred. This is a common theme in most specific questions: You are instructed to find particular text and then *use* that text to prove a choice.

Everyday use of the word *inference* often refers to something that is suggested by facts, but is not definitively certain. For example, if you see someone carrying an umbrella outside, you would likely infer that the person is expecting rain that day. But on the GRE, you can only infer that the person has *some reason* to carry an umbrella. **Any GRE inference should stick so closely to stated text that it feels provable from the text.**

The next two examples in the table (select a sentence and specific purpose) are the logical inverse of the first two. These questions do not task you with using the information, but instead ask how the author of the passage used the information. These questions strongly benefit from the type of analysis presented in Chapter 4: GRE Paragraphs.

The final example (word in context) asks you to identify the intended meaning of a word in the sentence and could almost be considered Sentence Equivalence in Reading Comprehension form. Your goal will be to select a word that could replace the quoted word without changing the original meaning of the sentence. As such, synonyms for the word in the question are your prediction.

Using the Specifics of a Specific Question

Imagine that in your initial scan you read the question *Robinson raises the issue of cultural bias to do which of the following?* You have no idea who Robinson is or how cultural bias is discussed. Don't expect to predict an answer or even understand the question before reading the paragraph! Instead, make a note of what is being asked. You might jot down the following note on your paper:

R: cult. bias why?

Unit Two: **Paragraphs and Passages**

When you reach the part of the passage that pertains to this question, do one thing: Make note of where in the passage this information is and make an effort to understand it within your work-in-progress interpretation. Do not stop reading to go answer the question! Many trap answers will seem tempting if you don't have the context of the entire paragraph. They're written that way intentionally, knowing some test takers will hunt for the relevant text and only skim the passage. If you think you can predict the answer partway through the passage, make a note of your prediction; then, continue reading the entire passage and working to understand the main idea. If the passage has multiple questions and you want to jump to this specific question to tackle first after you're done reading, that's fine. The order of the questions is up to you, but if you try to answer a question without the context of the entire passage, it will ultimately make the problem more harrowing and perhaps more frustrating.

Some specific questions won't provide enough detail for you to make a note. For example, the question "Which of the following can be inferred from the passage?" gives you no information about what to analyze while you read. When you see questions like that, anticipate that you'll spend more time on process of elimination with the answer choices and that the question may take a little longer than average.

To answer these frustratingly indeterminate questions, first eliminate any answer choices that are opposed to or not mentioned in the passage. Of the remaining answers, you *will* need to return to the passage. Find key words in the answer choices that help you find the relevant part of the passage. Use your notes as a search tool, if necessary.

> *Strategy Tip:*
> For specific questions, use key words from the question or answer choices to find relevant parts of the passage.

In order to find the relevant parts of the passage, you may need to find a synonym for the key words in the question. For example, if the question addresses *natural disasters*, you may need to find a sentence that addresses *natural hazards or similar*. In a question with no key words, e.g., *Which of the following can be inferred from the passage?*, your only option for key words will be key words from each choice.

Once you find the key words in the passage, analyze the surrounding sentence or sentences to predict an answer to the question. Almost all specific questions can be proven from one or two sentences; a small handful require more than two proof sentences. You may have to revisit the text or, in longer passages, take a few notes to figure out what the sentences mean. That is expected because, after all, the goal was not to master those details while reading. If you are working on a question with context clues, such as the original example *Robinson raises the issue of cultural bias . . .* , do not look at the answer choices until you boil down the relevant sentence or sentences into a synopsis—work to keep it to just a few words. (If you took notes as described in Chapter 4: Don't Just Read, Do Something!, this part of the process will be easier.)

Then you can bring that synopsis back to the answer choices and hold it in your head as you eliminate choices and seek out a match.

> *Strategy Tip:*
> For specific questions, craft a synopsis from one or two proof sentences and compare the choices to it.

If you struggle to summarize the relevant text or you cannot find relevant text at all, then you know that the question is hard. The remaining sections of this chapter will offer you some additional strategies to use when you encounter these situations. If you still have multiple choices remaining after prudent eliminations, it is time to guess. No one question is more important than the others, so pick an answer and move on, perhaps marking the question to return to should you have more time.

Common Wrong Answer Categories

Wrong answers on Reading Comprehension questions tend to fall into one or more of five broad categories. You do not need to categorize wrong answers as you eliminate them in timed attempts. On the test, do not spend time pondering the category of an answer choice that you know is blatantly wrong. But take the time to categorize as many wrong answers as you can during untimed review: You will find that the test writers repeat these archetypes very often, sometimes even in wrong answers within the same question. And if you become adept at this categorization, the wrongness of the wrong choices becomes more apparent, more quickly, on the actual test.

As another benefit to this analysis, you might recognize a pattern in your own dubious answer selections. For example, you might discover upon review that you frequently choose Direct Contradiction answers. With this realization, you can incorporate one more double check into your process to look for that particular sort of error.

1. **One Word Wrong**
    - Just one word (or maybe two) is incorrect; this includes extreme words
    - Very common in general questions
2. **Out of Scope**
    - Introduces an unsupported assertion that has no evidence in the passage
    - Might be "real-world plausible" (that is, the answer might be true, or at least believable, in the real world)—however, if the answer is not supported in the passage, it is out of scope
3. **Direct Contradiction**
    - States the exact opposite of something asserted in the passage
    - Paradoxically attractive because it relates to the passage closely; if you miss one contrast or switchback in the trail, you can easily think a direct contradiction is the right answer
4. **Mix-Up**
    - Scrambles together different words or phrases from the passage, but the meaning of the choice does not reflect what the passage said
    - Tries to trap the student who simply matches language, not meaning
5. **True but Irrelevant**
    - True according to the passage, but does not answer the given question
    - May be too narrow or simply unrelated

Unit Two: **Paragraphs and Passages**

Summary of Strategies for Answer Choice Eliminations

In the correct answer choice, every word must be completely true and within the scope of the passage. If you cannot justify *every* word in the answer choice, eliminate it. For example, consider the following answer choices:

(A) The colonists resented the king for taxing them without representation.
(B) England's policy of taxation without representation caused resentment among the colonists.

The difference in these two answer choices lies in the word *king* versus the word *England*. Although this seems like a small difference, it is the key to eliminating one of these answer choices. If the passage does not mention the *king* when it discusses the colonists' resentment, then the word *king* cannot be justified, and the answer choice can be eliminated.

> *Strategy Tip:*
> Justify *every* word in the answer choice.

Extreme words, such as *all* and *never*, tend to broaden the scope of an answer choice too much or make it too extreme. The GRE typically uses moderate language and ideas. Avoid wantonly selecting answer choices that sound confident, but go too far. Occasionally you are justified in picking an extreme choice, but the passage must back you up 100 percent.

> *Strategy Tip:*
> Only choose an answer with an extreme word if the passage itself uses similarly extreme language.

Many Reading Comprehension questions ask you to infer something from the passage. An inference is an informed deduction. Reading Comprehension inferences rarely go far beyond what is stated in the passage. In general, infer so little that the inference seems obvious.

It is often surprising how simplistic GRE inferences are. If an answer choice answers the question and can be confirmed by language in the passage, it will be the correct one. Conversely, eliminate answer choices that require any logical stretch or leap. When you read *The passage suggests …* or *The passage implies …*, rephrase that language: *The passage states just a little differently …* You must be able to prove the answer, just as if the question asked you to look it up in the passage.

> *Strategy Tip:*
> As you work through answer choices, keep inferences close to the text.

Chapter 5: **Short Passages in Reading Comprehension**

Comprehensive Strategies for All Reading Comprehension

You now have seven effective strategies to use on Reading Comprehension questions on the GRE. Practice them frequently.

For general questions:

1. Articulate the main idea in your own words and eliminate answers. If you are stuck between two answer choices, use a scoring system to find the one that covers more of the breadth of the whole passage.

For specific questions:

2. Match key words in specific questions to key words (or synonyms) in the passage.
3. Defend your answer choice with one or two proof sentences.

For all questions:

4. Justify *every* word in your answer choice.
5. Justify *extreme* words in answer choices.
6. Choose an answer choice that infers as *little* as possible.

And do not forget:

7. Preview the questions before reading the passage.

Vocabulary Challenge

> Did you spot these vocabulary words? If not, go back and find them in context! (The word may be in a different form than listed here— "digressing" instead of "digress," for example.) Write your own definitions based on the evidence in the chapter.

1. perspicacious (*adj.*), p. 134
2. harrowing (*adj.*), p. 136
3. indeterminate (*adj.*), p. 136
4. prudent (*adj.*), p. 137
5. dubious (*adj.*), p. 137
6. wanton (*adj.*), p. 138

Unit Two: **Paragraphs and Passages**

A Short Introduction to the Problem Set

As you will see in this chapter's problem set, content-based Reading Comprehension questions can be presented in one of three formats: Select One, Select One or More, and Select-in-Passage.

Select One is the standard, five-answer multiple choice question for which you pick one answer. In that format, you can expect to see both general and specific questions. Jot down A through E on your scratch paper for these problems.

Select One or More questions offer three answer choices, multiple of which might be correct; jot down A through C on your scratch paper.

Select-in-Passage questions ask you to click the sentence in the passage that matches a certain description. If you're given one paragraph, number each sentence in that paragraph to keep track of your answer eliminations. (For example, if there are six sentences, jot down 1 through 6.) If you are given multiple paragraphs, first number each paragraph; when you have narrowed down to a single paragraph, number each sentence.

Both Select One or More and Select-in-Passage will typically be specific questions. For full descriptions of the two types, return to the Introduction: Verbal Question Formats in Detail. Ensure you can quickly recognize the format and the applicable strategies.

In the following problem set, you will first revisit two passages you've already seen, and attempt GRE questions on them for the first time. Then, you will apply the strategies you've learned to a completely new passage and question set.

For the purpose of practice and exposure to different question types, this chapter will review many questions on some passages. However, on the GRE, a passage will typically have only one to three questions associated with it.

Preview the questions for the passage, then read that passage. As you read, take notes if you wish. Aim for approximately 30 seconds or so for general questions and about one minute for specific questions (though some may take you longer). When you're done, review the problems and analyze the answer choices in order to learn how to get better next time.

Chapter 5: **Short Passages in Reading Comprehension**

Problem Set

> The next two passages are revisited from the problem set in Chapter 4: GRE Paragraphs. Review the passages and attempt the questions that follow, using the 4-step process.

Passage A: Arousal and Attraction

In 1974, psychologists Dutton and Aron discovered that male subjects who had just crossed a precarious wire-suspension bridge reacted to an attractive female interviewer differently than subjects who had instead crossed a low, solid bridge. Specifically, in response to a questionnaire that secretly measured sexual arousal, subjects from the wire-suspension bridge revealed significantly more sexual imagery than the others; moreover, a far greater fraction of wire-suspension subjects than of solid-bridge subjects contacted the interviewer afterward. Dutton and Aron explained their results in terms of misattribution. In their view, subjects crossing the wobbly bridge experienced physiological fear reactions, such as increased heart rate. Such reactions with ambiguous or suppressed causes are easily reinterpreted, in the presence of a potential partner, as sexual attraction. However, Foster and others later found that an unattractive interviewer is actually perceived as much less attractive by subjects physiologically aroused by fearful situations. Thus, the arousal is reinterpreted either as attraction or as repulsion, but in either case, the true cause is masked.

1. Based on the passage, which of the following could be reasonably assumed about passengers of a particularly turbulent flight?

    Select <u>all</u> that apply.

    | A | They would be likely to misattribute the cause of a sexual attraction they felt to a fellow passenger during a lull in turbulence.
    | B | They would be likely to misattribute the cause of a sexual attraction they felt to a fellow passenger a few days after the flight.
    | C | They would be more likely to find themselves viscerally disgusted by a baggage handler at their arrival gate whom they typically would have found merely unappealing.

> Review the following passages and attempt the questions that follow.

Passage B: Animal Treatment

In the early nineteenth century, educated Britons came to accept the then-novel notion that animals must be treated humanely, as evidenced by the outlawing of certain forms of domestic animal abuse, as well as the founding of the Society for the Prevention of Cruelty to Animals in 1824. This trend may be regarded as part of a broader embrace of compassionate ideals, such as abolitionism and alleviation of poverty. For instance, in 1785 the Society for the Relief of Persons Imprisoned for Small Sums persuaded Parliament to restrict that archaic punishment, and similar societies focused on various issues of humane treatment emerged around this time. However, a deeper explanation should be traced to socioeconomic conditions related to ongoing industrialization. Those protesting cruelty to animals were city dwellers who viewed animals as pets rather than as livestock, despite the ubiquity of horse transport. In fact, nature was no longer considered menacing, since society's victory over wilderness was conspicuous. Animals were to some extent romanticized as emblems of a bucolic, pre-industrial age.

Unit Two: **Paragraphs and Passages**

2. Based on the passage, which of the following is true about the first few decades of the nineteenth century?

    Select all that apply.

    | A | England was entering a more bucolic age of industry.
    | B | English society was becoming more compassionate towards some oppressed animals and humans.
    | C | Some viewed industrialization as a victory over wilderness.

3. Select the sentence that, according to the author, would best explain the early nineteenth-century trend towards more humane treatment of animals.

> The following problem set consists of a passage followed by a series of questions. On the GRE, you will typically see one to four questions associated with each passage. However, in this problem set, there are excessive questions so that you can gain more practice answering a variety of question types. (Remember that you can preview the questions!) As such, use the following modified timing guidelines:
>
> - **When reading passages**, spend approximately 1.5 minutes for medium-length passages. If a topic is more complex or detailed, spend less time on the details; just get the main ideas and major twists.
> - **When answering questions**, spend approximately 30 to 45 seconds on General questions and approximately 45 to 60 seconds on Specific questions. Expect to spend the full time on Select-One-or-More and EXCEPT questions; these will almost always take longer.
>
> Finally, if you'd like, answer only three or four of the questions the first time you do the passage. You can then save the passage for a second pass (with the remaining three or four questions) later on in your study.

Passage C: Japanese Swords

Historians have long recognized the traditional Japanese sword, or *nihonto*, as one of the finest cutting weapons ever produced, but it has even been considered a spiritual entity. The adage "the sword is the soul of the samurai" reflects the sword's psychic importance, not only to its wielder, but also to its creator, the master smith. Not classically regarded as artists, master smiths nevertheless exerted great care in the process of creating swords, no two of which were ever forged exactly the same way. Over hundreds of hours, two types of steel were repeatedly heated, hammered, and folded together into thousands of imperceptible layers, yielding both a razor-sharp, durable edge and a flexible, shock-absorbing blade. Commonly, though optionally, the smith physically signed the blade; moreover, each smith's secret forging techniques left an idiosyncratic structural signature. Each unique finished product reflected the smith's personal honor and devotion to the craft, and today, the Japanese sword is valued as much for its artistic merit as for its historical significance.

4. The primary purpose of the passage is to
   - (A) challenge the observation that the Japanese sword is highly admired by historians
   - (B) introduce new information about the forging of Japanese swords
   - (C) identify the Japanese sword as an ephemeral work of art
   - (D) argue that Japanese sword makers were motivated by honor
   - (E) explain the value attributed to the Japanese sword

5. Each of the following is mentioned in the passage EXCEPT
   - (A) every Japanese sword has a unique structure that can be traced back to a special forging process
   - (B) master smiths kept their forging methodologies secret
   - (C) the Japanese sword was considered by some to have a spiritual quality
   - (D) master smiths are now considered artists by major historians
   - (E) the Japanese sword is considered both a work of art and a historical artifact

6. What could be inferred from the mention of an individual smith's secret forging techniques mentioned in the passage?
   - (A) The Japanese sword is the most important handheld weapon in history.
   - (B) The skill of the samurai is what made the Japanese sword so special.
   - (C) If a sword had a physical signature, other swords with that signature could be attributed to that sword's creator.
   - (D) Master smiths were more concerned about the artistic merit of their blades than about the blades' practical qualities.
   - (E) The Japanese sword has more historical importance than artistic importance.

7. Which of the following can be inferred about the words "structural signature" in this passage?
   - (A) They indicate the inscription that the smith places on the blade during the forging process.
   - (B) They imply the particular characteristics of a blade created by a smith's unique forging process.
   - (C) They suggest that each blade can be traced back to a known master smith.
   - (D) They reflect the soul of the samurai who wielded the sword.
   - (E) They refer to the unique curved shape of the blade.

8. The author most likely describes the forging process in order to
   - (A) present an explanation for a change in perception
   - (B) determine the historical significance of Japanese swords
   - (C) explain why each Japanese sword is unique
   - (D) compare Japanese master smiths to classical artists
   - (E) review the complete process of making a Japanese sword

Unit Two: **Paragraphs and Passages**

9. Select the sentence in the passage that best indicates that the author believes traditional Japanese swords are works of art.

10. Which of the following statements about Japanese swords is supported by the passage?

    Select all that apply.

    | A | There is a way to determine the creator of a given sword other than his signature on the blade.
    | B | They have been viewed in terms other than the purely material.
    | C | They have not always received the artistic recognition that they deserve.

Answers and Explanations

Vocabulary Challenge

1. perspicacious (*adj.*): having penetrating insight or good discernment

2. harrowing (*adj.*): painfully disturbing or distressing

3. indeterminate (*adj.*): not fixed or determined, indefinite; vague

4. prudent (*adj.*): wise in practical matters, carefully providing for the future

5. dubious (*adj.*): doubtful, questionable, suspect

6. wanton (*adj.*): reckless, vicious, without regard for what is right

Problem Set

> The first two passages are repeated from the Chapter 4: GRE Paragraphs problem set. If desired, refer to the Chapter 4 problem set explanations for additional instruction on taking notes for each passage.

1. Based on the passage, which of the following could be reasonably assumed about passengers of a particularly turbulent flight? Select <u>all</u> that apply.

   A. They would be likely to misattribute the cause of a sexual attraction they felt to a fellow passenger during a lull in turbulence.

   B. They would be likely to misattribute the cause of a sexual attraction they felt to a fellow passenger a few days after the flight.

   C. They would be more likely to find themselves viscerally disgusted by a baggage handler at their arrival gate whom they typically would have found merely unappealing.

This is a Select One or More question that asks you to extrapolate from the bridge example to an example involving an airplane. Despite the seemingly out-of-context setting, this should still be treated as an inference question: A turbulent flight would be almost exactly like crossing a wobbly bridge. Which of the choices are closest to the statements in the text itself? Your prediction might be "they would react more extremely immediately after the flight, but not really know why."

   A. **CORRECT.** This example is analogous to the one given in the passage. A passenger on a turbulent flight would still likely be experiencing "physiological fear reactions" even during a lull in the turbulence. This physiological arousal can be "reinterpreted either as attraction or repulsion," so any feeling of attraction is likely to be caused by the fear reaction.

   B. The passage stresses the manner in which the researchers interviewed subjects *immediately* after crossing the bridge, when the "physiological fear reactions" were still fresh. A few days after a turbulent flight, passengers would be unlikely to continue to experience those reactions.

   C. **CORRECT.** This example is analogous to the one given in the passage. A passenger coming off of a turbulent flight would likely still be experiencing "physiological fear reactions" that can cause repulsion as easily as attraction. The passage states that an "unattractive interviewer is actually perceived as much less attractive by subjects physiologically aroused by fearful situations."

Unit Two: **Paragraphs and Passages**

2. Based on the passage, which of the following is true about the first few decades of the nineteenth century? Select <u>all</u> that apply.

- [A] England was entering a more bucolic age of industry.
- [B] English society was becoming more compassionate towards some oppressed animals and humans.
- [C] Some viewed industrialization as a victory over wilderness.

This is a Select One or More question asking about the beginning of the nineteenth century. The passage mentions a few dates, all of which will be useful in determining what was true at the dawn of the nineteenth century. This is an inference question: The entire paragraph is about the early nineteenth century, so there is no single sentence you could point to for your answer. Examine the choices for key words, and compare those back to the paragraph.

- [A] The last sentence says that in the nineteenth century, animals became emblems of a "bucolic, pre-industrial age." The point is that that bucolic age was coming to an end at this time. This answer choice mismatches the details: "bucolic" is associated with the "pre-industrial age", not an age of industry.
- [B] **CORRECT.** The passage states that, in the early nineteenth century, some "forms of domestic animal abuse" were outlawed and society was also embracing "abolitionism and alleviation of poverty" (both of which are aimed at humans).
- [C] **CORRECT.** The author's "deeper explanation" relates the trends to "ongoing industrialization," as city dwellers came to view animals more as pets. The passage then states that "nature was no longer menacing, since society's victory over wilderness was conspicuous." Society, in this context, is the city dwellers who are living a more industrialized life.

3. Select the sentence that, according to the author, would best explain the early nineteenth-century trend towards more humane treatment of animals.

This is a Select-in-Passage question. The second sentence states: "This trend may be regarded as part of a broader embrace of compassionate ideals, such as abolitionism and alleviation of poverty." While this sentence would be tempting to select, as it provides one possible explanation for the phenomenon discussed, the author does not subscribe to this explanation. The author presents a "deeper explanation" in the fourth sentence of the paragraph: "However, a deeper explanation should be traced to socioeconomic conditions related to ongoing industrialization." This is the correct answer.

Chapter 5: **Short Passages in Reading Comprehension**

Answers to Passage C: Japanese Swords

> **Upon previewing the questions, here is an example of what you might jot down:**
>
> 1. main idea
> 2.
> 3. Au agree
> 4. structural signature
> 5. forging process why describe?
> 6. swords = art where?
> 7. sword facts
>
> Questions 4, 5, and 6 are specific enough that you can look for the answer to those as you read the passage. The other will take more focus on the answer choices. Question 2 has no context, so don't bother writing anything about it during your preview.
>
> **Upon reading the passage, here is one example of a possible set of notes for this passage:**
>
> 1. H: J sword = 1 of best cutting weapons, but even spiritual ← main idea
>   —Soul of Samurai
>   —Impt to smith too
> 2. —Smiths careful, swords unique
>   —Forging = complex
>   —Physical + structural signat

4. The primary purpose of the passage is to

- (A) challenge the observation that the Japanese sword is highly admired by historians
- (B) introduce new information about the forging of Japanese swords
- (C) identify the Japanese sword as an ephemeral work of art
- (D) argue that Japanese sword makers were motivated by honor
- (E) explain the value attributed to the Japanese sword

Unit Two: **Paragraphs and Passages**

To identify the primary purpose of the passage, examine the passage as a whole: the correct choice will reflect the main idea. Avoid answer choices that address only limited sections of the passage. The main idea of the passage (*the Japanese sword has been considered not just a fine weapon but a spiritual entity*) is established in the first two sentences; the purpose of the passage is to explain and support that main idea. Your prediction should resemble this main idea statement.

(A) The passage does not call into question the admiration that historians have for the Japanese sword.

(B) The middle of the passage discusses forging techniques, but none of the information is presented as new. Moreover, these forging techniques are not the overall focus of the passage.

(C) The Japanese sword is not identified as an ephemeral (passing) work of art in the passage.

(D) Japanese sword makers were indeed motivated by honor, at least in part, according to the last sentence, but this is not the overall purpose of the passage, much of which describes the Japanese sword's physical properties and reasons for its importance.

(E) **CORRECT.** The passage as a whole describes the immense value of the Japanese sword to both the samurai (the sword's owner) and the smith (its maker). The saying "the sword is the soul of the samurai" is referenced early to indicate this importance. Later portions of the passage detail the tremendous effort that is put into each sword, reflecting the importance of each one.

5. Each of the following is mentioned in the passage EXCEPT

(A) every Japanese sword has a unique structure that can be traced back to a special forging process

(B) master smiths kept their forging methodologies secret

(C) the Japanese sword was considered by some to have a spiritual quality

(D) master smiths are now considered artists by major historians

(E) the Japanese sword is considered both a work of art and a historical artifact

With no context clues in the question, use the answer choices themselves for key words. For an EXCEPT question (almost always a Specific question), use the process of elimination to cross out those details mentioned in the passage. Eliminate any answer choices you can remember, then use key words to seek out the remaining choices to verify that 4 of the 5 are present in the passage. You will not be able to make a prediction on this question: this will be entirely process of elimination.

(A) In the passage, this *unique signature* is referred to as a "structural signature" in the fifth sentence.

(B) The fifth sentence mentions the "secret forging techniques" used by each smith.

(C) The first sentence indicates that "the traditional Japanese sword…has even been considered a spiritual entity."

(D) **CORRECT.** The time and effort master smiths devote to making a sword is discussed, and the passage does indicate that the Japanese sword is valued for its artistic merit. However, the passage does not state that major historians consider master smiths themselves to be artists. *Major* historians are not referenced in the passage. Moreover, who values the Japanese sword for its artistic merit is not mentioned.

(E) In the last sentence, the passage indicates that "the Japanese sword is valued as much for its artistic merit as for its historical significance."

6. What could be inferred from the mention of an individual smith's secret forging techniques mentioned in the passage?

- (A) The Japanese sword is the most important handheld weapon in history.
- (B) The skill of the samurai is what made the Japanese sword so special.
- (C) If a sword had a physical signature, other swords with that same signature could likely be attributed to that sword's creator.
- (D) Master smiths were more concerned about the artistic merit of their blades than about the blades' practical qualities.
- (E) The Japanese sword has more historical importance than artistic importance.

This specific detail question refers to the next-to-last sentence: ". . .each smith's secret forging techniques left an idiosyncratic structural signature." The answer will reflect this sentence.

- (A) The opening sentence says: "Historians have long recognized the traditional Japanese sword…as one of the finest cutting weapons ever produced"; however, there is no indication that the Japanese sword is the *most* important handheld weapon in history.
- (B) This passage does not discuss the skill of the samurai warrior.
- (C) **CORRECT.** According to the passage, every master smith had a "structural signature" due to his own secret forging process. Therefore, if a physical signature is present on a blade, that blade's structural signature could then be associated with a master smith, whose *master* status implies the creation of numerous swords.
- (D) The passage mentions that each sword "reflected the smith's personal honor and devotion to craft"; however, there is no claim that master smiths emphasized their swords' artistic merit at the expense of practical qualities.
- (E) The final sentence indicates that the sword "is valued as much for it artistic merit as for its historical significance." According to the passage, the two attributes are essentially equally valued; the Japanese sword is not more valued for the historical aspect.

7. Which of the following can be inferred about the term "structural signature" in this passage?

- (A) They indicate the inscription that the smith places on the blade during the forging process.
- (B) They imply the particular characteristics of a blade created by a smith's unique forging process.
- (C) They suggest that each blade can be traced back to a known master smith.
- (D) They reflect the soul of the samurai who wielded the swords.
- (E) They refer to the unique curved shape of the blade.

Unit Two: **Paragraphs and Passages**

This question is a cross between a specific detail question and a word in context question. The correct answer will essentially rephrase the information in the sentence. The author states that "each smith's secret forging techniques left an idiosyncratic structural signature." The words *idiosyncratic* and *signature* imply the uniqueness of the smith's process. Be careful not to infer any additional information, particularly when the question refers to a specific sentence or phrase.

- (A) In the passage, such an inscription is referred to as a "physical signature," not a "structural signature."
- (B) **CORRECT.** The proof sentence indicates that each smith had his own process; the "structural signature" was unique to each smith (not necessarily to each individual blade).
- (C) This statement seems reasonable. However, the passage does not say whether all master smiths are currently "known." Certain swords with a "structural signature" may be of unknown origin.
- (D) The second sentence mentions the saying "the sword is the soul of the samurai," but does not say that the "structural signature" was the aspect of the sword reflecting the soul of the samurai who wielded it. The second paragraph explains that the sword "reflected the smith's personal honor and devotion to craft." This statement, however, does not justify the claim that the structural signature itself reflects the soul of the samurai who wielded it.
- (E) The passage does not discuss the shape of any Japanese blade.

8. The author most likely describes the forging process in order to
- (A) present an explanation for a change in perception
- (B) determine the historical significance of Japanese swords
- (C) explain why each Japanese sword is unique
- (D) compare Japanese master smiths to classical artists
- (E) review the complete process of making a Japanese sword

To answer this specific purpose question, pay attention to the emphasized content of the referenced sentence, in particular any reiterated points, and to the relationship that part has to other portions of the passage. Note that this sentence extends the discussion of how "no two of which were ever forged exactly the same way."

- (A) The final sentence mentions that Japanese swords are now appreciated more for their artistic merit, but no explanation as to why is provided.
- (B) The words "historical significance" close the passage, but the description of the forging process fails to explain or outline that significance.
- (C) **CORRECT.** The description of the forging process underscores the uniqueness of individual Japanese swords. One sentence mentions that "no two [swords] were ever forged in exactly the same way." Later, "structural signature" and "unique finished product" reinforce this point.
- (D) The passage explains that master smiths were not considered artists in the classical sense, and then goes on to point out the painstaking creation of each sword. This implicitly draws a parallel between the creation of the sword and classical artistry. However, the passage does not actually describe or discuss classical artists, nor does it set forth criteria for classical artists. There is no actual comparison to classical artists, despite the mention of "artistic merit." This answer choice goes too far beyond the passage.
- (E) Elements of the forging process are discussed, but the "complete" process of making a Japanese sword, such as making the handle, polishing the blade, etc., is not discussed in the paragraph.

Chapter 5: **Short Passages in Reading Comprehension**

9. **Select the sentence in the passage that best indicates that the author believes traditional Japanese swords are works of art.**

The passage first mentions the idea of art in the third sentence, but indicates that master smiths were *not* regarded as artists. After describing the meticulous forging process, the last sentence indicates that each sword is "unique" and is valued for its "artistic merit." The last sentence, then, best indicates that the author would consider these swords works of art.

The correct answer is the last sentence of the paragraph: "Each unique finished product reflected the smith's personal honor and devotion to the craft, and today, the Japanese sword is valued as much for its artistic merit as for its historical significance."

10. **Which of the following statements about Japanese swords is supported by the passage? Select all that apply.**

   A   There is a way to determine the creator of a given sword other than his signature on the blade.

   B   They have been viewed in terms other than the purely material.

   C   They have not always received the artistic recognition that they deserve.

This is an inference question of the Select One or More variety. Since the question references the entire paragraph rather than pointing to a specific detail, no prediction is possible. Tackle each answer choice as its own question.

   A   **CORRECT.** The second-to-last sentence says that "each smith's secret forging techniques left an idiosyncratic structural signature." This structural signature, then, could possibly be used to determine the creator of a given sword, even in the absence of a physical signature.

   B   **CORRECT.** The first sentence tells you that the Japanese sword "has even been considered a spiritual entity." In other words, it has been viewed in terms other than the strictly material.

   C   **CORRECT.** The last sentence tells you that "today, the Japanese sword is valued as much for its artistic merit as for its historical significance." Earlier in the passage, however, you were told that master smiths were "not classically regarded as artists." This means that those smiths viewed as artists today did not always receive the same recognition and neither did the swords they made.

CHAPTER 6
Argument-Based Reading Comprehension

In This Chapter ...

- Recognizing Argument-Based Passages
- Components of Argument-Based Passages
- Identifying the Components of an Argument
- Strategy for ABP Questions
- Taking Notes
- Useful Focal Points for All Question Types
- Question Types
- Vocabulary Challenge
- Problem Set
- Answers and Explanations

CHAPTER 6 Argument-Based Reading Comprehension

As discussed at the beginning of the previous chapter, some GRE passages are Argument-Based Passages (ABPs). ABPs consist of a brief argument, generally one to three sentences long, and a question relating to that argument. In this chapter, you will learn how to adjust your approach to RC for this passage type, and use that approach to answer various question types.

Here are your Chapter 6 vocabulary words:

>discrepancy (E)
>diverge (E)
>circumspect (A)
>germane (E)
>multifarious (A)
>circumscribe (A)

Recognizing Argument-Based Passages

Expect to see one to two ABPs per section, each accompanied by a single question. These individual questions should take about the same amount of time as similar questions on other RC passages. Though there aren't multiple questions to preview, still read the question before you read the passage, as it will tell you exactly what kind of ABP you're dealing with.

Similarly to the standard RC passages, arguments in ABPs are made up of premises, counterpoints, assumptions, and conclusions. Some arguments will also contain background information or context; this information helps you to understand the topic under discussion but is not actually part of the argument itself.

The Official Guide to the GRE® General Test does not differentiate between regular Reading Comprehension passages and Argument-Based Passages, but the difference is beneficial to your process. Your first job on any passage will be to categorize it.

How? Before you dive into the argument itself, read the question stem to determine what you've got.

Unit Two: **Paragraphs and Passages**

The following question types appear only on ABPs:

- Analyze Argument Structure: These questions will highlight a sentence or two in the passage and then ask you what purpose they're serving in the argument. Generally, when you see the word *argument*, think ABP.
- Strengthen and Weaken: If a question asks you to strengthen (support) or weaken (undermine) the argument, it's an ABP.
- Resolve a Paradox/Explain a Discrepancy: If the question asks you to resolve or explain something puzzling, then you've got an ABP.
- Find the Assumption: If a question asks you what is assumed by the argument or what the argument depends on, then you have a Find the Assumption ABP.

These question types appear only on RC passages:

- Main Idea, Tone, and Attitude: ABPs are generally too short to get across any kind of overall main point or tone.
- Look-Up Detail: Any question that begins "According to the passage" or asks what the author talked about in detail signals a regular RC passage.
- Author's Purpose: Some questions ask why the author mentioned a particular detail. If you see the language "in order to" in the question stem, then you know you've got a regular RC passage.
- Select-in-Passage or Select-One-or-More questions always signal a regular RC passage. ABP questions always ask you to choose exactly one answer choice from a listed set of five answers.

One question type can appear on both RC passages and ABPs. This chapter will focus on the presentation used for ABPs: a very brief paragraph followed by only one question.

- Inference: Any RC paragraph or passage can have a question that asks what is inferred, implied, or suggested—including ABPs. Here's the good news: The solution process for Inference is the same regardless of the passage type.

> *Strategy Tip:*
>
> For all RC questions, read the question stem itself to determine what type of question you have. If you have an ABP, jot down answer letters A through E to keep track of your eliminations.

Components of Argument-Based Passages

If you notice that the following discussion is eerily similar to what you read in Chapter 4: Components of Paragraphs, why yes…yes it is! Similar active reading habits are helpful across GRE Verbal, regardless of question type. If you already feel confident in breaking down paragraphs, merely skim the following paragraphs until the discussion of **assumptions**.

Premises provide support for the argument's conclusion. They may be facts, opinions, or claims. If they are opinions or claims, they will not be the overall claim the author is making; rather, they will be some intermediate claim the author is using to support the overall claim (conclusion). Some ABPs contain only premises: These paragraphs are used for questions that ask you to derive a conclusion or explanation based on those facts. In these instances, the question will not refer to the paragraph as an argument, but rather use language that indicates all the information in the paragraph is factual (e.g., *If the facts above are true, which of the following . . .* or *Which of the following provides an explanation for the surprising result described above?*)

The main idea of the argument is the conclusion, which is logically supported by the premises (and assumptions). Conclusions are in the form of an opinion or a claim; they are not pure facts. All arguments contain conclusions, so if the question references an argument, there will be a conclusion.

Counterpoints (or counter-premises) undermine or go against the conclusion. Occasionally, an argument will present both sides of an argument, with evidence to support both. The passage will still come down one way or the other in terms of an overall conclusion, but some of the provided evidence will be used as premises and some as counter-premises (supporting a kind of counter-conclusion).

Assumptions are unstated pieces of information that the argument requires to function. This is where you may need to adapt your process in ABPs. Whenever the question asks you to Strengthen, Weaken, or Find an Assumption, that's a clue that the passage is not stating a crucial element to the author's argument. Ask yourself: *What is this argument missing?*

> *Strategy Tip:*
>
> For all questions that pertain to an argument, pause and consider what unstated assumptions the argument has made.

Assumptions are often a factor the author didn't consider, such as an alternative explanation for a certain outcome that occurred or an additional outcome that might occur from a certain choice. Other assumptions can involve shifts in terminology: There is an example of this type of assumption in the argument regarding Melissa's GRE improvement in the next section.

Here's a simple example to illustrate:

> While the plot of the movie was compelling, the acting was atrocious. Thus, the movie will not win an Oscar.
>
> **Conclusion**: Thus, the movie will not win an Oscar.
> **Supporting premise**: The acting was atrocious.
> **Counterpoint**: The plot of the movie was compelling.
> **Assumption**: Atrocious acting prevents a movie from winning an Oscar (any kind of Oscar).

The paragraph evaluation elements discussed in Chapter 4: GRE Paragraphs still apply to Argument Structure Passages. The first word in the above example, "while," is a signal word to aid your evaluation of the relationships between the sentences.

Identifying the Components of an Argument

In order to do well on Argument-Based Passage questions, you must be able to identify the parts of an argument as described in the previous section. Consider the following argument and try to find the different pieces.

> Studying regularly is one factor that has been shown to improve one's performance on the GRE. Melissa took the GRE and scored a 150 on the Verbal section. If she studies several times a week, Melissa can expect to improve her score.

Unit Two: **Paragraphs and Passages**

In analyzing an argument, look first for the conclusion, which is the main idea of the argument. The conclusion is often at the end of the paragraph, and may be its own full sentence, but it does not have to be either. In this instance, the conclusion is at the end of the paragraph, but it is not a full sentence.

Conclusion: ". . . Melissa can expect to improve her score."

Note that the conclusion is just that she'll improve her score: This is the author's prediction, based on other given statements.

After finding the conclusion, identify the roles that the other statements play.

Premise: "Studying regularly is one factor that has been shown to improve one's performance on the GRE." This sentence supports the conclusion that Melissa can expect to improve her score.

Premise: "If she studies several times a week . . ." Studying several times a week is a given statement, and it is one reason the author predicts that Melissa can expect to improve her score.

Background: "Melissa took the GRE and scored a 150 on the Verbal section." This is good context for the argument, but has no direct bearing on whether Melissa can expect to improve her score.

The next step in the evaluation is where ABPs diverge from other RC passages and paragraphs. You need to identify what the author *assumes*. Here, there are multiple assumptions. The argument assumes that studying "several times a week" is the same as studying "regularly." Maybe "regularly" means every day! (This is an example of a "term shift" assumption: The author assumes that the term means a certain thing but there is no evidence to prove that this is the exact, correct meaning.) In that case, studying several times a week may not be enough.

The argument also assumes that there are not other factors involved. Yes, studying regularly is one factor that can improve performance on the GRE. But what if those studies are not organized or guided in any way, or are done in the midst of distraction? Maybe those factors would counterbalance any benefit of the regularity of the studies.

One more note: The conclusion was very, very carefully phrased in each step of this analysis. The conclusion was circumspect in avoiding more declarative language such as *will improve*. The original conclusion was less assertive, merely stating that Melissa *can expect* to improve. Take care with your conclusion statements, and do not insert language the author did not actually use.

Strategy for ABP Questions

In much the same way you tackled problems in Chapter 5: Short Passages in RC, you'll use a four-step process for every ABP you encounter:

Step 1: Identify the question type
Step 2: Deconstruct the argument
Step 3: State the goal
Step 4: Work from wrong to right

An overview follows; later, you'll go through the process in detail for each question type.

Step 1: Identify the Question Type

The vast majority of question stems will allow you to categorize a question into one of the types discussed previously. However, if the question stem is not immediately helpful or the question type is difficult to identify, do not dwell on the issue. Go ahead to the next step; afterward, you can reexamine the question.

Step 2: Deconstruct the Argument

Look for the conclusion, premises, counterpoints, and background. The question type will help you anticipate what to expect from the paragraph. (For example, if you've identified the question type, you'll know whether to look for a conclusion when reading the paragraph.) You may want to take notes while deconstructing; a few potential note-taking strategies will be discussed later.

Step 3: State the Goal

First, you probably won't be able to predict the exact language of the correct choice. Rather, you'll have a particular goal that you're trying to accomplish for each question type. Do not leave your goal a generic "weaken the argument" prediction. Instead, restate the question in terms of the argument whenever possible. For example, in a paragraph about climate effects on lobster populations, "Which choice makes it more likely that the lobster population will increase?" is more useful than "Which choice strengthens the argument?"

Step 4: Work from Wrong to Right

As on any RC question, process of elimination rules the day. (And those who don't follow process of elimination will *rue* the day! Sorry. . .we'll see ourselves out.) As a general rule, cross definitely wrong answers off first, and then compare any remaining tempting answers. Certain question types have common traps in the wrong answers:

Wrong Answer Category	Description	Commonly Found in Question Type . . .
Opposite Direction	This answer choice is germane to the argument, but has the opposite impact on the conclusion than the question requested (e.g., a Weaken question, but an answer that makes the argument more convincing, or an explain question, but the answer makes the situation more surprising).	Strengthen Weaken Explain
Wrong Focal Point	This answer choice focuses on background statements or counterpoints. Although this choice directly addresses a component of the paragraph, it fails in comparison to the common correct choice, which focuses on the argument's conclusion.	Strengthen Weaken Assumption
Too Extreme / Beyond the Scope	This wrong answer commonly contains absolute or overly broad language compared to the language in the paragraph.	Inference

Taking Notes

When dealing with Argument-Based Passages, you may wish to take some light notes as you do for regular Reading Comprehension passages. These notes will be even more abbreviated though, and they will focus on the flow of the information. What information leads to what conclusion, and what is the author assuming?

There are any number of ways to take notes; choose what you think would work best for your process. First, though, make sure you know what these notes are supposed to accomplish.

Your two main goals are as follows:

1. To classify each piece of information
2. To understand how the different pieces of information fit together

Option 1: Stream-of-Consciousness Notes

This option tends to work for people who jot down notes as they read. Read the first sentence (or part of a sentence), jot down a short note, and move on to the next sentence. At times, you may decide not to jot down a particular detail (e.g., background information may not be necessary to write down). Each new idea gets its own line.

When you're done, determine the conclusion if there is one. Place a C next to it (it's also a good idea to put a circle around the C). Put + (plus) signs next to any premises that support that conclusion. Put – (minus) signs next to any counterpoints that go against the conclusion.

Here's an example:

> Environmentalist: The national energy commission's current plan calls for the construction of six new nuclear power plants during the next decade. The commission argues that these plants are extremely safe and will have minimal environmental impact on their surrounding communities. However, all six nuclear power plants will be located far from densely populated areas. Clearly, the government is tacitly admitting that these plants do pose a serious health risk to humans.
>
> Which of the following, if true, most seriously weakens the environmentalist's claim of an unspoken government admission?

The left column shows sample notes. The right column, in italics, shows what someone may be thinking as they take these notes.

NEC plan: 6 NP next 10yr	*This is a fact, not a conclusion. I don't know yet whether it will support or go against the conclusion.*
NEC: v. safe, low enviro impact	*Okay, this group is claiming something.*
BUT NP not in pop areas	*Big contrast. Another fact.*
Gov admits NP = health risk	*Okay, this is the big claim.*

Now that you know what's going on, go back and add labels to each line:

    NEC plan: 6 NP next 10yr
– NEC: v. safe, low enviro impact
+ BUT NP not in pop areas
Ⓒ Gov admits NP = health risk

The first line is background information; these plants are going to be built. This fact doesn't work for or against the argument. The second line is information that goes against the conclusion. The author thinks these nuclear plants are bad, but the NEC thinks they will be safe. The third line is the author's sole premise and helps to support the author's conclusion. Since the NEC isn't placing any of these nuclear power plants in populated areas, the author concludes that the nuclear power plants must represent a health risk.

What does the author assume when drawing this conclusion?

One thing the author assumes is that there is no other reason why the nuclear power plants might be located in less populated areas. Perhaps the power plants need a lot of land and there isn't enough room in populated areas. If you think of that when reading the argument, you can add it to your notes:

[no other reason NP not in pop areas?]

Note the brackets; these can indicate that the argument itself doesn't mention this information. Rather, it's something you thought of yourself.

Option 2: The T-Diagram

This option tends to work for people who prefer to read the entire argument first and then jot down notes.

First, draw a large T on your scratch paper. Make it asymmetrical, leaving more room on the left side, which will be the "pro" side. In most arguments, you will have very little on the "con" side (to the right).

Step 1.

Second, read the argument and look for the conclusion. Once you find the conclusion, write it above the top line of the T, abbreviating heavily.

Step 2.

Conclusion

Third, add the rest of the argument information to the diagram. Write anything that supports the conclusion on the left side of the T ("pro" or "premise"), and write anything that goes against the conclusion on the right side of the T ("con" or "counterpoint").

Step 3.

Conclusion	
– Pro	– Con
– Pro	
– [Assumption]	

Finally, if you happened to think of any assumptions while reading, place them in brackets somewhere below the T. Make sure you can differentiate between information stated in the argument and your own thoughts when looking at your notes.

Here's how the environmentalist passage from above might look in T-diagram form:

plnts = ↑ hlth rsk	
plnts far frm pop areas	Comm: plnts safe, ↓ enviro impct
[No other reason for distance?]	

Note that this diagram contains different abbreviations from the first one. There is more than one way to write something down; use what works best for you.

How do I Know Whether My Notes are "Good"?

The above two options aren't the only ones. There are multifarious ways someone might choose to take notes. For example, some people are more visual and might feel most comfortable drawing or mapping out the information. You aren't obligated to follow one particular method; you can develop your own as long as you are accomplishing three goals:

1. If the argument does contain a conclusion, find and note it. The conclusion is the most important part of the argument.

2. If the argument contains any kind of *flow* of information (e.g., one thing leads to another or one thing goes against another), take note of how that information fits together.

3. Use simple and consistent ways to note important information. You don't need to designate the conclusion with a C, but you do need to designate the conclusion the same way every time. You don't want to spend time thinking about how to write something down or wondering what one of your abbreviations means.

If your notetaking style accomplishes those three goals at a minimum, then your process is good!

Useful Focal Points for All Question Types

Here are a few other approaches to try as you tackle the various question types in the next section.

Boundary Words in the Argument

For any question, it is helpful to focus your attention on the boundary words and phrases provided in the argument. These words and phrases specify what is being referred to, narrowing the scope of a premise or conclusion. For example:

Premise: The percentage of literate adults has increased.

The boundary word "percentage" circumscribes the scope of the premise. It restricts the meaning to percentage only, as opposed to the actual number of literate adults. For all you know, the actual number went down. The boundary word "adults" also limits the scope of the premise. It restricts the meaning to adults only, as opposed to the total population or children.

Here is another example:

> Conclusion: Controversial speech should be allowed, provided it does not incite major violence.

The sentences discusses an exception to the general rule that "Controversial speech should be allowed." The boundary word "major" limits the exception—controversial speech should *not* be allowed when it incites *major* violence, but the exception does not apply to speech that incites minor violence. Note that the argument doesn't define what constitutes major versus minor violence.

Boundary words and phrases are vital because they provide nuances to the argument, and these nuances will often be major factors in the answer choices. These details can single-handedly make some answer choices correct or incorrect. At the least, mentally note boundary words; if you write them down (recommended), you might underline them or capitalize them for emphasis. This will help you identify answer choices that try to trick you on the argument boundaries.

Extreme Words in the Argument

Another general strategy for all ABP questions involves extreme words and phrases in the body of the argument. Extreme words, such as *always*, *never*, *all*, and *none*, are the opposite of boundary words—they make the argument very broad or far-reaching.

Using extreme words opens up an argument unreasonably, making it very susceptible to strengthening or weakening. For example:

> Conclusion: Sugar is never healthy for anyone trying to lose weight.

The extreme word "never" unreasonably opens up this argument, placing no limitation on the claim that sugar is unhealthy. A more moderate conclusion would argue that sugar is often unhealthy or that excessive sugar is unhealthy. The extreme word "anyone" further opens up this argument. A more moderate conclusion might be that this claim applies to *most* people trying to lose weight. Note any extreme language used in premises or conclusions; any such words will likely be very useful in eliminating answer choices.

(The reason extreme words open an argument to attack is the same reason Too Extreme is one of the wrong answer traps listed earlier. Extreme words make a statement easier to question and harder to prove.)

Unit Two: Paragraphs and Passages

Boundary Words in the Answer Choices

Boundary words in the answers are just as important as boundary words in the body of the argument, though for a different reason. A correct answer choice must be 100 percent correct. As long as you interpret the words legitimately, such a choice must be valid no matter which way you interpret it. This principle provides an approach to evaluating answer choices. When you see boundary words in an answer choice, ask yourself, "What is the most extreme example I can think of that would still fit the wording of this answer choice?" Then, using the conclusion and the question asked, see whether your extreme example allows you to eliminate that answer choice.

For example, an answer choice might say:

(D) Some teachers leave the profession entirely within three years of beginning their teaching careers.

You might choose to address one of two different boundaries here. The word "Some" refers to some number of teachers but does not specify the size of the group. The phrase "within three years" refers to a period of time but does not specify the exact length of time.

If you choose to address the word "Some," you could say that 1 percent of teachers leave within three years or that 99 percent of teachers do so. Either way, the statistics still fit the criterion that some teachers do this. Suppose the conclusion asserted that new teacher turnover is having a major impact on the industry. If only 1 percent of new teachers leave within three years, then new teacher turnover will probably not have much of an impact.

Alternatively, you could interpret "within three years" to mean that many teachers in this category leave after 1 day of teaching. You could also imagine that many teachers in this category leave after 2 years and 364 days of teaching. Again, either way, the statistics still fit the criterion that new teachers leave the profession within 3 years of beginning their careers. Depending upon the conclusion and the question, you would then try to disprove answer choices by using these extreme interpretations.

Process of Elimination

It is important to eliminate answer choices on your scratch paper. Do *not* just eliminate answer choices in your head. As you go through many different questions during the test, it can be very difficult to remember which answer choices you have ruled out. You do not want to find yourself reevaluating answers that you have already eliminated or—even worse—accidentally choosing an answer that you meant to eliminate. By the end of the Verbal section of the GRE, your scratch paper will be filled with columns or rows of "A–E" (and a bit of "A–C" and "A–F" for the various question types that have three or six options) with incorrect answer choices crossed out and correct answers circled. Study this way when practicing as well; don't write in your books, since you can't write on the problem itself during the real test.

Even if you believe you have found the correct answer, always check all of the answer choices on Verbal questions. You may find that another answer choice is better, forcing you to rethink your initial choice.

Chapter 6: **Argument-Based Reading Comprehension**

Question Types

The following chart contains the same information presented in the section Recognizing Argument-Based Passages. It is presented here in chart form for your convenience as you examine the example problems later in this section.

Question Type	Example	How to Recognize
Strengthen the Conclusion	Which of the following, if true, most strongly supports the scientists' hypothesis?	In the question stem: *strengthen*, *support*, or similar Will often (but not always) include the words *if true*
Weaken the Conclusion	Which of the following, if true, most seriously undermines the mayor's claim?	In the question stem: *weaken*, *undermine*, or similar May ask what *supports* the idea that something will *not* be successful Will often (but not always) include the words *if true*
Find the Assumption	Which of the following is an assumption on which the argument depends?	In the question stem: either the word *assumption* or some word indicating that the answer choice is needed (e.g., *relies*, *depends*, or *requires*)
Analyze the Argument Structure	In the argument above, the two portions in boldface play which of the following roles?	In the question stem: *role* or similar In the argument: boldface font
Resolve a Paradox/Explain a Discrepancy	Which of the following pieces of evidence, if true, would provide the best explanation for the discrepancy?	In the question stem: *paradox*, *discrepancy*, *resolve*, or similar
Inference (This type can exist in both types of passages.)	Which of the following conclusions can best be drawn from the information above?	In the question stem: *conclusion*, *assertion*, *infer*, or similar Occasionally "is most strongly supported" by the paragraph Will often contain words indicating the paragraph is purely factual (e.g., "information" above)

165

Unit Two: Paragraphs and Passages

Strengthen, Weaken, and Find the Assumption Analysis

On Strengthen, Weaken, and Find the Assumption questions, your analysis is so similar that each will be discussed in the following argument example. Then, you will see a new example of each question type presented as the GRE would present them.

Step 1: Identify the Question Type

Each of the following could be questions for the paragraph that will follow:

- Which of the following statements would most reinforce the assertion that Shuai will win the tournament this year?
- Which of the following, if true, most weakens the author's conclusion?
- In making the above argument, the author is assuming which of the following?

Step 2: Deconstruct the Argument

Your first task is to find the conclusion. Also take note of the premises offered to support the conclusion and think about the gaps in the argument. What is the author assuming must be true in order to draw that particular conclusion?

You may or may not be able to brainstorm any concerns you have with the conclusion made by the author; it's worth spending about 15 to 20 seconds to try. Consider this argument:

> Shuai is the number one tennis player in the country. She lost in the final match of last year's national tennis championship, but she will win the tournament this year. Last year, an injury she suffered in the second set of the final match hampered her serve style.

The conclusion is that Shuai will win the tennis tournament this year; that is the author's prediction. What premises are you offered? Shuai is the number one tennis player in the country. And yet, there is a counterpoint: Shuai lost the final match of last year's tournament. Finally, the author offers information to qualify the impact of that counterpoint. Shuai's loss was (presumably) due to injury, not her skill level.

Brainstorm some issues you think the author should address. For example, has Shuai undergone physical conditioning this year to make her less prone to injury? Or conversely, is last year's injury the type of injury that is likely to recur during the physical stress of a tournament? Perhaps Shuai was ranked tenth last year, and her current number one ranking reflects her improved skills?

Step 3: State the Goal

For Strengthen questions, the correct answer will be a new piece of information that makes the conclusion at least a little more likely to be valid or true. It could be inserted into the argument as a new premise supporting the conclusion. Perhaps the answer might state that Shuai has undergone a surgery during the offseason to prevent recurring injury. Note this doesn't *prove* the conclusion; it merely makes it more convincing.

Find the Assumption questions are similar, with a small twist: The information supplies a needed link between the premise and conclusion. In this case, the assumption answer choice might state that there the likelihood of winning a tournament is strongly connected to the player's rank.

Finally, Weaken answers will contain a new piece of information that would make the conclusion a little less likely. Perhaps the answer choice would present something similar to, but opposite of, the Strengthen answer: Shuai's injury was of a type that, if it has happened once, becomes increasing likely to happen again the more physical stress is placed on the body.

Step 4: Work from Wrong to Right

Use an A–E chart on your paper to keep track of the answers. Mark a letter next to a choice (S, W, or A, for Strengthen, Weaken, and Assumption, respectively) if you believe that answer supplies a potential correct choice for that question type. Mark irrelevant choices with a "?" to indicate that you question whether that choice has any relevance at all to the argument. And finally, if you happen to realize that an answer choice is actually one of the common wrong answers described in the earlier section (four step process), mark it with an "X". If you cannot determine what mark to place next to a choice, do not stress: leave the corresponding answer choice letter unmarked on your page, and move on the next choice.

Try the following sample problems.

Strengthen Example

> At QuestCorp, many employees have quit recently and taken jobs with a competitor. Shortly before the employees quit, QuestCorp lost its largest client. Clearly, the employees were no longer confident in QuestCorp's long-term viability.
>
> Which of the following, if true, most strengthens the claim that concerns about QuestCorp's viability caused the employees to quit?
>
> (A) Employees at QuestCorp's main competitor recently received a large and well-publicized raise.
> (B) QuestCorp's largest client accounted for 40 percent of sales and nearly 60 percent of the company's profits.
> (C) Many prospective hires who have interviewed with QuestCorp ultimately accepted jobs with other companies.
> (D) Shortly before QuestCorp lost its largest client, that client was part of a corporate merger.
> (E) QuestCorp lost the client because QuestCorp is shifting focus to other markets out of that client's industry.

Step 1: Identify the Question Type

The "most strengthens" clearly indicates that this is a Strengthen the Conclusion question.

Step 2: Deconstruct the Argument

The question stem provides the conclusion: Concerns about Q's viability caused employees to quit. One set of notes might look like this:

+ Q lost client, then emp's quit, went to compet
Ⓒ emp's lost conf in Q viab

Step 3: State the Goal

The author assumes that the employees weren't quitting for some other reason. One way to strengthen the argument would be to show that there was some significant negative consequence because the largest client left.

Unit Two: **Paragraphs and Passages**

Step 4: Work from Wrong to Right

Use a chart to categorize and eliminate answer choices.

(A) Weaken or ?. If the competitor is offering more money, then perhaps that's why the employees switched companies; if so, this choice weakens the argument. Note that this choice doesn't actually say that the competitor is now paying more money than QuestCorp, so perhaps this information is irrelevant. Either way, this choice does not strengthen the argument.

(B) Strengthen. The largest client accounted for a very large percentage of both sales and profits. This piece of information does strengthen the idea that some employees may have lost confidence in QuestCorp's long-term viability.

(C) ?. The argument concludes something about QuestCorp employees, not people who interviewed with QuestCorp but ultimately accepted a job elsewhere.

(D) ?. While a corporate merger might explain why the client dropped QuestCorp, it does not indicate anything about whether QuestCorp's employees' perceptions of the company's long-term prospects.

(E) Weaken or ?. Arguably, this choice could weaken the argument, because QuestCorp's shift in focus could be to a market with better long-term potential. This choice does not state anything about the new market focus, however, so ultimately this could be considered a ? because there is not enough information to predict what impact this choice could have on either QuestCorp's growth or the employees perception of QuestCorp.

Note that choice A is one of the common wrong answer categories: Opposite Direction.

Answer choice (B) is correct.

Weaken Example

The national infrastructure for airport runways and air traffic control requires immediate expansion to accommodate the increase in private, smaller planes. To help fund this expansion, the Federal Aviation Authority (the FAA) has proposed a fee for all air travelers. However, this fee would be unfair, as it would impose costs on all travelers to benefit only the few who utilize the new private planes.

Which of the following, if true, would cast the most doubt on the claim that the proposed fee would be unfair?

(A) The existing national airport infrastructure benefits all air travelers.
(B) The fee, if imposed, will have a negligible effect on the overall volume of air travel.
(C) The expansion would reduce the number of delayed flights resulting from small private planes congesting runways.
(D) Travelers who use small private planes are almost uniformly wealthy or traveling on business.
(E) A substantial fee would need to be imposed in order to pay for the expansion costs.

Chapter 6: **Argument-Based Reading Comprehension**

Step 1: Identify the Question Type

The "cast the most doubt" and "if true" language indicate that this is a Weaken the Conclusion question.

Step 2: Deconstruct the Argument

The question stem indicates the conclusion: the proposed fee would be unfair. One set of notes might look like this:

Fee unfair
Cost for all, benefits only for priv planes

Step 3: State the Goal

The author assumes that the benefits will apply only to those flying in the private plans. One way to weaken the argument would be to show that there was some benefit for a greater group, or perhaps for all of the people who would be paying the fee.

Step 4: Work from Wrong to Right

Use an answer choice chart to categorize and eliminate answer choices.

(A) ?. The argument concerns a fee needed in order to expand the existing infrastructure. The status of the existing infrastructure is irrelevant to the argument.

(B) ?. A negligible impact is a very small impact. The fee, though, is intended to be used for infrastructure expansion. The argument makes no claim about what will happen with the overall volume of air travel.

(C) Weaken. This choice offers a benefit for all air travelers: if the expansion can reduce congestion, and therefore the number of delayed flights in general, then others besides the private plane travelers will benefit from the fee.

(D) ?. The wealth or employment status of the passengers does not address whether the fee benefits just these passengers versus all of the passengers.

(E) Strengthen or ?. The amount of the fee does not address whether the fee is unfair. If anything, you might argue that a very high fee is even more unfair, in which case this choice would strengthen the argument, not weaken it.

Note that choice E is one of the common wrong answer categories: Opposite Direction. Choice A is another common wrong answer category: its focus on the existing infrastructure only impacts the background information in the first sentence.

Answer choice (C) is the correct answer.

Unit Two: Paragraphs and Passages

Assumption Example

Many people who suffer from high blood pressure also have low levels of magnesium in their blood. Clearly, then, low magnesium levels contribute to high blood pressure.

Which of the following is an assumption made in the argument?

(A) There is no connection between trace chemical elements in the blood and blood pressure levels.

(B) Magnesium levels in the blood can contribute to various other health issues.

(C) The people in question did not have high blood pressure before their magnesium levels dropped below normal levels.

(D) Relatively minor changes in diet and lifestyle are enough to supplement magnesium intake.

(E) The medical costs associated with treating high blood pressure are significantly greater than those associated with treating magnesium deficiencies.

Step 1: Identify the Question Type

The question requests an assumption made by the argument.

Step 2: Deconstruct the Argument

The signal word "clearly" indicates a position held by the author. The previous sentence offers a fact in support of that position.

```
low mag causes HBP
HBP = low mag in blood
```

Step 3: State the Goal

The author assumes causation: There is an association between high blood pressure and low magnesium levels, but that does not prove that low magnesium causes the high blood pressure. There may not be a definitive link between the two. For a Find the Assumption, your goal is to find an answer choice that establishes a link between the two, and in the causal order desired: Low magnesium leads to high blood pressure.

Step 4: Work from Wrong to Right

(A) Weaken. This choice would counter the connection between magnesium and blood pressure needed by the argument. Eliminate answer A.

(B) ?. Does the argument require an assessment of other health issues? There is no indication that those other health issues would cause high blood pressure. Eliminate answer B.

(C) Correct. This choice addresses a link between high blood pressure and low magnesium, and offers the needed causal order: In order for high blood pressure to be caused by magnesium levels, the high blood pressure cannot exist before the low magnesium levels.

(D) ?. Does the argument need information on how to rectify low magnesium? While this information might be promising to someone who has high blood pressure, it has no impact on whether that high blood pressure was actually caused by the low magnesium levels. Eliminate answer D.

(E) ?. Does the argument need a comparison of treatment costs? This might provide a reason to treat low magnesium levels as early as possible, but this would not change the fundamental question of whether it is low magnesium that causes the high blood pressure. Eliminate answer E.

Note that choice A is one of the common wrong answer categories: Opposite Direction. In Find the Assumption questions, a weaken choice is the opposite of supplying a link between premise and conclusion.

Answer choice (C) is the correct answer.

Analyze the Argument Structure

Analyze the Argument Structure questions ask you to describe the role of a part or parts of the argument; these portions will be shown in bold font. The arguments tend to be complex, often with an argument/counterargument structure. Be prepared with guessing strategies (discussed next).

Step 1: Identify the Question Type

The question type will be immediately apparent because of the boldface font in portions of the argument. The question will typically ask what *role* the bold portions play in the overall argument.

Step 2: Deconstruct the Argument

The boldface portions can play one of three primary roles:

1. (C): The statement in boldface is the author's *conclusion*.
2. (S): The statement in boldface is a premise that *supports* the author's conclusion.
3. (E): The statement in boldface is *something else* (this could be a statement counter to the conclusion or it could be merely background information).

Find the author's conclusion, then classify each statement according to the categories C, S, or E. These arguments tend to be longer than average; note that the correct choice will not categorize the entire argument, just the two statements in bold font. Do not go to the answer choices until you have found the conclusion and categorized the statements.

Step 3: State the Goal

Your goal is to categorize the boldface statements and then to find an answer choice that matches your categorization. Note also whether the boldface statements are both aligned with the author's conclusion (C and S above) or not aligned with the author's conclusion (C vs E, or S vs E).

Step 4: Work from Wrong to Right

The wrong answers will provide descriptions of the wrong combination of categories. For example, you might decide that the first boldface is a conclusion (C) while the second is support (S). One wrong answer might describe the combination C, E, in that order, while another is E, C. Both would be incorrect if you are looking for the combination C, S.

Here is an example:

Mathematician: Recently, Zubin Ghosh made headlines when he was recognized to have solved the Hilbert Conjecture, postulated a hundred years ago. Ghosh posted his work on the Internet rather than submit it to established journals. In fact, **he has no job, let alone a university position**; he lives alone and has refused all acclaim. In reporting on Ghosh, the press unfortunately has reinforced the popular view that mathematicians are antisocial loners. But **mathematicians clearly form a tightly knit community**, frequently collaborating on important efforts; indeed, teams of researchers are working together to extend Ghosh's findings.

In the argument above, the two portions in boldface play which of the following roles?

(A) The first is an observation the author makes to illustrate a social pattern; the second is a generalization of that pattern.

(B) The first is evidence in favor of the popular view expressed in the argument; the second is a brief restatement of that view.

(C) The first is an example of a generalization that the author contradicts; the second is a reiteration of that generalization.

(D) The first is a counterexample to a generalization that the author asserts; the second is that generalization.

(E) The first is a judgment that counters the primary assertion expressed in the argument; the second is a circumstance on which that judgment is based.

Step 1: Identify the Question Type

The boldface font in the argument and the word "role" in the question stem indicate that this is an Analyze the Argument Structure question.

Step 2: Deconstruct the Argument

The author's conclusion is that mathematicians actually form a tightly knit community. The counterargument is that mathematicians are antisocial loners. Now, label each statement as either Conclusion (C), Support (S), or Something Else (E).

The first boldface represents an example that supports the *counter*argument; label this statement E. The second boldface represents the author's conclusion, C.

Step 3: State the Goal

You're looking for an answer that describes the first statement as an E and the second statement as a C. Note that these two statements are on opposite sides of the argument (the first goes with the counterargument and the second goes with the author's argument).

Step 4: Work from Wrong to Right

(A) This answer says that the author uses the first statement to illustrate a pattern. On the contrary, the author believes that the pattern described by the counterargument is not valid. Eliminate answer (A).

(B) The first portion of this answer is accurate: It supports the popular view, which goes against the view held by the author. The second half of this answer, though, is inaccurate. The second statement does not restate the popular view; rather, it provides the author's opposing view. Eliminate answer (B).

(C) The first portion of this answer is accurate: It supports an idea that the author contradicts. The second statement, though, is not "that generalization," or the popular view. Rather, the second statement reflects the author's opposing point of view. Eliminate answer (C).

Note that answers (A), (B), and (C) all describe the two statements as being on the same side of the fence. You're looking for the two statements to be on opposite sides of the fence.

(D) **CORRECT.** The author does assert something, and the first statement does go against that assertion; the first half of this answer is accurate. The second half of this choice refers to "that generalization," or the generalization that the author asserts. The author asserts their own conclusion, so the second half of this answer is also accurate. Leave this answer in.

(E) The first does counter the author's assertion, or conclusion, though note that this answer choice describes the first statement as a "judgment." It is not a judgment; rather, it's a fact or example. The second half of the choice says that the second boldface statement is based on the first statement; in fact, the second statement goes against the first one. Eliminate answer (E).

The correct answer is (D).

Alternative Approach for Argument Structure

If you have trouble with the above approach, or if you hit a very confusing or convoluted argument, you can try an alternative method for steps 2 through 4 that should help you to eliminate some answers (though you may not be able to eliminate all four wrong answers).

Step 2: Deconstruct the Argument

Read the passage and label each boldface statement as one of the following:

(F) Fact	A verifiable statement	
(O) Opinion	A minor claim, or an opinion of someone other than the author	
(C) Conclusion	The major claim of the author	

In the case of the previous problem, the first statement represents a Fact while the second statement represents the Conclusion.

Step 3: State the Goal

You're looking for F followed by C.

Step 4: Work from Wrong to Right

When working through the answers, look for words that can indicate the type of statement:

(F) Fact	= "evidence" "circumstance" "finding"
(O) Opinion	= "judgment" "claim" "position" (taken by someone else)
(C) Conclusion	= "position" (taken by the argument) "assertion" (of the author)

Do *not* dive very deeply into the content of the answer choices; rather, focus on moving pretty quickly and eliminating answer choices that do not match the Fact/Opinion/Conclusion classification. In the case of the previous problem, you can confidently eliminate answer (E) because a judgment is not the same thing as a fact. Answer (A) is questionable; an observation can be a fact, but facts are more often described as evidence or examples. If you had to guess, avoid (A) on this one.

Unit Two: **Paragraphs and Passages**

With this alternative method, you can avoid getting bogged down in the messy details and make a good guess without spending too much time, but you might not be able to eliminate all of the wrong answers.

If you can figure out how to categorize only one of the two boldface statements, then assess the corresponding half of the answer choices. Eliminate whatever answer choices you can, choose immediately from among the remaining answer choices, and move on.

Inference

Inference questions for ABPs are very similar to Inference questions for regular Reading Comprehension passages; the ABP versions differ from regular RC mainly in the length of the paragraph. As with any Inference question, you need to find the answer that logically follows, or must be true, based upon the information given in the argument.

It's critical to make a distinction between conclusions given in an argument and conclusions (or inferences) given in answer choices. When an ABP provides a conclusion for you in the argument itself, that conclusion is pretty faulty. It's an arguable statement, or claim, that is only partially supported by the premises of the argument, and you can find lots of gaps in the argument.

By contrast, if you are asked to draw a conclusion or to infer something yourself, that conclusion must be able to be *proven* from the given premises. The conclusion will not require you to make any additional assumptions at all, even tiny ones. The correct answer to an Inference question is *not* a claim or an arguable statement, but must be verifiably true based on the information given in the argument.

Step 1: Identify the Question Type

The question stem may appear in a number of forms:

- If the statements above are true, which of the following must be true?
- Which of the following conclusions can best be drawn from the information above?
- The statements above, if true, best support which of the following assertions?
- Which of the following can properly be inferred from the statement above?
- (A full paragraph of text, ending with . . .) Students typically study five days a week. Therefore, _____ .

The last is an example of a Fill-in-the-Blank format. The word "Therefore" signals that the correct answer is the conclusion of the argument.

Step 2: Deconstruct the Argument

Inference questions do not contain a conclusion in the paragraph. The paragraph will contain only premises and these premises will be primarily factual (though some might be more on the opinion or claim side). As with the other question types, jot down some light notes. If you can brainstorm any possible conclusions, do so—but remember that you might not think of what the correct answer will actually say.

Consider the following simplified example:

Samantha and Isabel are the only two people in the dining room. They are both over 50 years old.

What can be safely inferred from these facts? That is, what absolutely *must* be true as a result?

Must be true: There is no one under 50 years old in the dining room.

This conclusion may not seem very meaningful or important in a real-world sense, but this is what the correct answer to an Inference question is like. Avoid grand conclusions in these problems. A correct answer might simply restate one or more of the premises, using synonyms. Sometimes, a correct answer might be a mathematical or logical deduction.

Step 3: State the Goal

You need to find the answer choice that must be true given some or all of the information found in the argument. (Note that the correct answer is not required to use *all* of the given information.)

Step 4: Work from Wrong to Right

Eliminate any answers that require additional assumptions or outside information in order to be true. The wrong answers will all include something that doesn't have to be true.

Consider the following example:

> In certain congested urban areas, commuters who use public transportation options, such as trains and subways, spend approximately 25 percent less time in transit, on average, to reach their destinations than commuters who travel by car. Even individuals who drive their entire commute in carpool lanes, which are typically the least congested sections of roadways, still spend more time, on average, than commuters who use trains and subways.
>
> The statements above, if true, best support which of the following assertions about commuting in the congested urban areas mentioned above?
>
> (A) Waiting in traffic accounts for approximately 25 percent of the commuting time for individuals who drive to their destinations.
> (B) Walking between a subway or train station and one's final destination does not, on average, take longer than walking between one's car and one's final destination.
> (C) Using carpool lanes does not, on average, reduce driving time by more than 25 percent.
> (D) Individuals who commute via public buses spend approximately 25 percent more time in transit than those who commute using public trains or subways.
> (E) Subways and trains are available in the majority of congested urban areas.

Step 1: Identify the Question Type

The word "assertion" coupled with the fact that the assertion is in the answer choices indicates that this is an Inference question.

Step 2: Deconstruct the Argument

One set of notes might look like this:

> Pub trans (trn, sub): ~25% < t than ppl using car
> Even true for carpool

Step 3: State the Goal

You're looking for something that must be true using at least some of the presented information. It might be tempting to conclude that people *should* use public transportation—but note that this doesn't have to be true. Don't introduce opinions or real-world logic.

Step 4: Work from Wrong to Right

(A) While waiting in traffic probably does account for *some* of the commuting time, there's no reason why it must account for approximately 25 percent of that time. This might be an appropriate answer for a Strengthen question, but not for an Inference question. Eliminate answer (A).

(B) Careful! This one is tempting initially because it might cause someone to think, "Oh, wait, did they account for the time it takes to get from the subway to work or your house? Maybe this is it!" The difficulty here is that this length of time does not have to be similar to the length of time it takes to walk from the car to the final destination. The argument compares the overall commute time, not the time for smaller pieces of the commute. Eliminate answer (B).

(C) The argument does mention that "even" when someone uses a carpool lane, which should save time, it's still faster to take public transportation. Given that info, if public transportation also takes about 25 percent less time than using a car, then it actually must be the case that using a carpool lane does not (on average) save more than 25 percent of car commuting time. If it did, then carpooling might actually be faster than taking public transportation. Leave this answer in.

(D) The argument does not make a comparison between different forms of public transportation. Rather, it compares all of public transportation to all commuting by car. Eliminate answer (D).

(E) Tricky! Again, this one might make someone think, "Oh, they're assuming that public transportation is actually available." Note first that this argument is assuming nothing at all—it does not contain a conclusion and, by definition, only arguments containing conclusions also have assumptions. Next, the argument provides actual data for areas that do have public transportation, so that's the only concern. Finally, the argument never specifies that these areas must have subways and trains specifically (buses are also public transportation), nor does it specify that a "majority" of these areas have public transportation. In fact, the argument refers only to "certain congested urban areas."

Note that choice (E) is one of the common wrong answer categories: Too Extreme / Beyond the Scope. While it may not seem that a statement about the "majority" of congested urban areas, for a paragraph that only mentions "certain" congested areas, that is too extreme.

The correct answer is (C). Note that the correct answer addressed only one narrow part of the situation. It did not assume anything or go at all beyond the scope of the information given in the argument.

Resolve a Paradox

This question type poses two seemingly contradictory premises and asks you to find the answer choice that best reconciles them.

Step 1: Identify the Question Type

The question will often, though not always, indicate what the discrepancy is or provide a keyword pointing to the discrepancy in the argument. For example:

- Which of the following statements, if true, would best explain the sudden drop in temperature?
- Which of the following, if true, most helps to resolve the paradox described above?

Step 2: Deconstruct the Argument

Like Inference paragraphs, Paradox paragraphs do not contain a conclusion in the paragraph: it will contain only premises, and these premises will be primarily factual. Jot down some light notes, and articulate the paradox to yourself.

Consider the following simplified example:

> According to researchers, low dosages of aspirin taken daily can significantly reduce the risk of heart attack or stroke. Yet doctors have stopped recommending daily aspirin for most patients.

What? That doesn't make any sense! If aspirin is beneficial, why wouldn't doctors recommend it for patients?

There must be some other reason why they wouldn't want patients to take aspirin. Perhaps there are some other side effects that are worse than the possible benefits.

Step 3: State the Goal

Your goal is to find an answer that explains why the surprising facts given in the argument are not so paradoxical after all. The correct answer should resolve whatever paradox caused you to think, "Wait, that doesn't make sense!" If you insert the correct answer into the argument, someone who reads it would then say, "Oh, I see! Now it makes sense why they've stopped recommending aspirin."

Step 4: Work from Wrong to Right

As with all ABPs, read through each answer. Eliminate choices that do not explain or resolve the paradox. Often, some wrong answers on Resolve a Paradox questions will make the paradox even *more* confusing.

Consider the following example:

> In a recent poll, 71 percent of respondents reported that they cast votes in the most recent national election. Voting records show, however, that only 60 percent of eligible voters actually voted in that election.
>
> Which of the following pieces of evidence, if true, would provide the best explanation for the discrepancy?
>
> (A) The margin of error for the survey was plus or minus 5 percentage points.
> (B) Fifteen percent of the survey's respondents were living overseas at the time of the election.
> (C) Prior research has shown that people who actually do vote are also more likely to respond to polls than those who do not vote.
> (D) Some people who intend to vote are prevented from doing so by last-minute conflicts on election day or other complications.
> (E) Polls about voting behavior typically have margins of error within plus or minus 3 percentage points.

Step 1: Identify the Question Type

The word "discrepancy" in the question stem indicates that this is a Resolve the Paradox question.

Step 2: Deconstruct the Argument

> Poll: 71% of ppl said they voted
> Rec: 60% of eligible voters voted

Step 3: State the Goal

The goal is to find something that resolves the apparent discrepancy in these two numbers. First, the people who responded to the poll might not be the same group of people who were eligible to vote. Alternatively, there might be a reason why people said they voted when they actually didn't. Possibly there is some other reason to explain what happened.

Unit Two: **Paragraphs and Passages**

Step 4: Work from Wrong to Right

(A) This choice begins promisingly by discussing a margin of error. However, a margin of error of 5 percentage points will not close the 11-percentage point gap between the two statistics in the argument. Eliminate this choice.

(B) Fifteen percent is larger than the 11-point discrepancy in the argument. The percentage, however, applies to the percentage of respondents living overseas at the time of the election. If absentee ballots are allowed, then these people could still have voted. This choice doesn't definitively resolve the paradox, so eliminate it.

(C) If people who do vote are also more likely to respond to polls, then those people are overrepresented in the polling results. That is, they represent a greater proportion of the people answering the poll than they do of the overall population; this explains why a greater percentage of poll respondents said they had voted. Keep this answer in.

(D) This is probably true in the real world, but it does not explain the discrepancy in the statistics presented in the argument. The 60 percent figure represents people who actually did vote, not those who intended to vote but didn't. Eliminate this choice.

(E) This choice does not explain the discrepancy in the statistics presented in the argument; this poll might not have the same margin of error of "typical" polls. Even if you do adjust for a 3 percent margin of error, 11 percent still represents a substantial gap. Eliminate this choice.

The correct answer is (C). Incorrect choice (E), in this instance, is a common wrong answer category: Opposite Direction. If the typical margin of error is only 3 percent, then the existence of an 11 percentage point gap in these polls is more surprising, not less.

Vocabulary Challenge

> Did you spot these vocabulary words? If not, go back and find them in context! (The word may be in a different form than listed here—"digressing" instead of "digress," for example.) Write your own definitions based on the evidence in the chapter.

1. discrepancy (*n*), p. 156
2. diverge (*v*), p. 158
3. circumspect (*adj.*), p. 158
4. germane (*adj.*), p. 159
5. multifarious (*adj.*), p. 162
6. circumscribe (*v*), p. 163

Chapter 6: **Argument-Based Reading Comprehension**

Problem Set

> Use the four-step process taught for all ABPs, as well as any specific techniques recommended for that question type (e.g., the answer choice chart to track your eliminations). Consider all five answer choices before you make your final decision.

1. John was flying from San Francisco to New York with a connecting flight in Chicago on the same airline. Chicago's airport is one of the largest in the world, consisting of several small stand-alone terminals connected by trams. John's plane arrived on time. John was positive he would make his connecting flight 30 minutes later because _____ .

    Which of the following most logically completes the argument above?

    (A) John's airline is known for always being on time
    (B) a number of other passengers on John's first flight were also scheduled to take John's connecting flight
    (C) at the airport in Chicago, airlines always fly into and out of the same terminal
    (D) John knew there was another flight to New York scheduled for one hour after the connecting flight he was scheduled to take
    (E) the airline generally closes the doors of a particular flight 10 minutes before it is scheduled to take off

2. Media Critic: Network executives have alleged that television viewership is decreasing due to the availability of television programs on other platforms, such as the internet, video-on-demand, and mobile devices. These executives claim that **declining viewership will cause advertising revenue to fall so far that networks will be unable to spend the large sums necessary to produce programs of the quality now available**. That development, in turn, will lead to a dearth of programming for the very devices that cannibalized television's audience. However, technology executives point to research that indicates that **users of these platforms increase the number of hours per week that they watch television** because they are exposed to new programs through these alternative platforms. This analysis demonstrates that networks can actually increase their revenue through higher advertising rates, due to larger audiences lured to television through other media.

    The portions in boldface play which of the following roles in the media critic's argument?

    (A) The first is an inevitable trend that weighs against the critic's claim; the second is that claim.
    (B) The first is a prediction that is challenged by the argument; the second is a finding upon which the argument depends.
    (C) The first clarifies the reasoning behind the critic's claim; the second demonstrates why that claim is flawed.
    (D) The first acknowledges a position that the technology executives accept as true; the second is a consequence of that position.
    (E) The first opposes the critic's claim through an analogy; the second outlines a scenario in which that claim will not hold.

3. In the last year, real estate prices, such as those for houses and condominiums, have gone up an average of 7 percent in the city of Galway but only 2 percent in the town of Tuam. On the other hand, average rents for apartments have risen 8 percent in Tuam over the last year but only 4 percent in Galway.

   Which of the following is an inference that can be reasonably drawn from the premises given above?

   (A) In the last year, the ratio of average apartment rents to average real estate prices has increased in Tuam but fallen in Galway.
   (B) Tuam has experienced a greater shift in demand toward the rental market than Galway has.
   (C) It has become easier for Galway real estate to be bought and sold, whereas it has become easier for Tuam real estate to be rented.
   (D) The supply of rental apartment units has decreased more in Tuam than in Galway.
   (E) The average amount spent on housing is higher in Galway than it is in Tuam.

4. Due to the increase in traffic accidents caused by deer in the state, the governor last year reintroduced a longer deer hunting season to encourage recreational hunting of the animals. The governor expected the longer hunting season to decrease the number of deer and therefore decrease the number of accidents. However, this year the number of accidents caused by deer has increased substantially since the reintroduction of the longer deer hunting season.

   Which of the following, if true, would best explain the increase in traffic accidents caused by deer?

   (A) Many recreational hunters hunt only once or twice per hunting season, regardless of the length of the season.
   (B) The deer in the state have become accustomed to living in close proximity to humans and are often easy prey for hunters as a result.
   (C) Most automobile accidents involving deer result from cars swerving to avoid deer, and they leave the deer in question unharmed.
   (D) The number of drivers in the state has been gradually increasing over the past several years.
   (E) A heavily used new highway was recently built directly through the state's largest forest, which is the primary habitat of the state's deer population.

Chapter 6: **Argument-Based Reading Comprehension**

5. Political Analyst: After a coalition of states operating under a repressive regime collapsed, some hoped that freedom would bolster the population of the largest state, Algan, but as a result of dislocation and insecurity, the Algan population continues to dwindle at the rate of 700,000 a year. The government proposes to address the problem with a wide range of financial incentives, along with investments in improved healthcare, road safety, and the like. These are positive measures, but **they have been tried before, to little avail**. A better plan to reverse the population decline is to improve Algan's governance in both the public and the private sphere. **If a greater part of the population participated in important decisions and shared in Algan's wealth, then larger families would result.** In addition, if corruption and greed among the elite were curbed, public health would improve, and average life expectancy would increase.

   The two boldfaced statements serve what function in the argument above?

   (A) The first is the main point of the analyst's argument; the second is a premise that supports the first.
   (B) The first is a premise that undermines an alternative to the analyst's proposal; the second is a premise that supports the analyst's main claim.
   (C) The first is a premise that contradicts the main point made by the analyst; the second is the main point of the argument.
   (D) The first is a premise that supports a proposal; the second is that proposal.
   (E) The first is a conclusion that the argument endorses; the second is a premise that opposes that conclusion.

6. Displayco is marketing a holographic display to supermarkets that shows three-dimensional images of certain packaged goods in the aisles. Displayco's marketing literature states that patrons at supermarkets will be strongly attracted to goods that are promoted in this way, resulting in higher profits for the supermarkets that purchase the displays. Consumer advocates, however, feel that the displays will be intrusive to supermarket patrons and may even increase minor accidents involving shopping carts.

   Which of the following, if true, most seriously weakens the position of the consumer advocates?

   (A) The holographic displays are expensive to install and maintain.
   (B) Many other venues, including shopping malls, are considering adopting holographic displays.
   (C) Accidents in supermarkets that are serious enough to cause injury are rare.
   (D) Supermarkets tend to be low-margin businesses that struggle to achieve profitability.
   (E) Studies in test markets have shown that supermarket patrons quickly become accustomed to holographic displays.

Unit Two: **Paragraphs and Passages**

7. Brand X designs and builds custom sneakers, one sneaker at a time. It recently announced plans to sell "The Gold Standard," a sneaker that will cost five times more to manufacture than any other sneaker that has ever been created.

   A prediction that The Gold Standard shoe line will be profitable would require which of the following assumptions?

   (A) At least some consumers would be willing to spend enough money on sneakers to allow Brand X to charge prices for The Gold Standard that would exceed the cost to manufacture the sneaker.

   (B) Of the last four new sneakers that Brand X has released, three have sold at a rate that was higher than projected.

   (C) A rival brand recently declared bankruptcy and ceased manufacturing shoes.

   (D) The market for The Gold Standard will not be more limited than the market for other Brand X shoes.

   (E) The Gold Standard is made using canvas that is more than five times the cost of the canvas used in most sneakers.

8. With information readily available on the internet, consumers now often enter the automobile retail environment with certain models and detailed specifications in mind. In response to this trend, CarStore has decided to move toward a less aggressive sales approach. Despite the fact that members of its sales personnel have an average of 10 years of experience each, CarStore has implemented a mandatory training program for all sales personnel, because _____.

   (A) the sales personnel in CarStore have historically specialized in aggressively selling automobiles and add-on features

   (B) the sales personnel in CarStore do not themselves use the internet often for their own purposes

   (C) CarStore has found that most consumers do not mind negotiating over price

   (D) information found on the internet often does not reflect sales promotions at individual retail locations

   (E) several retailers that compete directly with CarStore have adopted "customer-centered" sales approaches

Chapter 6: **Argument-Based Reading Comprehension**

9. Government restrictions have severely limited the amount of stem cell research that companies in the United States can conduct. Because of these restrictions, many U.S.-based scientists who specialize in the field of stem cell research have signed long-term contracts to work for foreign-based companies. Recently, the U.S. government has proposed lifting all restrictions on stem cell research.

   Which of the following statements can most properly be inferred from the information above?

   (A) Some foreign-based companies that conduct stem cell research work under fewer restrictions than some U.S.-based companies do.
   (B) Because U.S.-based scientists are under long-term contracts to foreign-based companies, there will be a significant influx of foreign professionals into the United States.
   (C) In all parts of the world, stem cell research is dependent on the financial backing of local government.
   (D) In the near future, U.S.-based companies will no longer be at the forefront of stem cell research.
   (E) If restrictions on stem cell research are lifted, many of the U.S.-based scientists will break their contracts and return to U.S.-based companies.

10. Traditionally, public school instructors have been compensated according to seniority. Recently, the existing salary system has been increasingly criticized as an approach to compensation that rewards lackadaisical teaching and punishes motivated, highly qualified instruction. Instead, educational experts argue that, to retain exceptional teachers and maintain quality instruction, teachers should receive salaries or bonuses based on performance rather than seniority.

    Which of the following, if true, most weakens the conclusion of the educational experts?

    (A) Some teachers express that financial compensation is not the only factor contributing to job satisfaction and teaching performance.
    (B) School districts will develop their own unique compensation structures that may differ greatly from those of other school districts.
    (C) Upon leaving the teaching profession, many young, effective teachers cite a lack of opportunity for more rapid financial advancement as a primary factor in the decision to change careers.
    (D) A merit-based system that bases compensation on teacher performance reduces collaboration, which is an integral component of quality instruction.
    (E) In school districts that have implemented pay for performance compensation structures, standardized test scores have dramatically increased.

Unit Two: **Paragraphs and Passages**

Answers and Explanations

Vocabulary challenge

1. discrepancy (*n*): difference or inconsistency

2. diverge (*v*): differ, deviate; branch off or turn aside, as from a path

3. circumspect (*adj.*): cautious, prudent; careful to consider the circumstances and consequences

4. germane (*adj.*): relevant and appropriate, on-topic

5. multifarious (*adj.*): diverse, having a lot of variety

6. circumscribe (*v*): strictly limit a role, range of activity, or area

Problem Set

1. **(C):**

    John was flying from San Francisco to New York with a connecting flight in Chicago on the same airline. Chicago's airport is one of the largest in the world, consisting of several small stand-alone terminals connected by trams. John's plane arrived on time. John was positive he would make his connecting flight 30 minutes later, because _____.

    Which of the following most logically completes the argument above?

    (A) John's airline is known for always being on time

    (B) a number of other passengers on John's first flight were also scheduled to take John's connecting flight

    (C) at the airport in Chicago, airlines always fly into and out of the same terminal

    (D) John knew there was another flight to New York scheduled for one hour after the connecting flight he was scheduled to take

    (E) the airline generally closes the doors of a particular flight 10 minutes before it is scheduled to take off

Step 1: Identify the Question Type

The blank in this Fill-in-the-Blank question is preceded by the word "because," most commonly signaling a Strengthen question, but you'll need to read the argument to be sure. The beginning of that sentence contains the conclusion, so this is indeed a Strengthen question.

Step 2: Deconstruct the Argument

The Chicago airport is busy and very large, consisting of several small stand-alone terminals. Despite this, John thinks he will make his connecting flight.

Step 3: State the Goal

The correct answer choice will make it a little more likely that John's conclusion is valid. The information needs to support the idea that he'll make the connecting flight despite the size of the airport.

Chapter 6: **Argument-Based Reading Comprehension**

Step 4: Work from Wrong to Right

(A) ?. This is a general observation about the timeliness of John's airline, but it does not provide any new information—the argument already states that John's particular flight arrived on time. The fact that his connecting flight will probably depart on time might even weaken the argument.

(B) ?. The argument doesn't give any reason to believe that the airline would delay John's second flight just to allow more passengers to catch the flight. Even if this situation might be conceivable in the real world, if more additional assumptions are needed to demonstrate relevance, look for a better choice.

(C) **CORRECT.** Strengthen. Since John's connecting flight is on the same airline, John will not have to take a tram to another terminal in order to reach his connecting flight. The premises describe the individual terminals as "small." If he can walk to his next flight in a small terminal, then 30 minutes is likely enough time to make the connection.

(D) ?. This choice is out of scope. The argument concludes that John will make his current flight; the later flight has no bearing on John's ability to catch the flight on which he is currently booked.

(E) X. If anything, this choice weakens the idea that John will catch the connecting flight by shortening the length of time he has to get to the second flight's gate. He now has only 20 minutes, not 30.

2. **(B):**

Media Critic: Network executives have alleged that television viewership is decreasing due to the availability of television programs on other platforms, such as the internet, video-on-demand, and mobile devices. These executives claim that **declining viewership will cause advertising revenue to fall so far that networks will be unable to spend the large sums necessary to produce programs of the quality now available**. That development, in turn, will lead to a dearth of programming for the very devices that cannibalized television's audience. However, technology executives point to research that indicates that **users of these platforms increase the number of hours per week that they watch television** because they are exposed to new programs through these alternative platforms. This analysis demonstrates that networks can actually increase their revenue through higher advertising rates, due to larger audiences lured to television through other media.

The portions in boldface play which of the following roles in the media critic's argument?

(A) The first is an inevitable trend that weighs against the critic's claim; the second is that claim.

(B) The first is a prediction that is challenged by the argument; the second is a finding upon which the argument depends.

(C) The first clarifies the reasoning behind the critic's claim; the second demonstrates why that claim is flawed.

(D) The first acknowledges a position that the technology executives accept as true; the second is a consequence of that position.

(E) The first opposes the critic's claim through an analogy; the second outlines a scenario in which that claim will not hold.

Step 1: Identify the Question Type

The boldface font indicates that this is an Analyze the Argument question. Note that the question stem references the "media critic's argument"—this is the conclusion you want.

Unit Two: **Paragraphs and Passages**

Step 2: Deconstruct the Argument

The first three sentences describe the network executives' argument: Alternative viewing platforms will cause fewer people to watch TV, resulting in lower advertising revenues. The networks then won't have enough money to continue producing high-quality programming, so everyone will lose, even the people who are watching on alternative viewing platforms.

The fourth sentence begins with the word "However." The argument goes on to indicate that technology executives have research that contradicts the network executives' view. The media critic then concludes that the networks can actually *increase* their advertising revenues.

Label each statement C for Conclusion, S for Support, or E for Something Else. (Refer to the Argument Structure questions for a review on this approach.) The first boldface portion opposes the critic's position by predicting smaller audiences; label it E. The second boldface lends support to the critic's conclusion by citing evidence that alternative media platforms lead their users to watch more television; label this one S.

Step 3: State the Goal

The correct answer will first describe an E and then an S. More specifically, it will describe a point of support for the executives' argument, but then a point of support for the media critic's argument.

Step 4: Work from Wrong to Right

(A) The first boldface statement does weigh against the critic's claim, but it is a prediction, rather than an inevitable trend. The second boldface statement is a premise supporting the claim; it is not the conclusion itself.

(B) **CORRECT.** The first boldface statement's prediction about shrinking audiences and falling revenue is counter to the critic's conclusion about a potential increase in network revenue is contrary to the. Also, the critic's argument does depend upon the second boldface statement's assertion that users of alternative devices actually watch more hours of television.

(C) The first boldface statement opposes the critic's claim, rather than clarifies it. The second boldface statement supports the critic's claim; it does not indicate that the critic's claim is flawed.

(D) The argument does not indicate whether the technology executives accept or deny the prediction of the network executives. (Given, though, that the technology executives think that people will watch more television, not less, it doesn't seem likely that the technology executives will agree with the network executives.) The second boldface statement contradicts the first one; it does not follow as a consequence.

(E) The first boldface statement offers a prediction, not an analogy. The second boldface statement is in agreement with, not in opposition to, the critic's claim.

3. **(A):**

In the last year, real estate prices, such as those for houses and condominiums, have gone up an average of 7 percent in the city of Galway but only 2 percent in the town of Tuam. On the other hand, average rents for apartments have risen 8 percent in Tuam over the last year but only 4 percent in Galway.

Which of the following is an inference that can be reasonably drawn from the premises given above?

(A) In the last year, the ratio of average apartment rents to average real estate prices has increased in Tuam but fallen in Galway.

(B) Tuam has experienced a greater shift in demand toward the rental market than Galway has.

(C) It has become easier for Galway real estate to be bought and sold, whereas it has become easier for Tuam real estate to be rented.

(D) The supply of rental apartment units has decreased more in Tuam than in Galway.

(E) The average amount spent on housing is higher in Galway than it is in Tuam.

Step 1: Identify the Question Type

The word "inference" indicates that this is an Inference question. Expect to see only premises in the argument.

Step 2: Deconstruct the Argument

One set of notes might look like this:

Past yr: RE $ > 7% in G but 2% in T
          Avg rent > 4% in G but 8% in T

Notice two things. First, the argument gives only percentages, not real numbers; you can't conclude anything that involves real numbers, including which town has higher rents or home prices. Second, rents are increasing at a faster rate in Tuam but home prices are increasing at a faster rate in Galway.

Step 3: State the Goal

What must be true according to the given information?

Unit Two: **Paragraphs and Passages**

Step 4: Work from Wrong to Right

- (A) **CORRECT.** While it isn't possible to conclude anything about real numbers, you can use percentages to determine something about ratios. In Tuam, rents have gone up at a faster rate (8 percent) than have real estate prices (2 percent). Thus, the ratio of average rents to average real estate prices must have grown in that city—the numerator has grown faster than the denominator. In contrast, Galway rents have gone up at a slower rate (4 percent) than real estate prices (7 percent). Thus, the ratio of average rents to average real estate prices has decreased in Galway.

- (B) It's conceivable that a shift in demand towards renting has driven the rise in rent prices in Tuam. But there are other potential explanations as well. (For instance, a decline in the supply of rental units could explain it.) Without more evidence, this can't be inferred.

- (C) Similarly, this might be true but does not have to be. The premises do not indicate whether Galway real estate is easier or harder to be bought and sold or whether Tuam real estate is easier or harder to be rented. The premises simply indicate the growth in prices and rents, which could be for any number of causes.

- (D) Again, it is not necessarily true that the supply of rental units has decreased more in Tuam than in Galway. Just like B and C, this is one possible explanation for the data in the passage. But there is no evidence for this explanation in particular.

- (E) The premises indicate nothing about the actual amounts of money spent in the two towns. You are given only percentage growth rates.

4. **(E):**

Due to the increase in traffic accidents caused by deer in the state, the governor last year reintroduced a longer deer hunting season to encourage recreational hunting of the animals. The governor expected the longer hunting season to decrease the number of deer and therefore decrease the number of accidents. However, this year the number of accidents caused by deer has increased substantially since the reintroduction of the longer deer hunting season.

Which of the following, if true, would best explain the increase in traffic accidents caused by deer?

- (A) Many recreational hunters hunt only once or twice per hunting season, regardless of the length of the season.

- (B) The deer in the state have become accustomed to living in close proximity to humans and are often easy prey for hunters as a result.

- (C) Most automobile accidents involving deer result from cars swerving to avoid deer, and they leave the deer in question unharmed.

- (D) The number of drivers in the state has been gradually increasing over the past several years.

- (E) A heavily used new highway was recently built directly through the state's largest forest, which is the primary habitat of the state's deer population.

Step 1: Identify the Question Type

The words "explain" and "if true" signal that this is a Resolve a Paradox question.

Chapter 6: **Argument-Based Reading Comprehension**

Step 2: Deconstruct the Argument

Attempting to decrease the number of deer in his state, a governor extended the recreational hunting season. However, despite extending the hunting season, the number of accidents caused by deer has not declined—instead, it has increased substantially.

Step 3: State the Goal

You need to find the answer choice that explains why the accidents have increased rather than decreased as expected. Perhaps another influence is bringing more deer into the region. Perhaps many accidents are caused by deer fleeing the hunters, in which case more hunting could actually lead to more accidents.

Step 4: Work from Wrong to Right

(A) If the longer hunting season doesn't change the amount of times hunters go hunting, the policy might not be effective at reducing accidents. But, it doesn't explain why the number of accidents would *increase* instead.

(B) If the deer are "easy prey," then the governor's extension of the hunting season should be *effective* in reducing the deer overpopulation. This does not explain the increase in traffic accidents.

(C) Careful! This does explain how accidents occur but does not explain why there are more accidents this year, after the governor put in place a plan designed to reduce accidents.

(D) This answer choice does help to explain why car accidents involving deer might be increasing. However, it does not explain a substantial increase in accidents from just last year to this year. Both the extent of the increase and the time frame serve to make this answer choice an unsatisfactory explanation. It's the closest answer so far, but keep reading.

(E) **CORRECT.** A new highway system built directly through the deer's primary habitat provides a specific explanation as to why the number of accidents involving deer has increased. More people are driving in the area where deer primarily live. Since the highway was recently built, and would significantly change the amount of interactions between drivers and deer, this is the correct choice.

5. **(B):**

Political Analyst: After a coalition of states operating under a repressive regime collapsed, some hoped that freedom would bolster the population of the largest state, Algan, but as a result of dislocation and insecurity, the Algan population continues to dwindle at the rate of 700,000 a year. The government proposes to address the problem with a wide range of financial incentives, along with investments in improved healthcare, road safety, and the like. These are positive measures, but **they have been tried before, to little avail**. A better plan to reverse the population decline is to improve Algan's governance in both the public and the private sphere. **If a greater part of the population participated in important decisions and shared in Algan's wealth, then larger families would result.** In addition, if corruption and greed among the elite were curbed, public health would improve, and average life expectancy would increase.

Unit Two: **Paragraphs and Passages**

The two boldfaced statements serve what function in the argument above?

(A) The first is the main point of the analyst's argument; the second is a premise that supports the first.

(B) The first is a premise that undermines an alternative to the analyst's proposal; the second is a premise that supports the analyst's main claim.

(C) The first is a premise that contradicts the main point made by the analyst; the second is the main point of the argument.

(D) The first is a premise that supports a proposal; the second is that proposal.

(E) The first is a conclusion that the argument endorses; the second is a premise that opposes that conclusion.

Step 1: Identify the Question Type

The bold font indicates that this is an Analyze the Argument Structure question. Expect two opposing points of view in the argument. Use the CSE or FCO technique to label the two boldface statements.

Step 2: Deconstruct the Argument

The analyst recounts a proposal by the Algan government to increase the Algan population. The analyst dismisses the plan with the implication that, because the measures have not worked in the past, they will not work now. The analyst then offers a "better plan" (the analyst's conclusion) and offers two premises (the two if-then statements) in support of this better plan.

Step 3: State the Goal

The first boldface statement dismisses the government's plan; as such, it is in support of the analyst's conclusion. Label it with an S. The second boldface directly supports the analyst's proposal; it is also an S.

Step 4: Work from Wrong to Right

(A) The first statement is not itself the main point of the argument, which is to propose a new plan for the state. The second statement is a premise in support of the argument's proposal, not in support of the first statement.

(B) **CORRECT.** The first statement does undermine the alternative proposal made by the government. The second statement does support the analyst's conclusion by showing one way in which better governance might lead to a population increase.

(C) The first statement does not contradict the analyst's conclusion; rather, it undermines the government proposal. The second statement is not the conclusion itself; rather, it supports the conclusion by explaining why, in the analyst's opinion, the new plan would work.

(D) The first statement is a statement *against* the government's proposal, rather than a statement in *support* of a particular proposal. The second bolded statement is arguably part of the author's proposal, but it is not supported by the first bolded statement.

(E) The first statement is not by itself the analyst's conclusion. The second statement is indeed a premise, but it does not oppose the first statement.

Chapter 6: **Argument-Based Reading Comprehension**

6. (E):

Displayco is marketing a holographic display to supermarkets that shows three-dimensional images of certain packaged goods in the aisles. Displayco's marketing literature states that patrons at supermarkets will be strongly attracted to goods that are promoted in this way, resulting in higher profits for the supermarkets that purchase the displays. Consumer advocates, however, feel that the displays will be intrusive to supermarket patrons and may even increase minor accidents involving shopping carts.

Which of the following, if true, most seriously weakens the position of the consumer advocates?

(A) The holographic displays are expensive to install and maintain.

(B) Many other venues, including shopping malls, are considering adopting holographic displays.

(C) Accidents in supermarkets that are serious enough to cause injury are rare.

(D) Supermarkets tend to be low-margin businesses that struggle to achieve profitability.

(E) Studies in test markets have shown that supermarket patrons quickly become accustomed to holographic displays.

Step 1: Identify the Question Type

This is a Weaken the Conclusion question. Find the conclusion and look for an answer that makes this conclusion at least a little less likely to be valid. Note that the question stem specifically references the conclusion of the "consumer advocates."

Step 2: Deconstruct the Argument

One set of notes might look like this:

D: 3D goods → cust want → > profits
CA: bad, accident

The company, Displayco, points out the potential benefits of its new technology: increased profits for the stores. The advocates, though, point out a possible negative effect: shopping cart accidents. Note that the advocates don't deny that stores will increase their profits; rather, they offer other reasons for avoiding use of the technology. At the very least, then, the advocates assume their concerns outweigh the possible benefits of increased profits.

Step 3: State the Goal

Find an answer that makes the advocates' conclusion less likely to be valid, so an answer that decreases the chance of the displays being intrusive to patrons or causing shopping cart accidents.

Step 4: Work from Wrong to Right

(A) This answer choice may weaken Displayco's claim that the stores will have better profits, but it does not weaken the *advocates*' argument. This choice does not influence whether patrons will find the displays intrusive and distracting.

(B) The potential adoption of holographic displays by other venues does not impact the concerns of consumer advocates that the displays will be intrusive and distracting. It could be the case that holographic displays will be intrusive and distracting in all of these other venues as well. Alternatively, the argument might not apply to other venues where there might not be potential for minor shopping cart accidents.

(C) This seems true in the real world, so it can be tempting. But the consumer advocates' argument did not claim that the minor accidents would result in injury. Minor accidents can be bothersome to patrons without causing injury.

(D) While this choice might help Displayco to convince supermarkets to use its product, you were asked to weaken the consumer advocates' concerns. The struggles of supermarkets to achieve profitability is not relevant to the consumer advocates' concerns.

(E) **CORRECT.** If studies in test markets have shown that patrons quickly become accustomed to holographic displays, then patrons are much less likely to find the displays intrusive after an initial adjustment period. And if patrons become used to the displays, the displays are less likely to increase the frequency of minor shopping cart accidents. Note that this choice does not completely dismiss the advocates' concerns; rather, the concerns are diminished just a little bit.

7. **(A):**

Brand X designs and builds custom sneakers, one sneaker at a time. It recently announced plans to sell "The Gold Standard," a sneaker that will cost five times more to manufacture than any other sneaker that has ever been created.

A prediction that The Gold Standard shoe line will be profitable would require which of the following assumptions?

(A) At least some consumers would be willing to spend enough money on sneakers to allow Brand X to charge prices for The Gold Standard that would exceed the cost to manufacture the sneaker.

(B) Of the last four new sneakers that Brand X has released, three have sold at a rate that was higher than projected.

(C) A rival brand recently declared bankruptcy and ceased manufacturing shoes.

(D) The market for The Gold Standard will not be more limited than the market for other Brand X shoes.

(E) The Gold Standard is made using canvas that is more than five times the cost of the canvas used in most sneakers.

Step 1: Identify the Question Type

The question stem asks you to "which of the following assumptions" is required to believe that The Gold Standard shoe line will be profitable. This is best categorized as a Find the Assumption question.

Step 2: Deconstruct the Argument

The passage states only that the costs of manufacturing this shoe are exceptionally high, and does not make a formal argument. In this case, the conclusion is sneakily buried in the question stem itself. The question asks you to analyze "A prediction that The Gold Standard shoe line will be profitable." That prediction is the conclusion.

Step 3: State the Goal

Find an assumption that helps to confirm that The Gold Standard is profitable. What's the missing link between the shoes' high production costs and the prediction that they will be profitable nonetheless? Typically, if costs are exceptionally high, the only way a profit can be made is if revenue is also exceptionally high.

Step 4: Work from Wrong to Right

(A) **CORRECT.** This answer choice supplies the needed connection to reach the conclusion, namely, a confirmation that the company will receive a high amount of revenue to compensate for their high costs.

(B) The results of past releases are not necessarily indicative of the case at hand. And while this info might increase your faith in Brand X, it is not required for the conclusion that Brand X has had successful sales in the past.

(C) One can argue that this is good for Brand X, in that it will mean that there is one less competitor, or that this is bad for Brand X, in that it is indicative of a sagging sneaker market. In either case, there is no direct connection between this rival brand and the potential profitability of The Gold Standard.

(D) It's possible for The Gold Standard to be profitable regardless of whether its market is larger or smaller than Brand X's other shoe lines. So, this is not a required assumption.

(E) This helps to explain why the costs might be high, but it does not provide the needed link between high cost and revenue.

8. **(A):**

With information readily available on the internet, consumers now often enter the automobile retail environment with certain models and detailed specifications in mind. In response to this trend, CarStore has decided to move toward a less aggressive sales approach. Despite the fact that members of its sales personnel have an average of 10 years of experience each, CarStore has implemented a mandatory training program for all sales personnel, because _____.

(A) the sales personnel in CarStore have historically specialized in aggressively selling automobiles and add-on features

(B) the sales personnel in CarStore do not themselves use the internet when making their own purchase decisions

(C) CarStore has found that most consumers do not mind negotiating over price

(D) information found on the internet often does not reflect sales promotions at individual retail locations

(E) several retailers that compete directly with CarStore have adopted "customer-centered" sales approaches

Unit Two: **Paragraphs and Passages**

Step 1: Identify the Question Type

The word "because" just before the blank signals a possible Strengthen question, but you'll have to read the argument to be sure. The "Despite X, CarStore has implemented Y, because [answer]" structure indicates that this is actually a somewhat less common type: Resolve a Paradox.

Step 2: Deconstruct the Argument

The argument describes CarStore's decision to move toward a less aggressive sales approach in response to consumers coming into the stores with all kinds of information they have already found on the internet. Surprisingly, despite the fact that its sales personnel are very experienced, CarStore is implementing a mandatory training program. Why?

Step 3: State the Goal

Find an answer that explains why CarStore would require its very experienced sales team to go through a mandatory training program.

Step 4: Work from Wrong to Right

(A) **CORRECT.** If the sales personnel at CarStore have historically specialized in aggressive sales tactics and promoting add-on features, but CarStore wants to move to a less aggressive approach, then the sales team will need to learn new sales tactics. This explains the need for a mandatory retraining program.

(B) Though it may be helpful for the sales personnel of CarStore to use the internet to research car details so that they can relate to many of their customers, this choice refers to the sales team using the internet to research their own purchases, not necessarily for cars. The mandatory training must have something to do with the job of selling cars, so this choice is not relevant enough to the situation.

(C) If consumers do not mind negotiating over price, a less aggressive sales approach may not be necessary. This does not resolve the discrepancy, and can even be considered to make the discrepancy more severe.

(D) Similarly to C, if information found on the internet is often incomplete, it might make it less necessary for CarStore to adopt new tactics in response to the proliferation of online information. Again, if anything this makes the discrepancy more severe.

(E) What is a "customer-centered" sales approach? This choice might imply that competitors are already using the less aggressive approach, which might help explain why CarStore must adopt it as well. But it does not further explain why even experienced salespeople would need new training.

9. **(A):**

Government restrictions have severely limited the amount of stem cell research that companies in the United States can conduct. Because of these restrictions, many U.S.-based scientists who specialize in the field of stem cell research have signed long-term contracts to work for foreign-based companies. Recently, the U.S. government has proposed lifting all restrictions on stem cell research.

Which of the following statements can most properly be inferred from the information above?

(A) Some foreign-based companies that conduct stem cell research work under fewer restrictions than some U.S.-based companies do.

(B) Because U.S.-based scientists are under long-term contracts to foreign-based companies, there will be a significant influx of foreign professionals into the United States.

(C) In all parts of the world, stem cell research is dependent on the financial backing of local government.

(D) In the near future, U.S.-based companies will no longer be at the forefront of stem cell research.

(E) If restrictions on stem cell research are lifted, many of the U.S.-based scientists will break their contracts and return to U.S.-based companies.

Step 1: Identify the Question Type

The word "inferred" indicates that this is an Inference question type. There won't be a conclusion in the argument.

Step 2: Deconstruct the Argument

Two things have already occurred: the U.S. government has restricted stem cell research for companies in the United States, and U.S.-based scientists in this field have thus chosen to work instead for foreign-based companies. One thing has been proposed: the U.S. government is considering lifting the restrictions on this type of research.

(A) **CORRECT.** If U.S.-based scientists signed contracts with foreign-based companies *specifically because of restrictions* in the United States, then the new companies with which these scientists signed must operate under fewer restrictions. Therefore, at least some foreign companies must work under fewer restrictions than some American companies do.

(B) Even if a significant number of foreign professionals are displaced from their jobs because of the U.S.-based scientists working abroad, there's no guarantee that they would move to the United States to work. In general, avoid inferences that predict the future, unless that future outcome is virtually guaranteed based on the passage.

(C) This passage is about government restrictions in the United States; the source of the financial backing required for stem cell research is out of scope, and it is far too extreme to infer that any aspect of stem cell research is true in all parts of the world.

(D) You are not given any information regarding America's current or future position in terms of stem cell research. Though government restrictions and scientists switching companies could be issues related to a company's prosperity, you are given no information about America's position in stem cell research or how it has been impacted by restrictions.

(E) Though this is a reasonable expectation, it is impossible to conclude for certain that it will happen. Similar to other answers above, do not pick answers that predict a future outcome without specific evidence for it.

Unit Two: **Paragraphs and Passages**

10. **(D):**

Traditionally, public school instructors have been compensated according to seniority. Recently, the existing salary system has been increasingly criticized as an approach to compensation that rewards lackadaisical teaching and punishes motivated, highly qualified instruction. Instead, educational experts argue that, to retain exceptional teachers and maintain quality instruction, teachers should receive salaries or bonuses based on performance rather than seniority.

Which of the following, if true, most weakens the conclusion of the educational experts?

- (A) Some teachers express that financial compensation is not the only factor contributing to job satisfaction and teaching performance.
- (B) School districts will develop their own unique compensation structures that may differ greatly from those of other school districts.
- (C) Upon leaving the teaching profession, many young, effective teachers cite a lack of opportunity for more rapid financial advancement as a primary factor in the decision to change careers.
- (D) A merit-based system that bases compensation on teacher performance reduces collaboration, which is an integral component of quality instruction.
- (E) In school districts that have implemented pay for performance compensation structures, standardized test scores have dramatically increased.

Step 1: Identify the Question Type

The words "weaken" and "if true" indicate that this is a Weaken the Conclusion question. Look for the conclusion made by the "educational experts."

Step 2: Deconstruct the Argument

The argument is concerned with how public school teachers are compensated. According to the argument, educational experts claim that a system of teacher compensation based on performance rather than seniority would help to retain exceptional teachers and maintain quality instruction.

What are the experts assuming? Can "performance" actually be measured in a meaningful way? Should it be based on how much the students like the teacher? A fun but incompetent teacher might be beloved by students. A challenging teacher might receive lower teacher ratings even though their students learn more.

Step 3: State the Goal

The correct answer to this Weaken question will make the experts' conclusion at least a little less likely to be valid. Look for something that will make the performance-based salary system less likely to improve teacher retention and quality instruction.

Chapter 6: **Argument-Based Reading Comprehension**

Step 4: Work from Wrong to Right

(A) ?. The fact that other factors also contribute to job satisfaction and teaching performance neither weakens nor strengthens this argument. Either way, the teachers are getting paid; the issue is whether that pay should be based on performance or seniority.

(B) ?. Nothing in the argument indicates that one universal system of compensation must be adopted in order to implement this plan. It is very possible that several effective models of performance-based pay could be developed and implemented successfully.

(C) X. This choice indicates that many young, effective teachers are extremely frustrated by the traditional pay structure, in which financial advancement is directly tied to seniority. This bolsters the experts' argument: these young but effective teachers who are leaving the profession might stay longer if they had better opportunity for advancement based on performance.

(D) **CORRECT.** Weaken. This choice indicates that collaboration among teachers is integral to high-quality instruction and that a system of compensation based on teacher performance reduces collaboration. Thus, the effect of a merit-based system of pay might undermine quality instruction, which is one of the two stated goals of the educational experts.

(E) X. The educational experts' argument in favor of performance-based compensation is bolstered, not weakened, if standardized test scores have dramatically risen in school districts that have instituted such pay structures.

CHAPTER 7
Multi-Blank Text Completion

In This Chapter...

- Two- and Three-Blank Text Completions
- Start with the Easier (or Easiest) Blank
- Tricky Aspects of Multi-Blank Text Completion
- More on Traps in Text Completion
- Vocabulary Challenge
- Problem Set
- Answers and Explanations

Chapter 7 Multi-Blank Text Completion

Multi-blank Text Completion questions will build on your one-blank Text Completion skills, requiring you to adapt those skills to questions that often contain multiple sentences and less concrete truth. In this chapter, you will learn the similarities and differences between multi-blank Text Completion questions and their one-blank counterparts, as well as strategies to handle these more complicated questions effectively.

Here are your Chapter 7 vocabulary words:

> discrete (A)
> apposite (A)
> paucity (E)
> prohibitive (E)
> reticent (E)
> nettled (A)

Two- and Three-Blank Text Completions

Expect four or five out of the seven Text Completion questions that appear across the two Verbal sections to have more than one blank. Consider the following example:

In the twentieth century, the United States witnessed a nearly (i) _____ ascent to ever greater wealth, leaving its leaders (ii) _____ of publicly acknowledging budgetary limitations.

Blank (i)		Blank (ii)
A portentous	D	chary
B pertinacious	E	capable
C unremitting	F	guilty

In sentences with multiple blanks, the blanks themselves and the answer choices are labeled with lowercase Roman numerals.

Below the sentence, the first column contains the choices—*portentous, pertinacious,* and *unremitting*—for the first blank. The second column contains the choices—*chary, capable,* and *guilty*—for the second blank.

Your choice for the first blank is independent of your choice for the second blank. That is, if you correctly choose *unremitting* for the first blank, you are not simultaneously choosing *guilty* for the second blank. You must instead make a discrete decision for the second blank. In addition, *there is no partial credit.* You must get both words right or you receive no credit for your response. Fortunately, this fact is somewhat offset by the fact that, for each blank, there are only three options rather than five.

Unit Two: Paragraphs and Passages

The baseline approach to multi-blank Text Completion, as it was for one-blank Text Completion, is to **use proof from the sentence to predict answers for the blank**. However, there are a few of ways in which making predictions for multi-blank questions can play out differently:

- Two- and especially three-blank TC questions often consist of multiple sentences, and a blank that appears in one sentence can rely on proof from another sentence.
- Similarly, a prediction you're able make for one blank will often serve as proof for the other blank.
- Because there are often multiple sentences, pronouns (*this*, *these*, *that*, *it*, *they*, etc.) and transition words will be frequently used to reference ideas brought up in previous sentences. Think of these as additions to your list of direction markers. For more on these words and how they inform an understanding of paragraphs, see Chapter 4: Signals and Pronouns.
- The presence of multiple blanks leaves less room for concrete truth, making it sometimes difficult to come up with specific predictions for the blanks.

One more pleasant feature of two-blank and three-blank problems is that, while they may *seem* harder because they are generally longer, there are often more clues for you to use. Also, having multiple blanks means you get to choose which blank to tackle first. . .and some blanks are easier to predict for than others.

Start with the Easier (or Easiest) Blank

Don't force a prediction for the first blank simply because it comes first. Read the entire prompt first, consider all of the blanks, and figure out which one has the clearest proof. Write down your prediction for that blank, and use that prediction as extra proof for the harder blank(s).

An Example with Two Blanks

Take a look at this example:

> Even seasoned opera singers can be (i) _____ performing in Rome, where audiences traditionally view (ii) _____ performers as a birthright, passed down from heckler to heckler over generations.

Blank #2 is easier. Why? Compare the proof for each blank:

	Content Clues and Direction Markers	Interpretation
Blank (i)	Even seasoned opera singers Performing in Rome	The blank focuses on how *opera singers* can feel when performing in Rome, but the only thing you know about those opera singers so far is that they're *seasoned*. *Even* is a reversal marker in most cases, so the blank should in some way contradict *seasoned*, but *novices* probably doesn't seem like a great fit. Read on.
Blank (ii)	a birthright, passed down from heckler to heckler over generations	Whatever goes in this blank is seen as a *birthright* and is therefore linked to the *generations* of hecklers referenced in the last part of the sentence. This is significantly more concrete proof than was given for the first blank, and it supports a prediction like <u>heckling</u>.

This sentence offers more definitive proof for the second blank than for the first blank, so start your prediction process there. With that prediction in hand, making a prediction for the first blank becomes more feasible. The blank describes how opera singers feel about performing in Rome, and the only information you have about Rome is that performers get heckled there. Therefore, it's most likely the case that the opera singers are <u>nervous about</u> appearing there.

Your paper might now look like this: nervous about. . .heckling

On your paper, draw a grid to keep track of your take on the answer choices for both blanks:

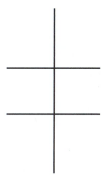

Or, if you prefer, write:

A   D

B   E

C   F

Finally, compare your predictions to the answer choices and mark your paper:

	Blank (i)		Blank (ii)
A	intrepid about	D	extolling
B	daunted by	E	lionizing
C	tempered by	F	badgering

Here is an example of what a student might have written down for this question. In this scenario, the student wasn't sure about *tempered by* and didn't know exactly about *lionizing* but felt that it wasn't quite right.

	nervous about	heckling
	✗	✗
	✓	~
	?	✓

This student would pick *daunted by* and *badgering*, which are the correct responses.

Unit Two: Paragraphs and Passages

> *Strategy Tip:*
>
> Some blanks will be harder to predict for than others. Predict for easier blanks first, and you'll have more concrete proof to use to determine the harder blanks.

An Example with Three Blanks

Take a look at the following three-blank TC question and try to identify the easiest blank:

Perceptions of the (i) _____ role of intellectual practices within modern life underlie the familiar stereotypes of the educated as self-appointed elites in ivory towers. This mischaracterization may be rooted in a (ii) _____ of the aims of academia, but it is unlikely to be (iii) _____ unless teachers take efforts to address it directly.

Blank (i)		Blank (ii)		Blank (iii)	
A	incongruous	D	dissemination	G	espoused
B	refractory	E	confounding	H	dispelled
C	salubrious	F	corroboration	I	promulgated

While this problem has three blanks instead of two and is made up of more than one sentence, the method is largely the same: Start with the easiest blank. The easiest blank is often the one surrounded by the most text—that is, the one that is farthest from the other two blanks and thus has the most potential proof located near it. Here, the first blank seems promising:

Perceptions of the (i) _____ role of intellectual practices within modern life underlie the familiar stereotypes of the educated as self-appointed elites in ivory towers.

The blank describes the *role of intellectual practices*, which underlies stereotypes about *self-appointed elites in ivory towers*. So the word describing the role should be related to the idea that intellectuals are perceived as separate from the majority of those in *modern life*. A good prediction for Blank (i) would be <u>disconnected</u>.

The second sentence references this perception of intellectuals and then seeks to explain the root cause. It's clear from *This* that the narrator is calling back to the situation described in the first sentence, and *mischaracterization* makes it clear that the narrator of this sentence believes that the take on intellectuals presented there is incorrect. As *the aims of academia* is also a reference to intellectuals, the best prediction for Blank (ii) would be <u>misunderstanding</u> or <u>mischaracterization</u>. (You can recycle wording from elsewhere in the sentences where apposite.)

The last part of the problem has a couple of reversal markers in *unlikely* and *unless*. Break it down into individual parts, taking care with the markers and substituting actual nouns in for reference language:

If teachers *don't* address it (the *mischaracterization*) directly . . .

. . . the mischaracterization will continue . . . (reasonable inference)

. . . *so* the mischaracterization is *unlikely* to be <u>ended</u>.

Chapter 7: **Multi-Blank Text Completion**

On your paper, you might have:

disconnected   misunderstanding   ended

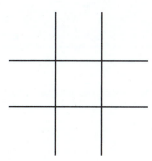

Or, if you prefer:

disconnected misunderstanding ended

A   D   G

B   E   H

C   F   I

Consider your choices and mark your paper appropriately:

Blank (i)		Blank (ii)		Blank (iii)	
A	incongruous	D	dissemination	G	espoused
B	refractory	E	confounding	H	dispelled
C	salubrious	F	corroboration	I	promulgated

Your notes for this question might look like this:

disconnected misunderstanding ended

✓	✗	~
?	✓	✓
✗	✗	✗

The correct answer is *incongruous*, *confounding*, and *dispelled*.

Unit Two: **Paragraphs and Passages**

Tricky Aspects of Multi-Blank Text Completion

This section will cover a few ways the GRE can up the difficulty level further on multi-blank text completion. Many of these *can* occur on single-blank questions, but are more likely to occur in longer sentences or full paragraphs, and therefore more likely in multi-blank questions.

Phrases in the Blanks

Double-blank and triple-blank questions can sometimes have choices that are phrases rather than single words. These questions tend to be less about knowing difficult vocabulary words than about being able to work out the meaning of the sentence(s).

Try this question:

(i) _____ subject of the sermon, her words possessed a (ii) _____ quality few could fail to find utterly enchanting. It was only when her conclusion devolved into (iii) _____ that the congregation began to fantasize about returning to the comfort of home.

	Blank (i)		Blank (ii)		Blank (iii)
A	In spite of the insipid	D	euphonious	G	a fallacious slew of prevarications
B	Notwithstanding the salubrious	E	euphemistic	H	an unending string of digressions
C	Because of the inauspicious	F	eulogistic	I	a sanctified series of assignations

Attack the easiest blank first. That might be the last one, since it's the only blank in its sentence. And indeed, the sentence provides clues: The sermon's conclusion *devolved into* whatever goes in the blank, and *the congregation began to fantasize about returning to the comfort of home*. Both bits of proof tell you that the sermon went off track in some way, but it's unclear exactly how. Rather than add to the story, for now keep your prediction appropriately vague, along the lines of <u>something bad</u>.

Now that you have mentally completed the last sentence, it might help to paraphrase it before using the information to work backward and analyze the rest of the sentence: *It was only when the conclusion went bad that the people wanted to leave.* The phrase *It was only when* serves as a reversal, signaling that before things went bad, they must have been pretty good, which in turn means that the first sentence must be describing the sermon favorably. That's backed up by the *utterly enchanting* at the end of the sentence, though due to the reversal markers (in bold below), some untangling will still be useful here:

Her words possess <u>some kind</u> of quality.

Few could *fail* to find this quality enchanting.

If many could *fail* to find this quality enchanting, her words would possess a <u>bad</u> quality . . .

. . . so if *few* could *fail,* her words must possess a <u>good</u> quality.

The second blank should be something good; recycle the word <u>enchanting</u>.

Finally, come to the first blank. It's pretty hard to fill in this one without glancing at the answer choices, but at least try to figure out a general category of what you'll be looking for. Whatever goes in this blank is about the *subject of the sermon*, and this whole part is followed by something nice about the words used in the sermon. These two parts of the sentence will go either in the same direction (that is, the *subject of the sermon* will also be *enchanting*) or in an opposite direction (that is, the *subject of the sermon* will be unenchanting even though the *words* themselves were *enchanting*).

You might have something like this on your paper:

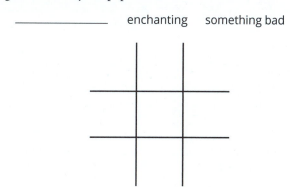

Now go to the choices, proceeding in order from the blank for which you have the clearest prediction to the blank for which you have the least clear prediction.

In Blank (ii), only *euphonious* works. The root *eu* means "good," but that's not too helpful here, since all three words use that root. However, *euphemistic* (substituting inoffensive words in for more explicit or hurtful ones) doesn't make sense, and *eulogistic* (full of praise, especially for a deceased person) also doesn't match the idea of *enchanting*. Bonus points if you recognized that *eulogistic* was a theme trap, as a *eulogy* is something that a sermonizer would likely deliver in other circumstances.

For Blank (iii), the third choice includes *sanctified*, a theme trap meaning "holy," and *assignations*, which are romantic meetups, so it's definitely out. However, the other two answer choices both offer something bad. At this point, rephrase each of those answer choices into simpler terms and consider which is a better fit for the content clues in the sentence. *A fallacious slew of prevarications* is basically a bunch of lies, and *an unending string of digressions* is a bunch of tangents. The question to resolve is which one would more likely lead people to *fantasize about returning to the comfort of home*. It can be helpful to imagine yourself in both situations and think of how you might react. A sermon that descends into a bunch of lies would probably provoke a more extreme or specific reaction than simply fantasizing about going home. On the other hand, a sermon that descends into a bunch of tangents would likely cause some impatience, which in turn could plausibly lead to fantasizing about going home. Go with *an unending string of digressions*.

The choices for Blank (i) require a bit more analysis in that they all contain direction markers. The first two choices contain the reversal markers *In spite of* and *Notwithstanding*, so for them to be right, they would have to contain a word that contrasts *euphonious*, the choice for Blank (ii). *In spite of the insipid* makes sense, as *insipid* is a good contrast for *euphonious* and *enchanting*. By contrast, *Notwithstanding the salubrious* doesn't work because *salubrious* (healthy) is a good thing, making it a poor contrast for the second part of the sentence. The third choice starts with *Because of*, a straight-ahead marker, but *inauspicious* (unfavorable) is a bad thing, making this choice incongruous with the second part of the sentence as well. Only *In spite of the insipid* works.

The answer is *In spite of the insipid, euphonious*, and *an unending string of digressions*.

Unit Two: Paragraphs and Passages

> *Strategy Tip:*
>
> When a blank won't yield to attempts at prediction, settle for a vague prediction (i.e., *something good / something bad*) and let the answer choices carry you the rest of the way.

Heavy Use of Markers

Take a look at this example:

> Although Paula claimed not to be (i) _____ that she was not selected for the scholarship, we nevertheless worried that our typically sanguine friend was not entirely (ii) _____ by the decision.

This sentence is just chock-full of switchbacks. Count the reversal signals: "Although . . . not . . . nevertheless . . . typically . . . not entirely . . ."

It's easy to lose your way in a thicket of reversals, especially under exam pressure. How many wrongs make a right?

The familiar process of chopping up the sentence and processing it in small chunks works well in these cases, even if there are multiple blanks. As always, start with the most concrete part of the story—a thing that actually happened. Then add one chunk of the sentence at a time to the story. Change complicated reversals and other signals to simple words, such as *but* and *so*.

As you go, emotionally punctuate each part of the story. Exaggerate the switchbacks in your mental voice, as if you were telling a story you really cared about. Finally, as you think about the whole, discard unnecessary elements so that you don't have to hold everything in your head at once.

For the previous example sentence, the breakdown might go like this:

> Our friend Paula is *typically* sanguine (optimistic).
>
> She was not selected for a scholarship.
>
> She was probably unhappy about this. (reasonable inference)
>
> She claimed NOT to be <u>something</u>.
>
> *But* we still worried that
>
> she was NOT entirely <u>something</u> by the decision.

Something like <u>unhappy</u> would be appropriate for the first blank and <u>pleased</u> would work for the second.

It looks like a lot of work, but with practice, your brain can generate this train of thought in seconds; by contrast, keeping the sentence in its original form makes it a lot harder to understand.

Now break down a few more challenging sentence types.

Not Enough Concrete Proof

Sometimes the GRE will construct sentences in such a way as to make predicting specific words for the blanks particularly difficult. This is most common in two-blank Text Completions, in which a paucity of proof is not necessarily prohibitive to success. In problems that don't give you enough information to predict specific answers, **predict the relationship between the blanks instead**. Consider the following example:

No one expected Salazar to (i) _____, given his long track record of (ii) _____.

Despite the fact that this sentence is relatively simple, it's impossible to make a specific prediction for either of the blanks. For instance, the first blank could be fail if the second blank were success, but the correct pairing could just as easily be eat and fasting, speak and reticence, fly and not flying, or a thousand other things. In these cases, the best thing to do is to predict a relationship between the blanks. The second half of the sentence points to Salazar's long track record of something, and this track record is presented as a reason that *no one expected* something else. It makes sense that the two blanks would be opposites. And while that might not seem like a lot to go on, in such cases the GRE will provide only one set of opposites in the answer choices.

Unfamiliar Style or Content

The GRE uses uncommon constructions and unfamiliar topics in TC in much the same way that it does in Reading Comprehension. Consider the following example:

That such a _____ of precedent would be countenanced was itself unprecedented in the court, a bastion of traditionalism.

The sentence starts with a *that* clause, a hallmark of a very academic writing style. If that sounds weird (and it probably does), add in *The fact* to make "The fact that such a _____ of precedent..."

Also, the content is about a legal matter. Add in the difficult vocabulary (*precedent, countenanced, bastion*), and it's no wonder that the sentence is forbidding.

In these cases, **swap in simpler words and phrases**.

The meaning of the sentence is something like, *The fact that such a _____ of previously established examples would be tolerated was a brand-new and surprising instance of a very traditional court going against tradition.*

A good prediction here would be something like *rejection*.

Red Herring Clues

A red herring is something that seems to offer a nice bit of proof but is actually only there to confuse you. Such traps occasionally appear on Text Completion questions, so be careful that all the proof you're using is *actually* proof.

(Fun fact: "Red herring" is an expression for something that seems like it's going to be important, but turns out to be just a distraction. The expression arose when criminals started rubbing herring—a type of fish—on trails to distract the hunting dogs chasing after them. Okay, back to the GRE!)

By (i) _____ observing social behavior, anthropologists (ii) _____ strict, though implicit, codes of conduct.

Unit Two: **Paragraphs and Passages**

Here, the word *strict*, despite its propinquity to the second blank, turns out to be less important to the meaning of that blank than *implicit*. Decoy answers for the second blank might be *follow* or *denounce*—that is, they might try to give you plausible options for how the *anthropologists* in question could react to *strict codes of conduct*. Such answers would represent story traps, however, as none of the proof elsewhere in the sentence provides any indication of how the *anthropologists* feel about *strict codes of conduct*.

By contrast, the *implicit* (hinted at or unspoken) nature of the behavior is more germane to the overall meaning of the sentence because the first part of the sentence deals with *observing social behavior*, a prospect that's definitely more complicated if the behavior is *implicit* (but has no clear relationship to the strictness of the behavior). Indeed, the implicit nature of this behavior would require assiduous observation to detect. A good prediction word for the first blank would be <u>assiduously</u>.

You may find that even with a solid prediction in hand for the first blank, the second blank is hard to make a specific prediction for. This will often be the case when the blanks represent verbs. Given the central role verbs play in sentences, it can be difficult to get a handle on a sentence's intended meaning when the sentence lacks a verb. In these cases, rely on the answer choices to help supply clarity to the sentence.

> *Strategy Tip:*
> When sentences get tricky, break them into smaller, easier to understand chunks—even if you end up needing *a lot* of chunks.
>
> If a sentence is still too abstruse to make specific predictions, **predict the relationship between the blanks** or **cheat off the answer choices**.

More on Traps in Text Completion

The previous section examined some aspects of Text Completion that can make it difficult to interpret the sentence's meaning and make predictions for the blanks. This section goes into more depth on some of the most common traps among answer choices. For a more exhaustive list of the traps that will appear in fill-in-the-blank questions on the GRE, see Chapter 3: Traps in TC and SE.

Theme Trap

This trap has already appeared in a few examples, but here it takes center stage. Give the following problem a try:

> The event horizon (or boundary) of a black hole represents both (i)_____ and intangibility; space travelers would pass through this literal "point of no return" so (ii)_____ that the precise moment at which their fate was sealed would almost certainly not be registered.

Blank (i)		Blank (ii)	
A	constellation	D	indiscernibly
B	irrevocability	E	universally
C	infallibility	F	cosmically

Which is the easier blank? Most would agree that the second blank is easier. A good part of the proof is that *the precise moment. . .would certainly not be registered*, and the lack of any signal to the contrary tells you that your prediction should agree with that proof. So you might fill in something like without registering (again, recycling language from the sentence itself).

Now turn to the first blank. It's directly connected to the *event horizon of a black hole*, and it's something different from *intangibility*. That's not a lot to go on. Luckily, the second part of the sentence contains a more complete description of the *event horizon*, referencing it as *this literal "point of no return"* and focusing on how a space travelers' fate would be sealed as they passed through. Because *intangibility* isn't related to this later information about the event horizon, it's likely that whatever goes in the first blank *is* related to that description. A good prediction might be no return or unreturnability. (It's totally fine to make up your own words when predicting an answer—as long as your prediction makes sense to you.)

Now match your predictions to the answer choices. Only *indiscernibly* fits *without registering* for Blank (ii), and only *irrevocability* fits *no return*, making this pair of answers correct.

A **theme trap** is an answer choice that shares a theme or field (such as medicine, sports, etc.) with the sentence. Since you naturally associate the trap word with the subject matter of the sentence, the choice sounds okay on its own and somehow seems to make sense in the sentence, even though it doesn't really fit with the proof for the blanks.

Notice the trap language in the choices: *constellation, universally, cosmically*. Like the sentence itself, these words all relate to space, but they have no actual relation to the meanings that the proof for the blanks demands. Be disciplined and follow the strategy every time, and you'll avoid traps like this.

Close But Not Close Enough Trap

Like theme traps, these appear in the answer choices, especially when the correct answer is a word that the GRE knows will be unfamiliar to most test-takers. Try this problem:

Marie was nettled by her sister's constant jocularity and preferred a(n) _____ approach to life.

A	miserable
B	indignant
C	waggish
D	staid
E	sycophantic

It may have been pretty straightforward for you to identify the proof (*nettled, jocularity,* and *preferred* all play a part) and see that Marie is against *constant jocularity*, or joking behavior. A safe prediction might be serious.

Now go through the answer choices. *Miserable* and *indignant* both have the negative inflection we're looking for, but they're not great matches for serious, and they might be too extreme. Just because Marie doesn't like her sister's constant joking, that doesn't mean she's *miserable* or *indignant* in her outlook on life. Perhaps you don't know what *waggish* or *staid* mean, and you don't totally remember *sycophantic* either, but you're sure it doesn't mean *serious*.

So your paper might look like this:

serious

A ∼
B ∼
C ?
D ?
E ✗

The **close but not close enough trap** occurs when a wrong answer choice is in the ballpark of what you want but slightly off the mark in its meaning, connotation, degree, or usage. This trap is at its most dangerous when the trap answer is familiar and the correct answer is unfamiliar.

In the sentence above, while you may not love *miserable* or *indignant*, the total unfamiliarity of the words in answers (C) and (D) can make you loath to choose them. Overcome this reluctance. If your prediction is based on clear proof in the sentence, the GRE will give you an answer that fits it; you shouldn't have to stretch an answer to make it work. Here, as it turns out, the correct answer is *staid*, which means "serious; sedate by temperament or habits." This is a better counterpoint to *jocularity* than either *miserable* or *indignant*.

It takes confidence to pick a word you don't know! To build that confidence, when you review your work on TC questions, keep track of problems on which you fall for a close but not close enough trap and should have picked the unfamiliar word instead. Use those questions to calibrate your sensitivity to these traps and bolster your confidence in picking a mystery word.

> *Strategy Tip:*
>
> Even the most pernicious traps can be avoided by making proof-based predictions and sticking to them. Pay attention to these traps as you study Text Completion and Sentence Equivalence, and make a special note of it when you fall into one. Knowing which traps you're susceptible to can help obviate those traps in the future.

Vocabulary Challenge

> Did you spot these vocabulary words? If not, go back and find them in context! (The word may be in a different form than listed here— "digressing" instead of "digress," for example.) Write your own definitions based on the evidence in the chapter.

1. discrete (*adj.*), p. 201
2. apposite (*adj.*), p. 204
3. paucity (*n*), p. 209
4. prohibitive (*adj.*), p. 209
5. reticent (*adj.*), p. 209
6. nettle (*v*), p. 211

Problem Set

As you do these questions, look for the proof, and start from the easier (or easiest) blank. Write down your own predictions, write out the letters A B C or make a grid, and use process of elimination.

That said, specific predictions are often harder to come by in multi-blank Text Completions. If you find it difficult to come up with a fill-in for a blank, try to guess its spin or its relationship to other blanks in the problem, and then proceed to the answer choices. Eliminate answers that don't agree with the proof in the sentence; choose those with the strongest connections to the proof.

As always, look up any unfamiliar words as you review the questions and add them to your vocabulary list.

1. Richardson's (i) _____ handling of the (ii) _____ scandal successfully prevented what seemed poised to become the ruination of her coalition.

	Blank (i)		Blank (ii)
A	penitent	D	fretful
B	adroit	E	looming
C	heterogeneous	F	ecumenical

2. The (i) _____ forces were just barely held at bay by a loyalist battalion (ii) _____ by its allies' reinforcements.

	Blank (i)		Blank (ii)
A	revolting	D	obviated
B	outclassed	E	bolstered
C	fascistic	F	sapped

3. (i) _____ by circumstance, the entrepreneur once known for his overweening (ii) _____ was now seen by others as the possessor of a broken spirit and timid demeanor.

	Blank (i)		Blank (ii)
A	Unaffected	D	pretension
B	Humbled	E	liberality
C	Exalted	F	wealth

4. Though he had been largely successful in his attempts to adopt a more (i) _____ lifestyle, he was not above occasionally indulging his proclivities for (ii) _____ dishes.

	Blank (i)		Blank (ii)
A	truculent	D	odious
B	salutary	E	sodden
C	frugal	F	unwholesome

Unit Two: Paragraphs and Passages

5. The discovery that exposure to allergens through the mother's diet during the last trimester could lead to complications during the first year after birth (i) _____ the U.K. Department of Health to (ii) _____ dietary recommendations for expecting mothers.

Blank (i)			Blank (ii)	
A	prompted		D	intuit
B	instigated		E	codify
C	lulled		F	officiate

6. Fearful of being seen as (i) _____, the Bieber Appreciation Society took pains to include (ii) _____ voices in its monthly newsletter.

Blank (i)			Blank (ii)	
A	enthusiasts		D	tantamount
B	detractors		E	critical
C	toadies		F	conciliatory

7. The fact that bringing together criminals and their victims for a moderated conversation has been shown to vastly reduce rates of (i) _____ might be explained by the fact that those who commit crimes can only do so by convincing themselves their actions have no (ii) _____.

Blank (i)			Blank (ii)	
A	violence		D	inconsistencies
B	recidivism		E	aberrations
C	malfeasance		F	ramifications

8. The (i) _____ of monks and abbots in Eastern Christianity were typically of plain black modest cloth, indicating their spiritual indifference to matters of this world in favor of a commitment to a (ii) _____ mindset. In this regard, the contrast with the (iii) _____ garments of Buddhist monks is striking.

Blank (i)		Blank (ii)		Blank (iii)	
A	vestiges	D	mundane	G	iridescent
B	habiliments	E	dogmatic	H	drab
C	paragons	F	transcendent	I	flowing

9. In many criminal trials, it emerges that the defendant (i) _____ some kind of abuse as a child. However, these biographical revelations should not have any effect on how the jury apportions (ii) _____. An excuse is not a justification, and the criminal justice system wasn't constructed to help balance the (iii) _____ of someone's life.

Blank (i)		Blank (ii)		Blank (iii)	
A	appreciated	D	culpability	G	ledger
B	exploited	E	history	H	imprisonment
C	suffered	F	insanity	I	verdict

10. The university president argued that top universities should not (i) _____ education as an academic (ii) _____; discouraging our brightest students from pursuing teaching careers does a disservice to the next generation of students by (iii) _____ them of the opportunity to learn from the cream of the crop.

Blank (i)		Blank (ii)		Blank (iii)	
A	disdain	D	recommendation	G	denigrating
B	proscribe	E	tome	H	degenerating
C	circumvent	F	discipline	I	divesting

11. Seeing its only alternative to be a (i) _____ diplomacy unbecoming of political visionaries—as members of the so-called National Liberation Organization saw themselves in those days—the militant branch veered toward a policy of (ii) _____ aggression against its perceived rivals.

Blank (i)		Blank (ii)	
A	wheedling	D	supine
B	freewheeling	E	unremitting
C	verdant	F	superfluous

12. A (i) _____ ran through the crowd of protesters chanting slogans and threats when the queen made the sudden announcement—only a fortnight after vowing not to give in to the popular demands for her departure—that she would abdicate the throne, (ii) _____ a period of disorder and confusion.

Blank (i)		Blank (ii)	
A	frisson	D	marring
B	murmur	E	precipitating
C	panegyric	F	diluting

13. A perfectionist in all things, Joseph expected to immediately become a (i) _____ and was downtrodden indeed when he remained (ii) _____ despite his best efforts.

Blank (i)		Blank (ii)	
A	hack	D	novel
B	musician	E	inane
C	virtuoso	F	inept

14. (i) _____ is unlikely to be an asset to someone (ii) _____ by liars and fabulists.

Blank (i)		Blank (ii)	
A	Credulity	D	forsaken
B	Duplicity	E	brooked
C	Ingenuity	F	beset

Unit Two: Paragraphs and Passages

15. While she was known to all her friends as quite the (i) _____, legendary for humorous stories from her years spent driving a taxi, her private behavior belied this (ii) _____ image.

	Blank (i)		Blank (ii)
A	sage	D	belligerent
B	prevaricator	E	pedantic
C	raconteur	F	genial

16. The common opinion at the court had it that her droll utterances as often as not (i) _____ attitudes unbecoming of a lady. This reputation cost her the attentions of some gentlemen, above all thanks to their fear of being bested by her (ii) _____.

	Blank (i)		Blank (ii)
A	eluded	D	subtlety
B	derided	E	doggerel
C	evinced	F	repartee

17. While courage is anything but unimportant—and his character is indeed (i) _____—a cartoon mouse with a (ii) _____ for excessive violence is hardly an appropriate mascot for a children's charity.

	Blank (i)		Blank (ii)
A	mettlesome	D	penchant
B	impetuous	E	kinship
C	heady	F	largess

18. The double-dealing ambassador's political (i) _____ and backpedaling looked all the worse when compared to the (ii) _____ straightforwardness of his Australian counterpart.

	Blank (i)		Blank (ii)
A	plutocracy	D	occlusive
B	bugaboo	E	ostensible
C	sleight of hand	F	intransigent

19. The most (i) _____ puzzle was in determining how to deliver the antisense strand to the right place at the right moment, after the virus had penetrated the cell but before it had replicated and escaped to infect other cells. To accomplish this, the synthetic strand had to be potent enough to be effective and to resist rapid (ii) _____ inside the body, allowing it time to accomplish its task.

	Blank (i)		Blank (ii)
A	recalcitrant	D	desiccation
B	pedestrian	E	degradation
C	monolithic	F	compunction

20. The Russo-Turkish War (i) _____ Albanians, placing before them the (ii) _____ prospect of a division of their lands among competing powers. This, above all, served to bring Albanian nationalism surging out of its former (iii) _____, culminating in a successful bid for independence only a few decades later.

Blank (i)		Blank (ii)		Blank (iii)	
A	rankled	D	evanescent	G	latency
B	enervated	E	pernicious	H	insularity
C	debased	F	transient	I	lucidity

21. Though she acknowledges that modern farming practices are more (i) _____ than traditional agriculture, she nonetheless argues that this difference represents no real (ii) _____. Perhaps more worrying, however, is her insistence that similar claims can be advanced regarding the treatment of farmers by an often (iii) _____ social hierarchy.

Blank (i)		Blank (ii)		Blank (iii)	
A	expensive	D	progress	G	iniquitous
B	efficient	E	disincentive	H	halcyon
C	polluting	F	countermand	I	stratified

22. The (i) _____ of the word *assassin* is (ii) _____ in philological circles, as the word comes from a sect of brutal killers believed to have smoked the drug hashish before going on a mission. The topic is equally attractive to historians, as the (iii) _____ of the sect, which dates to before the First Crusade in the 11th century, remains a mystery.

Blank (i)		Blank (ii)		Blank (iii)	
A	introduction	D	notorious	G	provenance
B	derivation	E	unheralded	H	legend
C	circumlocution	F	enigmatic	I	bane

23. Statistics often need to be (i) _____ for their real meaning: In the last decade, while both the population and the amount of meat eaten annually in the nation remained (ii) _____, the growing gap between rich and poor meant that the wealthy few were eating more meat than ever while the masses suffered from a (iii) _____ of foodstuffs of all kinds.

Blank (i)		Blank (ii)		Blank (iii)	
A	plumbed	D	plastic	G	deceleration
B	calculated	E	static	H	dearth
C	designed	F	demographic	I	glut

Unit Two: Paragraphs and Passages

24. Although Cage supported the expanded reliance on electronically produced (i) _____, most of his early music is surprisingly (ii) _____. His "Music for Marcel Duchamp," a prepared-piano work from 1947, never rises above mezzo-piano, offering instead (iii) _____ melody that maintains its softness throughout.

Blank (i)		Blank (ii)		Blank (iii)	
A	timbre	D	strident	G	a noisome
B	murmur	E	auspicious	H	an undulating
C	clangor	F	subdued	I	an erstwhile

25. The tokens given by the aristocrat, while (i) _____, still served as a reminder that the power of the Crown continued to be held in some esteem even in such (ii) _____ political times.

Blank (i)		Blank (ii)	
A	sardonic	D	mercurial
B	nugatory	E	jocund
C	sumptuous	F	magisterial

26. Having built up to a (i) _____, the shelling stopped as suddenly as it had begun; gazing at the drooping barrels of the artillery, one might be forgiven for thinking they were rendered (ii) _____ by the pathetic sight of their (iii) _____ targets.

Blank (i)		Blank (ii)		Blank (iii)	
A	pique	D	sidereal	G	ethereal
B	crescendo	E	doleful	H	affluent
C	euphony	F	erroneous	I	haggard

27. Despite having capably engineered and overseen the return of several stray dioceses that had broken away under his predecessor's (i) _____, the bishop had a modest quality that (ii) _____ the (iii) _____ of his position.

Blank (i)		Blank (ii)		Blank (iii)	
A	diligence	D	construed	G	tenuousness
B	epaulet	E	belied	H	audacity
C	laxity	F	derided	I	eminence

28. The (i) _____ of "surds"—irrational roots—with the Pythagoreans' faith that all phenomena in the universe could be expressed through harmonious ratios of whole numbers led the cult to (ii) _____ any mention of their existence to the uninitiated.

Blank (i)		Blank (ii)	
A	absurdity	D	condone
B	incongruity	E	proscribe
C	imperilment	F	palliate

Chapter 7: **Multi-Blank Text Completion**

29. Architectural (i) _____ such as Koolhaas recognized Hadid's talents early and encouraged their development. By 1977, only a few years after their initial encounter, she had perfected her (ii) _____ style, inspired equally by such disparate styles as Malevich's sparse constructivism and the flowing calligraphy of her native Arabic.

	Blank (i)		Blank (ii)
A	cognoscenti	D	fungible
B	fledglings	E	malleable
C	neophytes	F	heterogeneous

30. Aleister Crowley, despite being given to wildly fantastic claims—he insisted, for instance, that the founding book of his religion was dictated to him by a divine being who visited his hotel room wearing sunglasses and a trench coat—had his share of (i) _____ followers. It is hard to know whether these were spurred on or dissuaded by the (ii) _____ cast on him by the popular press, whose dubbing him "the wickedest man in the world" was, to be fair, hardly (iii) _____ given the relative harmlessness of his eccentricities.

	Blank (i)		Blank (ii)		Blank (iii)
A	sober	D	disadvantages	G	glib
B	sordid	E	gauntlets	H	peevish
C	skeptical	F	aspersions	I	condign

31. The Biblical portrayal of (i) _____ times preceding the great deluge stands in stark contrast to the ancient Greek representation of the (ii) _____ past as a Golden Age from which humanity has slowly descended into godless chaos. Such observations can easily give rise to the notion that stories about the past are less faithful attempts at reconstruction than (iii) _____, expressing both our cultural fears and hopes.

	Blank (i)		Blank (ii)		Blank (iii)
A	flagitious	D	proximate	G	allegories
B	dubious	E	antediluvian	H	equivocations
C	rustic	F	obscure	I	platitudes

32. Seeing digestive irregularity as perhaps the (i) _____ of preventable illness, such twelfth-century physicians as Moses Maimonides aimed the bulk of their (ii) _____ pamphlets at the prescription of prophylactic dietary regimens, offering advice that often appears risible to modern sensibilities.

	Blank (i)		Blank (ii)
A	most significant cause	D	maleficent
B	only panacea	E	didactic
C	sine qua non	F	tenable

Unit Two: Paragraphs and Passages

33. Not trusting his (i) _____ attire to impress the suave, sharply dressed executive, despite the latter's frequent professions of a fondness for rural life, Francis reduced himself to near (ii) _____ through costly new wardrobe acquisitions. If only he had known that the executive was secretly ashamed of her (iii) _____ showboating, which she only indulged to conceal her financial ruin.

Blank (i)		Blank (ii)		Blank (iii)	
A	rustic	D	penury	G	bombastic
B	natty	E	malaise	H	runic
C	exclusive	F	lethargy	I	sartorial

34. (i) _____ is generally unlikely to gain a reputation for reliability; Garth's poorly disguised excuses for his frequent absences, however, were improbably interpreted by his (ii) _____, hypochondriac employer as a sign of great foresight and (iii) _____.

Blank (i)		Blank (ii)		Blank (iii)	
A	An embezzler	D	casuistic	G	insipidity
B	A malingerer	E	imposing	H	sagacity
C	A pilferer	F	credulous	I	temerity

35. Perhaps unjustifiably, history has (i) _____ the movement's leader to the extent that his considerable moral shortcomings—his (ii) _____ misogyny, for example—are (iii) _____ and, if mentioned at all, are seen as little more than peccadilloes.

Blank (i)		Blank (ii)		Blank (iii)	
A	lionized	D	diffident	G	mere relics
B	extirpated	E	incorrigible	H	widely praised
C	impugned	F	reformed	I	rarely discussed

36. The new film chronicles exploitation and iniquity as the dark side of its overarching theme of (i) _____. The film succeeds in creating an immediately sympathetic protagonist, and it does well to showcase the elimination of all her longtime abusers in the end, granting the audience the (ii) _____ they've been awaiting for two hours. Despite the satisfying upheaval, however, the ponderous plot en route to this (iii) _____ leaves much to be desired.

Blank (i)		Blank (ii)		Blank (iii)	
A	fairness	D	catharsis	G	embellishment
B	slavery	E	revelation	H	denouement
C	injustice	F	inconclusiveness	I	platitude

Chapter 7: Multi-Blank Text Completion

37. Although (i) _____ is frequently used to give otherwise insubstantial work (ii) _____ of profundity, even Wallgot's most charitable readers were known to sneer at the breadth of his references.

Blank (i)		Blank (ii)	
A	stringency	D	an iota
B	insularity	E	a veneer
C	eclecticism	F	a medley

38. She rarely bothered to (i) _____ her lengthy tomes, but their surprising popularity with the public empowered her to avoid editorial complaints through (ii) _____ threats to sign a contract with a different publisher.

Blank (i)		Blank (ii)	
A	emend	D	impuissant
B	allay	E	preemptive
C	edify	F	toothsome

39. In future discounting, subjects place a lower value on events in the distant future than on (i) _____ ones, explaining the common tendency to (ii) _____ present pleasures even at the expense of a likely (iii) _____ of future detriments.

Blank (i)		Blank (ii)		Blank (iii)	
A	atavistic	D	avert	G	malady
B	remote	E	rescind	H	proliferation
C	proximate	F	protract	I	buttressing

40. She makes the facile claim that it is possible to deduce matters of fact from logic and, with just as little (i) _____ , aims to derive ethical and economic truths as well. The laws of logic, in her opinion, (ii) _____ her proclamation that "existence exists," which is very much like saying that the law of thermodynamics gave rise to the discovery that heat is hot.

Blank (i)		Blank (ii)	
A	syllogism	D	undergird
B	warrant	E	occlude
C	fallacy	F	galvanize

Unit Two: **Paragraphs and Passages**

Answers and Explanations

Vocabulary Challenge

1. discrete (*adj.*): separate, distinct, detached, existing as individual parts

2. apposite (*adj.*): highly appropriate, suitable, or relevant

3. paucity (*n*): scarcity, the state of being small in number

4. prohibitive (*adj.*): tending to forbid something, or serving to prevent something

5. reticent (*adj.*): not talking much; private (of a person), restrained, reserved

6. nettle (*v*): irritate, sting, or annoy

Problem Set

1. **(i) adroit; (ii) looming:** The first blank describes Richardson's "handling" of a situation, and the second blank describes a "scandal." Start, as always, with some concrete proof. There was something that "seemed poised to become the ruination" of Richardson's coalition (probably the scandal), but it was "successfully prevented" by "Richardson's handling." Well done, Richardson. The first blank needs to be a positive word, such as <u>successful</u>, so *adroit* (skilled, adept) fits well. Neither a *penitent* (sorry for sin) nor a *heterogeneous* (mixed; composed of differing parts) handling of the scandal is supported by proof in the sentence.

In predicting for the second blank, look for clues in the sentence that describe the scandal. All you know is that it "seemed poised" to ruin things—that is, it hadn't done so already. A word that means <u>about to happen</u> would make sense. *Looming* (taking shape as an impending event) is the most sensible match. Someone might be *fretful* (worried) over a scandal, but *fretful* doesn't make sense as a description of the scandal itself, and there are no indications in the sentence that the scandal was *ecumenical* (worldwide in scope).

2. **(i) revolting; (ii) bolstered:** The first blank describes "forces," and the second blank is connected to a "battalion." Given the thematic similarity between "forces" and "battalion," look to the word used to describe the battalion: "loyalist." If a loyalist battalion is holding some other forces at bay, those other forces must be <u>rebels</u>. You don't have any indication that the forces were *outclassed* (surpassed in quality) or *fascistic* (totalitarian, led by dictator). Don't be thrown off by the dual meaning of *revolting*—*revolting* can mean "disgusting," but it can also mean engaging in a literal revolt, such as against a government.

The second blank links the loyalist battalion to "its allies' reinforcements." Since allies and reinforcements are both good things to have when you're engaged in conflict, and since the loyalists have been able to hold the revolting forces at bay, the word must be something good, like <u>helped</u>. Only *bolstered* (supported) makes sense. *Obviated* (anticipated and made unnecessary) isn't supported by any proof in the sentence. *Sapped* (weakened, especially of energy) conflicts with the idea that allies would help the loyalists, making this an opposite trap.

3. **(i) humbled; (ii) pretension:** Both blanks in this sentence describe "the entrepreneur" in some way. The concrete truth in this sentence is that the entrepreneur is now "the possessor of a broken spirit and timid demeanor." This informs the second blank, which describes what the entrepreneur *was* known for before his spirit broke. The adjective "overweening" means "conceited" or "excessive," so a good prediction for the second blank might be <u>confidence</u>, albeit likely with a more negative spin. *Pretension* fits this.

Neither *liberality* (giving or spending freely; open-mindedness) nor *wealth* correctly oppose the idea of having a broken spirit or being timid.

Now move on to the first blank. It's in an awkward position in the sentence, so it's good to have as clear an idea as possible of what's going on in the rest of the sentence before working on this. Given how things turn out for the entrepreneur, a good prediction for this blank might be brought down or broken. The only answer that comes close is *humbled*. *Exalted* (held in high regard; in a state of extreme happiness) is the opposite of what the blank requires, and *unaffected* clashes with the meaning of the sentence: The entrepreneur has definitely been affected by circumstance, given the change in how he's perceived.

4. (i) salutary; (ii) unwholesome: The blanks in this sentence can be difficult to predict with certainty, as there aren't many concrete clues given in the sentence. When this happens in a two-blank TC question, settle for determining the relationship between the blanks rather than making a specific prediction. The reversal marker "though" offers a clue: The two parts of the sentence must contradict each other in some way. Since the first part describes something "successful," it would make sense if the word in the first blank, which describes the "lifestyle" he had been making efforts to adopt, were a good word, but it's not totally guaranteed—you'll need some information about the second blank before you can decide.

The second part of the sentence says that the person in question was "not above occasionally indulging" proclivities (inclinations or predilections) for some kind of dishes. Unpack it a little. If he *were* above indulging his proclivities, he wouldn't indulge them; since he's *not* above it, he must actually indulge these proclivities on occasion. Now, it can help to simplify the sentence a bit: Though he'd adopted some kind of lifestyle, he still sometimes indulged his liking for some kind of dishes. The two words need to be opposites.

Examine the answer choices. It's hard to imagine what kind of dishes could possibly be a counterpart to a *truculent* (ferocious, cruel, or savage) lifestyle, but regardless, none of the options for Blank (ii) is a good opposite. *Salutary* (conducive to health) does have a good counterpoint in the other blank: *unwholesome*. And *unwholesome* works to describe dishes, too, so this is looking like a pretty promising pair of answers. *Frugal* (thrifty) would work in Blank (i) if there were a word like "expensive" among the choices for the second blank, but neither *odious* (extremely repulsive) nor *sodden* (soaked) means anything like expensive.

5. (i) prompted; (ii) codify: Both blanks here represent verbs, which can make them particularly hard to predict. Unpack the sentence: There was a discovery, and this discovery did something to the "U.K. Department of Health." The discovery was that pregnancy complications are being caused and can be avoided. This is a health issue, so the Department of Health would definitely want to do something about. It's likely that the first blank means something like caused. Among the options for Blank (i), there are two that mean something like "caused": *prompted* and *instigated*. *Instigated* (urged, goaded, provoked, or incited) has a somewhat negative spin that means it's most often used before negative acts (instigate a fight, for instance). The more neutral *prompted* is a better fit, as it doesn't seem any urging or goading was necessary. *Lulled* (deceptively caused to feel safe) is the opposite of the reaction this sort of health discovery would elicit from the Department of Health.

The second blank will describe what the Department of Health was *prompted* to do by the discovery. Given that it would likely be important to get the word about this discovery out to "expectant mothers," a word like publish would make sense here. *Intuit* (understand or solve by instinct) isn't right, as there's no reason to intuit what has already been discovered. *Officiate* (act as an official in charge) wouldn't be used in this

Unit Two: **Paragraphs and Passages**

context, though it is a potential theme trap due to the Department of Health's official leadership status. Only *codify* (put into an explicit law or code) works.

6. (i) toadies; (ii) critical: The first blank describes "the Bieber Appreciation Society," which clearly exists to appreciate all things Bieber, and the second blank describes the "voices" that the society will soon include in its publication. These voices are going to be included specifically because the BAS has become "fearful" of being seen in a certain way, so the voices are probably meant to create the opposite impression. Therefore, the two blanks should be opposites.

Look at the options for the first blank. The answer choices are gentle, happily. There's no reason that the Bieber Appreciation Society would be "fearful" of being seen as *enthusiasts* (or they'd better consider a name change), and they're likely in no danger of being seen as *detractors* (people who criticize something)—this represents an opposite trap. Only *toadies* (servile followers) makes sense here, as it has a negative spin that fits "fearful" but that *enthusiasts* lacks.

In the second blank, *tantamount* (equivalent) doesn't make any sense, and *conciliatory* would be positive toward Bieber (so why would the Bieber Appreciation Society have trouble finding such voices?). Only *critical*, which in this context likely means "involving careful evaluation and judgment," works in offering a good contrast to *toadies* (because a toady is by definition uncritical).

7. (i) recidivism; (ii) ramifications: " Bringing together criminals and their victims" reduces the rates of something, and the second part of the sentence offers a potential explanation for why that reduction has been observed: The criminals convince themselves their actions have no something in order to commit the crimes in the first place. A good prediction for the second blank might be something like consequences or effect on others, as that would provide a good reason why making criminals face their victims might bring about a change. Both *inconsistencies* and *aberrations* mean something like "deviations from the norm," which doesn't work for this blank; *ramifications*, on the other hand, fits the "consequences" prediction.

The sentence doesn't give much to go on for the first blank except that it will probably be something bad. Unfortunately, all the options for Blank (i) are negative words, so a more subtle analysis will be needed. *Violence* could work, but nothing in the sentence suggests that these were necessarily violent criminals. *Recidivism* (a tendency to re-engage in crime or bad behavior) works really well here. If the criminals could only commit crimes when they believed their actions had no consequences, meeting the victims—the human consequences of their actions—would disabuse them of this belief, rendering them unable to commit more crimes. *Malfeasance* (crime or lesser wrongdoing) works better than *violence* in that criminals have by definition committed some kind of malfeasance; however, it doesn't fit as well as *recidivism*, which is specifically about *repeated* malfeasance.

8. (i) habiliments; (ii) transcendent; (iii) iridescent: The first blank is referring to something made of cloth, which is contrasted with the "garments of Buddhist monks." For this comparison to work, the first blank must mean something like garments. *Habiliments* (clothes associated with a particular profession or occasion) is the only choice that fits—*vestiges* (remaining traces of something) and *paragons* (the best exemplars of a usually good quality) are off the mark.

The contrast between the first sentence and the second sentence make the third blank the next easiest to predict for. Since the first sentence describes the Christian garments as being made of "plain black modest cloth," it would make sense if the garments of the Buddhist monks were not plain, bright and colorful, or immodest. *Iridescent* is a decent match for the second prediction. *Drab* (dull-colored) is an opposite trap, and *flowing* has no connection to the content clues in the first sentence.

The word in the second blank has nothing to do with clothing. Instead, it describes the "mindset" of the Eastern Christians. The only information in the sentences that touches on their mindset is the part about "their spiritual indifference to matters of this world." If they're indifferent to matters of this world, they're likely "in favor of a commitment to" something not of this world. *Mundane* (boring; relating to this world) is an opposite trap, and *dogmatic* (marked by absolute adherence to rules or principles) is a theme trap. *Transcendent* correctly indicates a focus on matters beyond the material plane.

9. (i) suffered; (ii) culpability; (iii) ledger: The first blank is a good place to start, as there aren't many words that could plausibly precede "some kind of abuse as a child." A prediction of suffered wouldn't go amiss, and indeed it's reflected in the answer choices. That said, there's not much in the way of content clues to support such a prediction, so look at the other answers for Blank (i) before you finalize the choice. *Appreciated* is pretty unlikely—nobody appreciates abuse. *Exploited* is a bit trickier, but the text never implies that the abuse was used to exploit anything.

For the second blank, you only need to know what a jury does: They apportion (assign) blame, which is a synonym of *culpability*. *History* doesn't make sense here, and *insanity* is a theme trap due to the frequency of insanity pleas in criminal trials.

The third blank is fairly hard to predict for, so go to the answer choices instead. The only option that can be "balanced" is *ledger* (a record of transactions, used here figuratively). You can't as clearly balance an *imprisonment* or a *verdict*, and neither word makes sense with the "of someone's life" that follows the blank. They're both theme traps.

10. (i) disdain; (ii) discipline; (iii) divesting: The concrete proof is that the "brightest students" are being discouraged from "pursuing teaching careers," something the sentence describes as a "disservice." This will help with the first blank, but it's still probably easier to predict for the third blank first, as there's much more concrete information in the second part of the sentence. If the brightest students aren't pursuing teaching careers, how does that affect the next generation of students? The next generation won't be learning from "the cream of the crop," a reference to the bright students who won't be pursuing teaching. A good prediction would be depriving. *Divesting* is a good synonym for "depriving." Don't fall for the traps of *denigrating* (defaming, belittling) and *degenerating* (deteriorating, declining), both of which fit with the overall negative theme but don't fit into the blank.

Back to the first part of the sentence now. The second part of the sentence has fully described a negative consequence of discouraging students from choosing to teach; therefore, it's justifiable to say that "top universities should not (i) discourage education as an academic (ii) pursuit." In Blank (i), *disdain* (look down on) is somewhat close in tone and effect to "discourage." *Proscribe* (ban) is much more extreme than "discourage," and *circumvent* (avoid via circuitous means) doesn't really fit. In Blank (ii) *discipline* (in this case, an area of study) is the closest match for the prediction pursuit in the context of academics. *Tome* (a large, usually academic book) is a theme trap, and *recommendation* is a story trap—you can sort of make it work, but the sentence isn't advocating for education to be recommended as a pursuit, just for it not to be discouraged.

11. (i) wheedling; (ii) unremitting: The first blank describes "diplomacy," and the second describes "aggression." Since the political organization is described as "militant," it would likely favor aggression against rivals, so check the answers for Blank (ii) to see if one of the words is consistent with that expectation. *Supine* (lying flat; passive) doesn't work to describe "aggression" and doesn't fit with "militant." *Unremitting* (not letting up) works in that it intensifies the aggression described. *Superfluous* (dispensable;

Unit Two: **Paragraphs and Passages**

redundant; more than what's needed) adds a strange spin to the sentence, in that it implies that the organization is going to somehow act with more aggression than it's able to use.

Returning to the first blank, the kind of "diplomacy" that the blank describes is characterized as "unbecoming" and is presented as an "alternative" to the aggression described later in the sentence (the information between the dashes in this sentence is a red herring). Therefore, the diplomacy in question must offer a contrast to aggression. It might best be described as weak. *Wheedling* (persuade through flattery) is decidedly *not* an aggressive approach, so it might work, but consider the other answers before making a decision. *Freewheeling* (acting without concern for rules or consequences) is not indicated by any proof in the sentence and isn't as clear a counterpoint to "unremitting aggression." *Verdant* (green, covered in vegetation) is totally unrelated to diplomacy. *Wheedling* might be considered a bit of a story trap in other circumstances, compared to *freewheeling* and *verdant* it's definitely the safest bet.

12. (i) frisson; (ii) precipitating: Start from the concrete truth: There are people who have been demanding the queen's departure for at least a fortnight, and the queen has announced her abdication (giving up a throne) to a crowd of those people, acceding to their demands. Thus, the protesters to whom the first blank is connected are getting what they want. Thrill may work well for the first blank, and among the answer choices, *frisson* fits. *Murmur* is definitely possible, but its neutrality makes it a less than ideal fit for the clues in the sentence (especially "chanting threats" and "popular demands"). A *panegyric* (formal speech or composition in praise of someone or something) is not something that would "run through the crowd," and certainly not in praise of the very queen the crowd wishes to depose.

For the second blank, one might expect a period of disorder to either begin or end with the act of abdication—after all, there's clearly been some disorder in the weeks leading up to this abdication, but there's also likely to be more disorder in the wake of such a political upheaval. Among the answers, *precipitating* (causing to begin) is the only possibility. *Marring* (damaging, disfiguring) doesn't work and is inappropriate in the context of something negative (*marring* tends to happen to something that would've been good otherwise, like a beautiful day *marred* by clouds). Similarly, *diluting* (making weaker by adding other elements to it) isn't really a thing that could be done to "a period" of time.

13. (i) virtuoso; (ii) inept: The overall message of the sentence is that Joseph "expected" to become one thing but, disappointingly, "remained" something else. Since Joseph is a "perfectionist," he probably expected to become perfect, or at least good, and was disappointed when he remained something like unskilled or bad. *Virtuoso* (highly skilled, especially in music or art) and *inept* (lacking competency) match those predictions well. A perfectionist would certainly not expect to become a *hack* (a dull, unoriginal writer), and while he might have expected to become a *musician*, one of the choices in Blank (ii) would have to mean "non-musician" for this to work, as the two blanks are definitely opposites.

As for the answers that are offered for the second blank, *novel* (new) would've offered a decent contrast to *hack* in Blank (i), but the spin of that pair is the opposite of what the sentence calls for (the first blank should be something good and the second something bad). *Inane* (silly) might have worked with an appropriate option in the first blank (such as "genius"), but it doesn't work as a contrast to *virtuoso*.

14. (i) Credulity; (ii) beset: For the first blank, you are looking for something that is unhelpful to a person connected in some way to "liars and fabulists" (*fabulists* are just very creative liars), but there's not enough concrete proof to grab onto in this sentence to make a confident prediction for either blank. Look to the answer choices for help. In Blank (i), *ingenuity* (inventiveness or cleverness) is basically always an asset no matter the circumstances, and it has less connection to "liars and fabulists" than the other two options. *Credulity* (a willingness to believe people too easily) and *duplicity* (deceptiveness) are both relevant to "liars and fabulists" clue. *Credulity* wouldn't be an asset to someone surrounded by liars, because a credulous person would be easy to take advantage of. *Duplicity* wouldn't be an asset for someone on some kind of crusade against liars and fabulists, as a duplicitous person would look like a hypocrite in such circumstances. See which of these options is offered in Blank (ii).

Forsaken (abandoned) doesn't match either of these needed meanings, so it can be eliminated it. It also carries an unhelpful spin suggesting that it would be preferable to be around liars (because you're usually *forsaken* by something positive). *Brooked* (tolerated) also isn't a great match for the predictions or for the context. But *beset* (surrounded or threatened persistently by) does match the prediction for what the blank would contain if *credulity* were chosen for the first blank.

15. (i) raconteur; (ii) genial: The first blank describes how a person "was known to all her friends." The concrete description of her in the sentence indicates that she was "legendary for humorous stories" from a certain set of life experiences. So she must be known as a storyteller or a funny person. A *raconteur* is someone who tells amusing stories, but there's no clear reason why her humorous stories would lead to her being known as a *sage* (wise or learned person) or a *prevaricator* (someone who tells false stories).

In the last part of the sentence, the reversal marker "belied" indicates that "her private behavior" is actually at odds with her public reputation. Someone who tells amusing stories would plausibly be considered *genial* (friendly and cheerful), but not *belligerent* (hostile and aggressive) or *pedantic* (overly concerned with small details or rules).

16. (i) evinced; (ii) repartee: The first sentence tells you that an opinion has formed about a lady's "droll utterances." That's not much to go on yet. Luckily, the second sentence immediately calls back to "the common opinion" by talking about "this reputation," and from this sentence you can confirm what you might have already suspected: The opinion about her is clearly negative, given that it has "cost" her something. Given that, the opinion at court must hold that her behavior *is* "unbecoming of a lady," so look for a word that means displayed. *Evinced* (demonstrated) works. Her utterances don't *deride* (ridicule) these attitudes, though that's a theme trap, nor *elude* (avoid) them, an opposite trap.

The second blank refers to some characteristic of the lady that gentlemen fear "being bested by," and since the only thing you know about the lady's character is that she makes droll (amusing and wry) utterances, they must be afraid of her drollness. *Repartee* (clever, quick, and witty banter) is the best fit—watch out, gentlemen. *Doggerel* (a comic poem) might work, but compared to *repartee*, it requires more assumptions to fit. *Subtlety* doesn't reflect any proof in the sentence.

17. (i) mettlesome; (ii) penchant: The dashes indicate that the first blank comes in a part of the sentence that is meant as an addendum to the first part of the sentence. There, you're told only that courage is important ("anything but" is a reversal marker), and the "indeed" just before the blank indicates that this cartoon mouse's character agrees with this principle. Therefore, the mouse must be courageous. *Mettlesome* does mean "courageous," and its positive spin fits well with this part of the sentence—it's only after this blank that negativity creeps into the sentence. As such, *impetuous* (impulsive or rash), which could be seen as an offshoot of courage but has a lightly negative spin, can't work. *Heady* (intoxicating; exhilarating) doesn't come close.

The second blank describes the mouse's relationship with "excessive violence." Whatever this relationship is, it's not a good look for a children's charity mascot. So the mouse may have a liking (or, if you're feeling fancy, a proclivity) for excessive violence. *Penchant* (a strong liking) is a perfect fit. *Kinship* (blood relationship) doesn't work—even if you interpret it figuratively, the correct idiom would have been "kinship with," not "kinship for." *Largess* (generosity) isn't a good fit.

Unit Two: **Paragraphs and Passages**

18. (i) sleight of hand; (ii) ostensible: The ambassador is "double-dealing" (duplicitous) and "backpedaling" (retreating from a position), so a good fit in the first blank would be something like deceitfulness. *Sleight of hand* (skillful deception) works. There is no indication that the ambassador had political *plutocracy* (government by the wealthy) or political *bugaboo* (something causing fear).

The tricky ambassador's "Australian counterpart" is straightforward and is compared favorably to the ambassador himself. So while it may prove difficult to predict an exact answer for the second blank, expect a positive adjective that can describe "straightforwardness." *Occlusive* (tending to close off) would conflict with being straightforward, and *intransigent* (uncompromising, obstinate) has too negative a spin. Only *ostensible* (seemingly true, but not necessarily true) is neither too negative nor at odds with any proof in the sentence. *Ostensible* works in a sentence about how politicians "looked," not necessarily about how they really were.

19. (i) recalcitrant; (ii) degradation: The first blank describes a puzzle that sounds quite complicated—delivering an "antisense strand," to the right place at just the right moment. Only *recalcitrant* (stubborn) is appropriate to describe a complicated puzzle; *pedestrian* (commonplace, uninspired) conflicts with the proof, and *monolithic* (large and indivisible) is not indicated by any piece of evidence and is usually used to describe groups.

The second blank is something that the strand must be strong enough to resist so that it has "time to accomplish its task." The strand needs time to work, so it needs to resist something like destruction. *Desiccation* (drying out) would *probably* be bad for the strand, but there is no indication in the sentence that drying out would prevent the strand from working, and *compunction* (uneasiness due to guilt) doesn't apply to strands. However, *degradation* (deterioration, breakdown) is something the strand would have to resist in order to work on the virus.

20. (i) rankled; (ii) pernicious; (iii) latency: The third blank is probably the easiest to predict for in this question, as it's the sole blank in a long sentence offering a lot of concrete proof to go on. There, the blank denotes the state "Albanian nationalism" had been in before it came "surging out." The blank should be something like dormancy. *Latency* (a state of being unexpressed) works here as a good counterpoint for the subsequent surging. *Insularity* (isolation) and *lucidity* (clarity) don't offer the same kind of counterpoint, though *insularity* is a theme trap because it's often associated with nationalism.

Back to the first blank. The war would have had some sort of negative effect on Albanians, given the prospects laid out in the second part of the sentence, but it's hard to make a very specific prediction. Worse still, all three answers are negative words, so the nuance of the words will be important. *Enervate* (weaken) doesn't quite fit, as the rest of the story describes an Albania that if anything has seen its resolve for independence strengthened. And while some aspects of the war might have *debased* (degraded) them, the prospect of division of their lands didn't do this. However, the war might have left the Albanians *rankled* (angered or resentful), given the strength and duration of the subsequent nationalistic surge.

Finally, expect another negative word in the second blank—a good prediction might be to recycle rankling for now. *Pernicious* (greatly destructive, deadly, injurious, or harmful) is a bit more extreme than *rankling*, but *evanescent* (fleeting; tending to vanish like vapor) and *transient* (quickly coming into and passing out of existence; transitory) aren't negative enough, and both have short-term meanings that conflict with the long time frame indicated by the decades-long struggle referenced in the second sentence.

21. (i) efficient; (ii) progress; (iii) iniquitous: The fact that the second sentence starts out with "Perhaps more worrying" is an indication that whatever was expressed in the main body of the preceding sentence was already somewhat worrying, and whatever's to come in the second sentence is also worrying. Start with Blank (iii), as it's in a longer sentence with fewer blanks. There's something worrying about "treatment of farmers by" some kind of "social hierarchy." The hierarchy in question must not be great for farmers, so look to the options for something negative. *Halcyon* (calm, peaceful) is positive, so that can be eliminated. *Stratified* (divided into classes) describes literally any hierarchy, but its tone isn't inherently negative, even if "social stratification" is commonly referenced as a problem in the real world. *Iniquitous* (unjust) offers the best fit.

Return to the first sentence now. The first sentence must be describing a worrying situation. It's broken down into two contrasting parts by the reversal marker "though" at the beginning. The second part of the first sentence is the worrying part (because it come right before the second sentence), so the first part must contain a bit of good news. Go into Blank (i) looking for a positive word. *Expensive* and *polluting* are both negative, leaving *efficient* as the only possible option.

Now that you know modern farming is more *efficient*, it's time to tackle the worrying part of the sentence. The reversal marker "no" just before the second blank means that, for this part of the sentence to be worrying, the word in the blank has to be a good thing. Predict something like improvement and head to the answers. *Progress* isn't always the same as improvement, but it's close, so keep it around. *Disincentive* (deterrent) and *countermand* (an order that revokes a previous order) aren't particularly positive, so go with *progress*.

22. (i) derivation; (ii) notorious; (iii) provenance: The first sentence comes in two parts linked with the straight-ahead marker "as." The second part of it contains concrete proof about where the word *assassin* comes from, so the first part should be about the same thing. A good prediction for the first blank would be origin. *Introduction* seems somewhat close to this prediction, but the proof in the sentence doesn't tell you anything about how the word was introduced to people. *Derivation* comes closer, as it specifically reflects the idea of tracing the origins and development of something. *Circumlocution* (roundabout or evasive speech; use of more words than necessary) represents a theme trap.

The second sentence states that "the topic is equally attractive to historians," and because historians and philologists are both academics, this would seem to merit a prediction of attractive for the second blank. However, there's no match for this among the words. Switch to process of elimination. Since the derivation is known, it follows that it isn't *enigmatic* (mysterious) or *unheralded* (unannounced, unsung); while *notorious* can sometimes have a negative connotation, it at least carries the denotation of "well known."

With the phrase "The topic," the second sentence is calling back to the topic of the first sentence: the derivation of the word *assassin*. However, while the derivation of the word is known, something about the sect presents a mystery. Because the sentence also discusses how the sect "dates to before the First Crusade in the 11th century," you can expect a word that means something like origin once again. *Provenance* is a synonym for origin or derivation. The *legend* of the sect must not be much of a mystery, given that it is summarized in this sentence, and the sentence indicates nothing about any *bane* (curse, affliction) that the sect might have been subject to.

23. (i) plumbed; (ii) static; (iii) dearth: The third blank is likely the easiest to predict for, as there's a lot of concrete information around it. There, a mention of the "growing gap between rich and poor" prefaces the part with the blank. The wealthy were "eating more meat than ever," so the masses—the poor side of the gap—must have suffered from a lack of foodstuffs. A *dearth* is exactly that: a lack. *Glut* (excessive supply) is an opposite trap, and *deceleration* (slowing down) could happen to the production or harvest of foodstuffs, but not to foodstuffs themselves.

The second blank is a bit trickier. The reversal marker "while" draws a contrast between this part of the sentence and latter part where the rich are eating more meat and the poor are eating less. The statistics about meat consumption must be contradicting that reality, and since the second blank is immediately preceded by "remained," a good prediction would be the same. *Plastic* (artificial; changeable) has some definitions that are unrelated and others that are somewhat opposite to this prediction. *Demographic* (related to structure of a population) is a theme trap. But *static* fits.

Finally, now that you know that the statistics about population and meat consumption obscured the growing gap, it would make sense to say that statistics need to be examined closely. *Plumbed*, which among other things means "explored fully," works. *Calculated* doesn't go far enough (the sentence is saying you need to do more than just calculate), and *designed* goes a bit too far (the sentence doesn't say people should design or invent statistics, just that they should study statistics thoughtfully).

24. (i) clangor; (ii) subdued; (iii) an undulating: The two parts of the first sentence should contradict each other, owing to the complementary reversal markers "although" and "surprisingly." Since both blanks describe the sound of Cage's music, you could go straight to the answer choices right away and see if there are any decent opposite pairs. Unfortunately, there are two pairs of opposites: *murmur* (a soft sound) contrasts *strident* (loud and harsh), and *clangor* (loud noise) contrasts *subdued* (soft and restrained). Concrete proof in the second sentence, which in the absence of other markers should be presumed to discuss Cage's early music in more detail, describes music that "maintains its softness throughout." Therefore, the pair to choose for the first two blanks is *clangor* and *subdued*. *Timbre* (the unique quality of a given instrument) and *auspicious* (promising or propitious) aren't a good pair, though *timbre* is a theme trap.

The third blank describes the melody of Cage's "Music for Marcel Duchamp." This music "never rises above mezzo-piano" (meaning a moderately low volume), and the melody "maintains its softness throughout." A good prediction for the blank would be gentle. Among the answers, only *undulating* (rising or falling smoothly in pitch, volume, or cadence) works in the last blank, particularly in the *pitch* sense. *Noisome* (noxious, harmful, or dangerous) and *erstwhile* (former) are unrelated to the sentence. Don't be distracted by the superficial similarity between *noisome* and "noise."

25. (i) nugatory; (ii) mercurial: The "while" in front of the first blank suggests that the description of the tokens that will go in the blank will contradict the surrounding description of the tokens. That description points to the fact that the tokens serve as a reminder of the Crown's power, so the blank should emphasize that the tokens may have no *real* power. Look for a word like powerless. *Nugatory* means "of no value," a decent fit, especially given that *sumptuous* (very costly, luxurious, or lavish) implies real value and *sardonic* (scornfully or derisively mocking) is unrelated.

The second blank is preceded by the reversal marker "even," so look for the blank to contrast what comes before the "even." There, it's stated that "the power of the Crown continued to be held in esteem," so these must be either changing political times or anti-monarchist political times. *Mercurial* (highly changeable or frequently changing) fits the first prediction. *Jocund* (cheerful, merry) political times are not indicated by any proof. *Magisterial* (having great authority; dictatorial) is a theme trap, and as it implies a strong government, it doesn't reflect the reversal called for by "even."

26. (i) crescendo; (ii) despondent; (iii) haggard: Before it suddenly stopped, the shelling had built up to something like a peak. *Crescendo* (climax; loudest point) is the choice that works best. *Pique* (a passing feeling of irritation at a perceived slight) sounds the same as *peak* (making it a vocabulary trap) but is unrelated to shelling. *Euphony* (a pleasing sound) doesn't match "shelling."

The second blank describes the "drooping barrels of the artillery," and specifically their reaction to a "pathetic sight." Both of these bits of proof support a prediction like sad, Only *doleful* (mournful) fits; *sidereal* (relating to the stars or constellations) and *erroneous* (wrong) are unrelated.

The third blank describes the "targets," who are elsewhere described as a sight so pathetic it leaves even artillery depressed. Look for a word that reflects this, like pathetic itself. The targets aren't likely to be *ethereal* (light, airy; heavenly, celestial) or *affluent* (rich), as these are both positive words. Instead, the targets are most likely *haggard* (worn out).

27. (i) laxity; (ii) belied; (iii) eminence: The first blank has the most concrete truth around it: The predecessor had some quality that allowed "several stray dioceses" to break away. A prediction like negligence or incompetence wouldn't go amiss. *Laxity* (looseness; leniency) is the only choice that comes close; *diligence* (perseverance; attentiveness) is the opposite of what is needed, and *epaulet* (a shoulder ornament typically worn on military uniforms) has no relationship.

The third blank will contain some characteristic of the bishop's position, but the rest of the sentence doesn't give much to go on except "modest." However, without the sentence's verb, which will be the answer for Blank (ii), it's hard to know what the third blank's relationship to "modesty" is. It's worth examining the answer choices to see if any might work as a plausible descriptor. There is no indication of *tenuousness* (uncertainty); it offers neither a clear relationship with "modesty" nor a description of the bishop's position that lines up with the sentence (if his position were tenuous, he might be about to lose that position). *Audacity* (recklessness, daring) works as a counterpoint to "modesty," but again, "the *audacity* of his position" doesn't quite fit, as a bishop's position isn't generally audacious and there's no proof to suggest that this one would be. *Eminence* (high rank, station, or status), on the other hand, would generally apply to a leader's position, and it's also a good counterpoint to modesty.

You can now turn to the second blank. You don't expect someone in a position of *eminence* to be "modest," so his modesty seems to disguise or contradict that *eminence*. *Belied*, the perennial GRE favorite, means exactly that. *Construed* (deduced; explained) is an opposite trap, and *derided* (mocked, ridiculed) doesn't work.

28. (i) incongruity; (ii) proscribe: Interpreting this sentence correctly will require some guesswork if you're not comfortable with the phrase "irrational roots," because the first blank describes the relationship between these roots and the belief that everything can be expressed "through harmonious ratios of whole numbers." The contrast of "irrational" and "harmonious" may lead you to predict contrast or even incompatibility for the first blank. It's difficult to be completely sure if you aren't familiar with surds, but you know whatever the blank is must be describing the relationship between surds and something harmonious. Check the answer choices. *Absurdity* (ridiculousness) and *imperilment* (endangerment) don't capture any clear relationship, but *incongruity* (lack of agreement) does, and in a way that makes sense.

For the second blank, if surds have *incongruity* with a tenet of the Pythagoreans' faith, the cult would likely be hesitant to mention them; they'd at the very least discourage any mention of surds to those outside the cult. *Condone* (accept, allow) does the opposite of what you need, and in addition to not fitting with the prediction, *palliate* (alleviate, diminish) also doesn't fit the context (you can't "palliate any mention" of something). *Proscribing* (forbidding) is more extreme than the prediction, but of these answer choices, it fits the best.

Unit Two: **Paragraphs and Passages**

29. (i) cognoscenti; (ii) heteromorphic: The first blank will be a word describing people such as Koolhaas, who recognized and encouraged the development of Hadid's nascent talents. This serves as the concrete proof for the blank: The word should indicate an ability to spot talent and foster it. Something like experts or mentors might work. *Cognoscenti* (people well informed about a subject) matches the first prediction. *Fledglings* (young, immature, or inexperienced people) and *neophytes* (beginners) are opposite traps—they might have been appropriate to describe Hadid at this point in the story, but not Koolhaas.

The second blank describes Hadid's style, which is further described as influenced by "disparate styles." Look for a word like eclectic. *Fungible* (replaceable) doesn't work, and while *malleable* (easily changed) could work, it contradicts the assertion that her style had been "perfected," which implies that her style is no longer developing. *Heterogeneous* (diverse in character or composition) does a better job of reflecting that her perfected style was a reflection of disparate influences.

30. (i) sober; (ii) aspersions; (iii) condign: The first blank is alone in a sentence full of proof, so it's likely an easy place to start. Acknowledge the truth between the dashes—that Crowley founded a religion and its angels have style—and then reread the sentence without that part. Crowley is "given to wildly fantastic claims," and "despite" that, he has some kind of followers. The blank must contrast the fantastic claims in some way, so a good prediction might be sensible. *Sober* (serious and sensible) is a good fit. *Sordid* (morally degraded or contemptible) is a theme trap, meant to appeal through its connection to Crowley's alleged wickedness. However, it doesn't offer a good counterpoint to fantastic claims. *Skeptical* is an opposite trap—if anything you'd *expect* people to be skeptical of wildly fantastic claims.

In Blank (ii), something is being "cast on him by the popular press," and it's not looking good: Crowley is being called wicked. Look for a word like criticisms or attacks. The negative coverage might be causing Crowley some *disadvantages* down the road, but it wouldn't typically be described as "casting" them on him. *Gauntlets* (open challenges) goes too far, as there's no evidence of anyone challenging him. Luckily, *aspersions* (attacks on someone's reputation) doesn't require any extra story to work.

The third blank connects the allegation of wickedness to Crowley's "relative harmlessness." This juxtaposition makes the allegation seem disproportionately harsh, but this shouldn't be your prediction: The reversal marker "hardly" before the blank makes merited or fair a better fit. Neither *glib* (fluent to the point of insincerity) nor *peevish* (discontented; ill-tempered) fits, though *peevish* represents an opposite trap. *Condign* (deserved or appropriate) fits, especially as it's most often used to describe punishments and other negative repercussions.

31. (i) flagitious; (ii) antediluvian; (iii) allegories: The first sentence makes a comparison between the "Biblical portrayal" of a period in the past and the "Greek representation" of what must be the same time (otherwise there'd be no common ground on which to base a comparison). Since the first part of the comparison specifies the time period (the "times preceding the great deluge"), choose something for Blank (ii) that means before the flood or distant. *Antediluvian* satisfies both predictions: It literally means "before the flood" but is therefore also used as a synonym for "ancient." *Proximate* is an opposite trap, and while *obscure* (hard to discover) almost works, in that all moments in the past are obscured by the veils of time, it's not as close to the concrete proof in the sentence as *antediluvian*.

The first blank is the other missing piece in the comparison between the two times: It contains the Biblical characterization of these times, which "stands in stark contrast" to the Greek representation of these times as a "Golden Age." The blank should be diametrically opposed to "Golden Age," so look for the word to be bad. Starkly bad. *Dubious* (warranting uncertainty or doubt) and *rustic* (rural; lacking refinement) don't match specific proof and aren't anywhere near as negative as *flagitious* (marked by vice).

For the third blank, look to the surrounding text for clues. The word should be something that contrasts "faithful attempts at reconstruction" but still expresses "cultural fears and hopes." It could be something like fictions, but it's probably best to just consider the answers. *Allegories* are fictional accounts with a moral or political meaning, and given the comparison between *flagitious* times and Golden Ages earlier in the problem, this is the best fit. *Equivocations* would make sense if we knew that the stories were intended to deceive or mislead, but it's hard to know their true intent, making this a story trap. There's no reason to believe these weren't good-faith attempts at expressing some cultural truth, even if allegorically. *Platitudes* (dull, trite statements or remarks) similarly introduces a connotation of banality not indicated by the text.

32. (i) most important cause; (ii) didactic: Start with the second blank in this case. It's a description of "pamphlets," which are otherwise noted in the sentence as offering prescriptions and advice. A good prediction would be advisory. *Maleficent* (malicious; intending or producing evil) is way off unless you make a lot of assumptions, and *tenable* (able to be held, maintained, or justified) doesn't quite work as a description of a pamphlet, though it might have worked for some of the advice contained within. *Didactic* (intended to instruct) works best.

The first blank contains phrases, but it's still worth trying to make a prediction before engaging with the answers. The blank is connecting "digestive irregularity" to "preventable illness." Whatever this connection is, it prompted medieval physicians to focus heavily on "prophylactic dietary regimens." It's reasonable to infer that these were meant to avert digestive problems, which in turn suggests that the physicians saw the prevention of those digestive problems as very important. That would make sense if digestive irregularity were a cause of preventable illness. *Most significant cause* is a good match. *Only panacea* (cure-all or remedy) doesn't work; Maimonides and the other physicians might have wanted a panacea for preventable illness, but they wouldn't say that digestive irregularity *was* the panacea. *Sine qua non* (an absolutely essential component) also doesn't quite fit, as its positive spin makes digestive irregularity seem like a desirable thing.

33. (i) georgic; (ii) penury; (iii) sartorial: The first blank describes Francis' attire, which Francis doesn't believe will impress the well dressed executive *despite* her "fondness for rural life." The best prediction would be rural. *Rustic* means exactly that, and has the added benefit of meaning "simply made," a good contrast to the sharpness of the executive's apparel. *Natty*, meaning "sharp and stylish," is an opposite trap. *Exclusive* would give his attire a unique and unobtainable air, which, while possibly true of his attire, isn't justified by the proof and is usually used in a positive sense.

Following the concrete truth forward, his discomfort with his *rustic* garb led Francis to some "costly new wardrobe acquisitions." It sounds like Francis spent a lot of money on clothes and in so doing "reduced himself to" something. The phrase negative spin of "reduced himself" and the concrete proof that he spent money support a prediction of poverty. *Penury* (destitution) is a more extreme synonym. *Malaise* (vague, general sense of unease or mental discomfort) and *lethargy* (state of sluggishness, inactivity, laziness, or indifference) are near-synonyms of each other, and neither follows from the proof "costly" as well as *penury* does.

The plot thickens in the second sentence. The suave executive was concealing her own "financial ruin" with some kind of "showboating." What kind of showboating makes sense? All you know about the executive is that she's suave, sharply dressed, and financially devastated. Given that showboating is usually done to flaunt something that others will find impressive and "suave showboating" seems like a mismatch, stylistic showboating makes the most sense. *Bombastic* (pompous; pretentious) and *runic* (mysterious or arcane) don't match this prediction and have no clear support from any of the proof in the sentence. *Bombastic* showboating makes sense in general, but there is more direct proof for the correct answer *sartorial* (relating to clothes or style), since she is known to be "sharply dressed."

34. (i) A malingerer; (ii) credulous; (iii) sagacity: The word in the first blank should be identified with unreliability, but all three options for Blank (i) are words for people who are unreliable in some way. Look to see which of the words identifies a kind of unreliability that has more proof in the sentence. To be *an embezzler*, Garth would need to steal money entrusted to him by his employer, and no proof suggests that he does. Indeed, there's no evidence that Garth has stolen anything, ruling out *a pilferer* as well. *A malingerer* (someone who fakes illness to elude duty or obligation) fits with Garth's "frequent absences" and his hypochondriac employer's seemingly positive reaction.

The second blank is a word that, alongside "hypochondriac," describes Garth's employer. The only other thing we know is that the employer seems inclined to believe Garth's ill-disguised lies. So the word should either be something akin to hypochondriac or gullible. The boss could maybe be *casuistic* (practicing clever but unsound reasoning) or *imposing* (grand and impressive in appearance), but *credulous* (prone to easily believing things) is the best fit for the proof and matches the second prediction.

The last blank is a word similar to "foresight," and only *sagacity* fits. *Insipidity* (boringness, dullness) and *temerity* (excessive confidence, audacity) both usually have negative connotation, and would require extra story elements to work.

35. (i) lionized; (ii) incorrigible; (iii) rarely discussed: The concrete proof in this sentence indicates that the leader had "considerable moral shortcomings" that are seen as "peccadilloes" (minor transgressions) if they're mentioned at all. Blank (iii) contains a phrase that should make sense as a lead-in to "if mentioned at all." A good prediction would be not usually mentioned. *Rarely discussed* is a good match. *Mere relics* is a theme trap with "history" but is incorrect, as *relics* are the parts of history that survive until latter days, whereas mentions of the leader's shortcomings seem to be increasingly uncommon. *Widely praised* offers superficial agreement with the correct answer for Blank (i) but doesn't agree with "if mentioned at all."

With Blank (iii) filled in, Blank (i) is easier to manage. It's a word that identifies history's treatment of this leader, and the concrete proof is that the leader's negative qualities are *rarely discussed* and excused when they are discussed. It seems history has been kind to this leader—too kind. A word like whitewashed would fit the proof well. *Lionized* (popularly approved or lauded) takes this idea and runs with it, whereas *extirpated* (removed completely) and *impugned* (called into question) contradict the proof in the sentence.

The second blank describes the leader's "misogyny," an example of one of his "considerable moral shortcomings." There's no other description of his misogyny in the sentence, rendering prediction difficult, though there's a chance that the word in the blank should have some overlap with considerable. There's no proof suggesting that his misogyny would be *diffident* (shy or timid) or *reformed* (corrected). *Incorrigible* (inveterate; irredeemable) requires less assumption than the other choices in that it suggests only that the misogyny likely went on for the duration of the leader's time in prominence. This corroborates the proposition that his moral shortcomings were "considerable."

36. (i) fairness; (ii) catharsis; (iii) denouement: The first blank identifies the "overarching theme" of the new film. Since this theme's "dark side" is "exploitation and iniquity," the theme itself may be a more positive version of these two ideas. Look for something like fairness or good treatment. The former is there, and as exploitation and iniquity are both by definition unfair, this must be the right answer. *Slavery* and *injustice* are both theme and opposite traps in that they agree with "exploitation and iniquity" rather than follow the content reversal marker "dark side."

The film showcases the elimination of all the sympathetic protagonist's abusers, a move that garners the approval of the sentence's narrator and grants the audience something they've awaited the entire time, in a "satisfying upheaval." Look for a word that means something like good ending or satisfaction—something positive. The audience hasn't been waiting for *inconclusiveness*, which contradicts the proof and is vaguely negative. Maybe it has been waiting for a *revelation*, but this adds to the story of the sentence rather than reflects it, as there's no indication of anything unknown or discovered. *Catharsis* (release from built-up emotions) is a good fit.

The final blank is preceded by "this," a pronoun calling back to something recently mentioned. This something is what the "ponderous plot" was leading up to, and as the previous sentence discussed the cathartic ending of the film, the blank should be something like conclusion. *Denouement*, the part of a narrative in which the plot resolves, is a perfect match for the context. A *platitude* (trite saying) wouldn't provide a "satisfying upheaval," and there is no indication that the conclusion of the film was an *embellishment* (an often untrue detail added to a story to make it more interesting).

37. (i) eclecticism; (ii) a veneer: The concrete truth in the sentence is after the comma, and it would benefit from some rephrasing: Wallgot makes such wide-ranging references that even his biggest fans think it's ridiculous. The first part of the sentence, which starts with the reversal marker "although," must contrast this concrete truth in some way, saying something like "Although making wide-ranging references can be a good thing. . ." So the first blank should be something like making wide-ranging references. *Stringency* (strictness) and *insularity* (the narrow point of view resulting from life in a closed off community) imply the opposite of wide-ranging, but *eclecticism* (drawing on a wide variety of sources) fits well.

With *eclecticism* in the first blank, there's more concrete truth for the second. This part of the sentence must be expressing something beneficial about eclecticism. Perhaps it gives insubstantial work an illusion of profundity. *An iota* (a minimal amount) could be tempting as it allows the eclecticism to "give" something to the work. But if even Wallgot's fans "sneered" at its references, it may be safer to assume that in truth the work still had no profundity at all. Keep it for the moment. *A medley* (a mixture), which represents a theme trap with *eclecticism*, has no support in the sentence. *A veneer* is a surface covering designed to make low-quality underlying materials appear more attractive that they actually are, which is to say *a veneer* is perfect for this sentence: Eclectic references won't give the book *actual* profundity, but they might seem substantial enough to disguise a lack of profundity.

38. (i) emend; (ii) preemptive: For the first blank, you are looking for something the writer *could* do to "her lengthy tomes" that would appease editors if she did it. Shorten seems like a reasonable prediction, as all you really know about the book is that it's long. However, none of the options for Blank (i) mean "shorten." Look for the answer that has the best connection to other proof in the sentence. Though it doesn't mean shorten, *emend* (make corrections to) is something that can be done to a text, and it would also help "avoid editorial complaints," giving it a connection to the proof in the sentence. *Allay* (alleviate; put to rest) is not something that can be done to a tome, and while many tomes may *edify* (instruct, especially morally) their readers, a tome can't *be* edified.

She may not be a fan of edits, but the author is popular with the public. This popularity gives her a certain amount of leverage with her editors, in that she can threaten to sign with another publisher whenever she wants to avoid their complaints. The second blank is a word describing these threats, but the sentence doesn't offer much characterization of the threats. See if one of the answers has a connection to

Unit Two: Paragraphs and Passages

the proof. *Impuissant* (powerless) clashes with the proof, as the ability to make these threats is one of the ways that the author has been "empowered" by her popularity. There's no proof for or against *toothsome* (tasty). On the other hand, *preemptive* (intended to prevent or forestall) is a great fit, as the threats are said help the author to "avoid editorial complaints."

39. (i) proximate; (ii) protract; (iii) proliferation: The first blank asks for a contrast with "distant future," so look for a word meaning not distant. *Proximate* means exactly that. *Atavistic* (manifesting or reverting to ancestral characteristics) seems to call more directly to the past; this seems like it could actually work as a counterpoint to "the distant future," but it adds a very particular spin (reversion or regression) that's not justified by the context.

The second blank is connected to "present pleasures," a callback to the *proximate* times that subjects are said to place a higher value on. This preference for present times means the second blank should be a word that's positive, like enjoy or appreciate. None of the words mean exactly that, but *avert* (avoid by turning away) and *rescind* (revoke) are both too negative to fit with the higher value the subjects place on present times. *Protract* (prolong) reflects the subjects' predilection for the present better.

The third blank is some kind of "expense" and is connected to "future detriments." The subjects place a low value on things in the distant future, so it's fair to infer they would *protract* present pleasures even if it meant incurring or accumulating future expenses. *Proliferation* (a rapid increase; a large number) fits the second prediction well. *Malady* (illness) makes no sense here, and while *buttressing* (reinforcing) has a tempting positive spin, it doesn't fit the context (*buttressing* is typically used for things you want to protect or fortify).

40. (i) warrant; (ii) undergird: It is clear from "facile claim" (superficial, lacking complexity) and the generally derisive tone of the sentence that the author does not think the "she" in question has argued her point well enough. That informs the first blank, which will be something that her argument has "little" of. A good prediction would be nuance or justification. *Warrant* fits the latter prediction. *Syllogism* (a common form of logical reasoning) is a theme trap, and *fallacy* (logical flaw) is both a theme trap and an opposite trap—if anything, the author of this sentence *does* think an error has been made.

The second sentence also equates two things: how the "laws of logic" affected her dubious proclamation and how the "law of thermodynamics" led to a dubious discovery. Given the parallel between these two parts of the sentence as well as evidence from the first sentence, the word in the blank should be something like led to. *Undergird* (provide the basis for) is a good match. *Occlude* (close, cover, or obstruct) doesn't fit at all. *Galvanize* (spur to action) might initially seem like a good fit, but it's not as good a match for "gave rise to" as *undergird*. *Galvanize* often implies a subtext of excitement or intrigue that isn't present in the passage.

CHAPTER 8

Reading Comprehension Problem Set

In This Chapter...

- Problem Set
- Answers and Explanations

Chapter 8 Reading Comprehension Problem Set

In this chapter, you will practice all the techniques you have learned for content-based reading comprehension.

Chapter 8: **Reading Comprehension Problem Set**

Problem Set

> The following problem set consists of passages accompanied by a series of questions for that passage. Just as on the real test, scan the questions before reading the passage.
>
> On the GRE, you will typically see one to four questions associated with each passage. However, in this problem set, each passage has additional questions so that you can gain more practice answering a variety of problem types. As such, use the following modified timing guidelines:
>
> - **When reading passages**, spend approximately 1.5 minutes for medium-length passages. If a topic is more detailed or complex, spend less time on the details; focus on the main ideas and major twists.
>
> - **When answering questions**, spend approximately 30 to 45 seconds on general questions and approximately 45 to 60 seconds on specific questions. Expect to spend the full time on Select-One-or-More and EXCEPT questions; these will almost always take longer.
>
> Finally, if you'd like, answer only three or four of the questions the first time you do a passage. You can then save the passage for a second pass (with the remaining three or four questions) later on in your studies.

Unit Two: **Paragraphs and Passages**

Passage F: Television's Inventor

In the early years of television, Vladimir Zworykin was considered the device's inventor, at least publicly. His loudest champion was his boss David Sarnoff, the president of RCA and the "father of television," as he was, and is, widely regarded. Modern historians agree that Philo Farnsworth, a self-educated prodigy who was the first to transmit live images, was television's technical inventor. But Farnsworth's contributions have gone relatively unnoticed, since it was Sarnoff, not Farnsworth, who put televisions into living rooms. More importantly, it was Sarnoff who successfully borrowed from the radio industry the paradigm of advertiser-funded programming, a paradigm still dominant today. In contrast, Farnsworth lacked business savvy and was unable to realize his dream of television as an educational tool.

Perhaps Sarnoff simply adapted his business ideas from other industries, such as newspapers, replacing the revenue from subscriptions and newsstand purchases with that of television set sales, but Sarnoff promoted himself as a visionary. Some critics argue that Sarnoff's construct has damaged programming content. Others contend that it merely created a democratic platform allowing audiences to choose the programming they desire.

1. The primary purpose of the passage is to

    (A) correct public misconceptions about Farnsworth's role in developing early television programs
    (B) debate the influence of television on popular culture
    (C) challenge the current public perception of Vladimir Zworykin
    (D) chronicle the events that led from the development of radio to the invention of the television
    (E) describe both Sarnoff's influence on the public perception of television's inception and the debate around the impact of Sarnoff's paradigm

2. It can be inferred from the second paragraph of the passage that

    (A) television shows produced by David Sarnoff and Vladimir Zworykin tended to earn negative reviews
    (B) educational programs cannot draw as large an audience as sports programs
    (C) a number of critics feel that Sarnoff's initial decision to earn television revenue through advertising has had a positive or neutral impact on content
    (D) educational programs that are aired in prime time, the hours during which the greatest number of viewers are watching television, are less likely to earn a profit than those that are aired during the daytime hours
    (E) in matters of programming, the audience's preferences should be more influential than those of the advertisers

3. According to the passage, the television industry, at its inception, earned revenue from

    (A) advertising only
    (B) advertising and the sale of television sets
    (C) advertising and subscriptions
    (D) subscriptions and the sale of television sets
    (E) advertising, subscriptions, and the sale of television sets

4. Select the sentence that provides factual evidence that Sarnoff's talents were more imitative than innovative.

5. Which of the following statements is supported by the passage?
   Select all that apply.

   | A | The advertising-funded model of television has damaged programming content.
   | B | The contributions of television's technical inventor were overshadowed by the actions of those who popularized the medium.
   | C | There is no way to definitively prove who invented the first television.

Unit Two: **Paragraphs and Passages**

Passage G: Life on Mars

    Because of the proximity and likeness of Mars to Earth, scientists have long speculated about the possibility of life on Mars. Roughly three centuries ago, astronomers observed Martian polar ice caps, and later scientists discovered other similarities to Earth, including length of day and axial tilt. But in 1965, photos taken by the *Mariner 4* probe revealed a Mars without rivers, oceans, or signs of life. Moreover, in the 1990s, it was discovered that unlike Earth, Mars no longer possessed a substantial global magnetic field, allowing celestial radiation to reach the planet's surface and solar wind to eliminate much of Mars's atmosphere over the course of several billion years.

    More recent probes have investigated whether there was once liquid water on Mars. Some scientists believe that the presence of certain geological landforms definitively resolves this question. Others posit that wind erosion or carbon dioxide oceans may be responsible for these formations. Mars rovers *Opportunity* and *Spirit*, which landed on Mars in 2004, have both discovered geological evidence of past water activity. These findings substantially bolster claims that there was once life on Mars.

6. The author's stance on the possibility of life on Mars can best be described as

    (A) optimistic
    (B) open-minded
    (C) skeptical
    (D) simplistic
    (E) cynical

7. The passage is primarily concerned with which of the following?

    (A) Disproving a widely accepted theory
    (B) Initiating a debate about the possibility of life on Mars
    (C) Presenting evidence in support of a controversial claim
    (D) Describing the various discoveries made concerning the possibility of life on Mars
    (E) Detailing the findings of the Mars rovers *Opportunity* and *Spirit*

8. Each of the following is a discovery mentioned in the passage EXCEPT

    (A) Wind erosion and carbon dioxide oceans are responsible for certain geological landforms on Mars.
    (B) Mars does not have a substantial global magnetic field.
    (C) Mars had water activity at some point in the past.
    (D) The length of day on Mars is similar to that on Earth.
    (E) The axial tilt of Mars is similar to that of Earth.

9. In the first paragraph, the author most likely mentions the discovery of polar ice caps to suggest that

    (A) until recently Mars's polar ice caps were thought to consist largely of carbon dioxide
    (B) Martian polar ice caps are made almost entirely of water ice
    (C) Mars has multiple similarities to Earth, including the existence of polar ice caps
    (D) Mars has only a small fraction of the carbon dioxide found on Earth and Venus
    (E) conditions on the planet Mars were once very different than they are at present

10. Each of the following can be inferred from the passage EXCEPT

    (A) the presence of certain geological landforms is not definitive proof that there was once life on Mars
    (B) similarities to Earth bolster the idea that a planet might be or have been capable of supporting life
    (C) the absence of a substantial global magnetic field on Mars suggests that it would be difficult to sustain life on Mars
    (D) the presence of water activity on Mars is related to the possibility of life on Mars
    (E) the claim that there was once water on Mars has only marginal support from recent discoveries

11. It can be inferred from the passage that which of the following characteristics of a planet would imply that it might support life?
    Select all that apply.

    [A] A significant global magnetic field
    [B] Evidence of liquid carbon dioxide on the planet's surface
    [C] The average daily level of sunlight reaching the planet's surface

12. Select the sentence in the passage that provides the best evidence that, at the given time, life did not exist on Mars.

Unit Two: Paragraphs and Passages

Passage H: Fossils

Archaeological discoveries frequently undermine accepted ideas, giving rise to new theories. Recently, a set of 3.3-million-year-old fossils, the remains of the earliest well-preserved child ever found, were discovered in Ethiopia. Estimated to be 3 years old at death, the female child was of the *Australopithecus afarensis* species, a human ancestor that lived in Africa over 3 million years ago. "Her completeness, antiquity, and age at death make this find of unprecedented importance in the history of paleo-anthropology," said Zeresenay Alemseged, a noted paleo-anthropologist, opining that the discovery could reconfigure conceptions about early humans' capacities.

Previously, *afarensis* was believed to have abandoned arboreal habitats. However, while the new fossil's lower limbs support the view of an upright stance, its gorilla-like arms suggest that *afarensis* was still able to swing through trees, initiating a reexamination of long-held theories of early human development. Also, the presence of a hyoid bone, a rarely preserved larynx bone that supports throat muscles, has dramatically affected concepts of the origin of speech. Although primitive and more ape-like than human-like, this fossil hyoid is the first found in such an early human-related species.

13. The organization of the passage could best be described as

    (A) discussing a controversial scientific discovery
    (B) contrasting previous theories of development with current theories
    (C) illustrating a general contention with a specific example
    (D) arguing for the importance of a particular field of study
    (E) refuting a popular misconception

14. The passage quotes Zeresenay Alemseged in order to

    (A) provide evidence to qualify the main idea of the first paragraph
    (B) question the claims of other scientists
    (C) provide evidence to support the linguistic abilities of the *afarensis* species
    (D) provide corroboration for the significance of the find
    (E) provide a subjective opinion that is refuted in the second paragraph

15. Each of the following is cited as a factor in the importance of the discovery of the fossils EXCEPT

    (A) the fact that the remains were those of a child
    (B) the age of the fossils
    (C) the location of the discovery
    (D) the species of the fossils
    (E) the intact nature of the fossils

16. It can be inferred from the passage's description of the discovered fossil hyoid bone that

    (A) *Australopithecus afarensis* was capable of speech
    (B) the discovered hyoid bone is less primitive than the hyoid bone of apes
    (C) the hyoid bone is necessary for speech
    (D) the discovery of the hyoid bone necessitated the reexamination of prior theories
    (E) the hyoid bone was the most important fossil found at the site

17. The impact of the discovery of the hyoid bone in the field of archaeology could be best compared to which one of the following examples in another field?

   (A) The discovery and analysis of cosmic rays lend support to a widely accepted theory of the origin of the universe.

   (B) The original manuscript of a deceased nineteenth-century author confirms ideas of the development of an important work of literature.

   (C) The continued prosperity of a state-run economy stirs debate in the discipline of macroeconomics.

   (D) Newly revealed journal entries by a prominent Civil War–era politician lead to a questioning of certain accepted historical interpretations about the conflict.

   (E) Research into the mapping of the human genome gives rise to nascent applications of individually tailored medicines.

18. Select the sentence that most distinctly undermines an accepted paleo-anthropological theory.

Unit Two: **Paragraphs and Passages**

Passage I: Chaos Theory

Around 1960, mathematician Edward Lorenz found unexpected behavior in apparently simple equations representing atmospheric air flows. Whenever he reran his model with the same inputs, different outputs resulted—although the model lacked any random elements. Lorenz realized that tiny rounding errors in his analog computer mushroomed over time, leading to erratic results. His findings marked a seminal moment in the development of chaos theory, which, despite its name, has little to do with randomness.

To understand how unpredictability can arise from deterministic equations, which do not involve chance outcomes, consider the non-chaotic system of two poppy seeds placed in a round bowl. As the seeds roll to the bowl's center, a position known as a point attractor, the distance between the seeds shrinks. If, instead, the bowl is flipped over, two seeds placed on top will roll away from each other. Such a system, while still not technically chaotic, enlarges initial differences in position.

Chaotic systems, such as a machine mixing bread dough, are characterized by both attraction and repulsion. As the dough is stretched, folded, and pressed back together, any poppy seeds sprinkled in are intermixed seemingly at random. But this randomness is illusory. In fact, the poppy seeds are captured by "strange attractors," staggeringly complex pathways whose tangles appear accidental but are in fact determined by the system's fundamental equations.

During the dough-kneading process, two poppy seeds positioned next to each other eventually go their separate ways. Any early divergence or measurement error is repeatedly amplified by the mixing until the position of any seed becomes effectively unpredictable. It is this "sensitive dependence on initial conditions" and not true randomness that generates unpredictability in chaotic systems, of which one example may be the Earth's weather. According to the popular interpretation of the "Butterfly Effect," a butterfly flapping its wings causes hurricanes. A better understanding is that the butterfly causes uncertainty about the precise state of the air. This microscopic uncertainty grows until it encompasses even hurricanes. Few meteorologists believe that we will ever be able to predict rain or shine for a particular day years in the future.

19. The main purpose of this passage is to

    (A) explore a common misconception about a type of complex physical system
    (B) trace the historical development of a scientific theory
    (C) distinguish a mathematical pattern from its opposite
    (D) describe the spread of a technical model from one field of study to others
    (E) contrast possible causes of weather phenomena

20. In the example discussed in the passage, what is true about poppy seeds in bread dough once the dough has been thoroughly mixed?

    (A) They have been individually stretched and folded over.
    (B) They are scattered in random clumps throughout the dough.
    (C) They are accidentally caught in tangled objects called "strange attractors."
    (D) They are bound to regularly dispersed patterns of point attractors.
    (E) They are in positions dictated by the underlying equations that govern the mixing process.

Chapter 8: **Reading Comprehension Problem Set**

21. According to the passage, the rounding errors in Lorenz's model

    (A) indicated that the model was programmed in a fundamentally faulty way
    (B) were deliberately included to represent tiny fluctuations in atmospheric air currents
    (C) were imperceptibly small at first, but tended to grow
    (D) were at least partially expected, given the complexity of the actual atmosphere
    (E) shrank to insignificant levels during each trial of the model

22. The passage mentions each of the following as an example or potential example of a chaotic or non-chaotic system EXCEPT

    (A) a dough-mixing machine
    (B) atmospheric weather patterns
    (C) poppy seeds placed on top of an upside-down bowl
    (D) poppy seeds placed in a right-side-up bowl
    (E) fluctuating butterfly flight patterns

23. It can be inferred from the passage that which of the following pairs of items would most likely follow typical pathways within a chaotic system?

    (A) Two particles ejected in random directions from the same decaying atomic nucleus
    (B) Two stickers affixed to a balloon that expands and contracts over and over again
    (C) Two avalanches sliding down opposite sides of the same mountain
    (D) Two baseballs placed into a device designed to mix paint
    (E) Two coins flipped into a large bowl

24. The author implies which of the following about weather systems?
    Select all that apply.

    [A] They illustrate the same fundamental phenomenon as Lorenz's rounding errors.
    [B] Experts agree unanimously that weather will never be predictable years in advance.
    [C] They are governed mostly by seemingly trivial events, such as the flapping of a butterfly's wings.

25. Select the sentence in the second or third paragraph that illustrates why "chaos theory" might be called a misnomer.

Unit Two: **Paragraphs and Passages**

Answers and Explanations

Answers to Passage F: Television's Inventor

    In the early years of television, Vladimir Zworykin was considered the device's inventor, at least publicly. His loudest champion was his boss David Sarnoff, the president of RCA and the "father of television," as he was, and is, widely regarded. Modern historians agree that Philo Farnsworth, a self-educated prodigy who was the first to transmit live images, was television's technical inventor. But Farnsworth's contributions have gone relatively unnoticed, since it was Sarnoff, not Farnsworth, who put televisions into living rooms. More importantly, it was Sarnoff who successfully borrowed from the radio industry the paradigm of advertiser-funded programming, a paradigm still dominant today. In contrast, Farnsworth lacked business savvy and was unable to realize his dream of television as an educational tool.

    Perhaps Sarnoff simply adapted his business ideas from other industries, such as newspapers, replacing the revenue from subscriptions and newsstand purchases with that of television set sales, but Sarnoff promoted himself as a visionary. Some critics argue that Sarnoff's construct has damaged programming content. Others contend that it merely created a democratic platform allowing audiences to choose the programming they desire.

Upon previewing the questions, here is an example of what you might jot down:

1. Main Idea

2. Infer from P2

3. How TV get rev?

4. Select: talent = imitative

5. Infer

The first question will come from your initial read. As you read, try to see how paragraph two fits into the context of the passage, and note when you see the discussion of revenue from TV or talent that is imitative. The fifth question will require using the answer choices before finding proof.

Here is one example of a possible set of notes for this passage:

1. Early TV, Z seen as invntr

    —Champ by Sarn (father of TV)

    BUT now hist agree: F = TRUE invntr

    —S: launched: advrs pay

    —F: not biz savvy, wanted TV = educ

2. S: visionary or adopter?

    + or – effect?

Simple Story: Farnsworth really invented TV, but he didn't know how to turn it into a business. Sarnoff used the radio model to make television big business. People have differing feelings about his role.

Chapter 8: **Reading Comprehension Problem Set**

1. **The primary purpose of the passage is to**

    (A) correct public misconception about Farnsworth's role in developing early television programs

    (B) debate the influence of television on popular culture

    (C) challenge the current public perception of Vladimir Zworykin

    (D) chronicle the events that led from the development of radio to the invention of the television

    (E) describe both Sarnoff's influence on the public perception of television's inception and the debate around the impact of Sarnoff's paradigm

The main idea is that even though Sarnoff did not invent the television, he was responsible for introducing television to the public and establishing a dominant paradigm. This is foreshadowed when Sarnoff is called "the father of television."

   (A) Farnsworth's influence on the development of the television itself is only mentioned in the first paragraph; Farnsworth's role in developing programs is never mentioned.

   (B) The impact of television is not discussed until the second paragraph. Although this paragraph debates whether or not Sarnoff's influence was a positive one, it does not address the influence of television on popular culture.

   (C) Vladimir Zworykin is only mentioned briefly in the first paragraph, so he is not the primary subject of the passage. Furthermore, even though the passage mentions the initial public perception, it says nothing about the current public perception of Zworykin.

   (D) The passage discusses events that occurred after the invention; there is no mention of the events that led up to the invention of the television.

   (E) **CORRECT.** The passage does describe how Sarnoff made television popular; some critics think that his role was positive while others think that it was negative. Notice that this is the only answer choice that mentions Sarnoff. He is featured prominently in every paragraph, so any answer choice representing the point of the passage should not mention other people while ignoring him.

2. **It can be inferred from the second paragraph of the passage that**

    (A) television shows produced by David Sarnoff and Vladimir Zworykin tended to earn negative reviews

    (B) educational programs cannot draw as large an audience as sports programs

    (C) a number of critics feel that Sarnoff's initial decision to earn television revenue through advertising has had a positive or neutral impact on content

    (D) educational programs that are aired in prime time, the hours during which the greatest number of viewers are watching television, are less likely to earn a profit than those that are aired during the daytime hours

    (E) in matters of programming, the audience's preferences should be more influential than those of the advertisers

Unit Two: **Paragraphs and Passages**

The second paragraph states that some critics viewed Sarnoff's approach negatively and others thought his approach embodied a democratic concept. The correct inference must follow from at least one of those statements.

- (A) There is no information about the television programs Sarnoff and Zworykin produced; in fact, you have not been told that they produced television shows. The paragraph is about the advertising revenue construct Sarnoff implemented, not about the television shows he produced.
- (B) It is implied that ratings for educational programs are, in general, not strong, but that does not mean that any one particular educational program cannot have higher ratings than one particular sports program. Beware of answer choices that contain absolutes such as *cannot*.
- (C) **CORRECT.** The passage states that "[o]thers contend that it created a democratic platform." This sentence, following immediately after the negative implications of "[s]ome critics argue . . ." states that there are mixed feelings among critics. Some view Sarnoff's decision as negative, but others view it as at least neutral, if not positive.
- (D) The passage does not differentiate programming based on what time television shows air, nor does it mention profitability.
- (E) The word "should" implies a moral judgment, and the answer is therefore out of the scope of the passage. The second paragraph does not indicate a belief as to who should influence programming choices.

3. **According to the passage, the television industry, at its inception, earned revenue from**

    - (A) advertising only
    - (B) advertising and the sale of television sets
    - (C) advertising and subscriptions
    - (D) subscriptions and the sale of television sets
    - (E) advertising, subscriptions, and the sale of television sets

In an attempt to trick you on a specific detail question such as this, the GRE will offer incomplete answers that incorporate language from throughout the passage but do not directly bear on the question at hand. Two sections in the passage discuss ways in which the television industry brought in revenue. The first paragraph mentions "advertiser-funded programming." The second paragraph states that Sarnoff borrowed from other business models by "replacing the revenue from subscriptions and newsstand purchases with that of television set sales."

- (A) This answer choice, with the word "only," would deny the revenue from television set sales.
- (B) **CORRECT.** Advertising and the sale of television sets are the two ways mentioned through which the industry could generate revenue.
- (C) Subscriptions are mentioned as a method for newspapers to earn revenue; the last paragraph states that television replaced this revenue with that earned by selling the sets themselves.
- (D) This choice does not mention advertising revenue; moreover, it incorrectly mentions subscription revenue.
- (E) This answer choice incorrectly mentions subscription revenue.

Chapter 8: Reading Comprehension Problem Set

4. **Select the sentence that provides factual evidence that Sarnoff's talents were more imitative than innovative.**

This question relates to Sarnoff's legacy as an imitator versus his legacy as an innovator. There are two plausible candidates. First, the second-to-last sentence of the first paragraph says that Sarnoff "successfully borrowed from the radio industry the paradigm of advertiser-funded programming." This sentence states a fact indicating that Sarnoff took a business model from another medium, which would be imitative rather than innovative.

The second possible answer is the first sentence of the second paragraph, which says, "Perhaps Sarnoff simply adapted his business ideas from other industries such as newspapers." However, the use of the word *perhaps* means that this is an idea of the author's, rather than a statement of fact. For this reason, this cannot be the answer.

The correct answer is the second-to-last sentence of the first paragraph: "More importantly, it was Sarnoff who successfully borrowed from the radio industry the paradigm of advertiser-funded programming, a paradigm still dominant today."

5. **Which of the following statements is supported by the passage? Select all that apply.**

   - [A] The advertising-funded model of television has damaged programming content.
   - [B] The contributions of television's technical inventor were overshadowed by the actions of those who popularized the medium.
   - [C] There is no way to definitively prove who invented the first television.

Expect to need extra time on Select One or More inference questions. This one, annoyingly, does not provide any clues about where to look in the passage. Use the key words in each statement to determine where to examine the passage.

- [A] While the last sentence says that some critics "argue that Sarnoff's construct has damaged programming content," this is not stated as a fact, only a possible opinion. Always be careful to differentiate between opinions and facts on RC passages.
- [B] **CORRECT.** The first paragraph indicates that Farnsworth was the technical inventor of television. That paragraph also says that "Farnsworth's contributions have gone relatively unnoticed, since it was Sarnoff who put televisions into living rooms."
- [C] Though the passage describes the ways in which both Zworykin and Farnsworth have been described as the progenitors of television, and though it makes a case that there remains a lively debate over who deserves the credit, this does not mean that there is "no way" of determining who invented the first television. Always be wary of extreme language like this when dealing with RC questions.

Unit Two: Paragraphs and Passages

Answers to Passage G: Life on Mars

Because of the proximity and likeness of Mars to Earth, scientists have long speculated about the possibility of life on Mars. Roughly three centuries ago, astronomers observed Martian polar ice caps, and later scientists discovered other similarities to Earth, including length of day and axial tilt. But in 1965, photos taken by the *Mariner 4* probe revealed a Mars without rivers, oceans, or signs of life. Moreover, in the 1990s, it was discovered that unlike Earth, Mars no longer possessed a substantial global magnetic field, allowing celestial radiation to reach the planet's surface and solar wind to eliminate much of Mars's atmosphere over the course of several billion years.

More recent probes have investigated whether there was once liquid water on Mars. Some scientists believe that the presence of certain geological landforms definitively resolves this question. Others posit that wind erosion or carbon dioxide oceans may be responsible for these formations. Mars rovers *Opportunity* and *Spirit*, which landed on Mars in 2004, have both discovered geological evidence of past water activity. These findings substantially bolster claims that there was once life on Mars.

Upon previewing the questions, here is an example of what you might jot down:

6. Was life on mars?

7. Main idea

8. List discoveries

9. P1 why "polar ice caps"?

10. Infer

11. Infer: what supports life?

12. Select: proof no life on Mars

The first two questions will involve an understanding from your first read. While you read the first paragraph, consider why the author mentions the polar ice caps. As you build your headline list, note discoveries and any details about what supports life.

Here is one example of a possible set of notes for this passage:

1. S: Mars close, simil to Earth → poss life on M
   —Sims (polar ice, day, tilt)
   —Diffs (no water, no more mag field)

2. Rec. focus: was there water?
   —Evid: yes/no, now <u>more</u> support for life on M ← main idea

Simple Story: Debate about life on Mars. Positives and negatives, but the big deal was the discovery of water, increasing the chance that there was life on Mars.

Chapter 8: **Reading Comprehension Problem Set**

6. **The author's stance on the possibility of life on Mars can best be described as**

   (A) optimistic
   (B) open-minded
   (C) skeptical
   (D) simplistic
   (E) cynical

This passage is concerned with the possibility of life on Mars. It details the various discoveries that have been made over centuries. The main idea is that, although not definitively proven, recent evidence shows there may have been life on Mars. The correct answer will reflect the tone of that main idea.

   (A) The author is neither optimistic nor pessimistic about the possibility of life on Mars.
   (B) **CORRECT.** Open-minded reflects the main idea: It is not proven, but there is new evidence to be considered.
   (C) There is no indication that the author of the passage is skeptical. The main idea is not as negative as this choice.
   (D) The author considers several different factors in the determination of life on Mars. The author's stance could not appropriately be described as simplistic.
   (E) Again, the author is more objective in tone and could not accurately be characterized as cynical.

7. **The passage is primarily concerned with which of the following?**

   (A) Disproving a widely accepted theory
   (B) Initiating a debate about the possibility of life on Mars
   (C) Presenting evidence in support of a controversial claim
   (D) Describing the various discoveries made concerning the possibility of life on Mars
   (E) Detailing the findings of the Mars rovers *Opportunity* and *Spirit*

This passage is primarily concerned with the possibility of life on Mars. The two paragraphs discuss various discoveries that have been made over the past few centuries. The passage concludes that recent findings substantiate claims that there was once life on Mars. However, scientists are still not certain. In determining the purpose or main idea of the passage, avoid extreme words and be able to defend every word, matching your choice to your prediction.

   (A) This passage does not set out to *disprove* the theory that there is life on Mars. It is also too extreme to suggest that this is a "widely accepted theory."
   (B) This answer choice is tempting because it is relatively neutral. However, the passage does not seek to initiate a debate; it is more concerned with documenting findings that pertain to life on Mars. In other words, the passage presents the findings that frame a debate; it doesn't initiate the debate itself.
   (C) The passage presents evidence in support of and against the possibility of life on Mars. It is too limited to suggest that the passage is primarily concerned with presenting evidence "in support of" life on Mars.
   (D) **CORRECT.** This answer choice avoids extreme words and best summarizes the purpose of the passage.
   (E) This answer choice is too specific. The passage does mention the Mars rovers *Opportunity* and *Spirit*, but it is inaccurate to suggest that the passage is primarily concerned with these two rovers.

8. Each of the following is a discovery mentioned in the passage EXCEPT

   (A) Wind erosion and carbon dioxide oceans are responsible for certain geological landforms on Mars.
   (B) Mars does not have a substantial global magnetic field.
   (C) Mars had water activity at some point in the past.
   (D) The length of day on Mars is similar to that on Earth.
   (E) The axial tilt of Mars is similar to that of Earth.

To address this specific detail question, point out specific evidence in the text to defend your answer choice. The passage discusses several discoveries; to answer this question, find the four choices which *are* discoveries specifically mentioned. A prediction for this question will not be possible, you must work from key words in the answer choices.

   (A) **CORRECT.** The passage does make mention of wind erosion and carbon dioxide oceans, but the author states that these are other possible explanations for certain geological landforms on Mars. The text states that some scientists "posit" that wind erosion and carbon dioxide oceans may have had an effect, but that is a hypothesis, not a discovery.
   (B) At the end of the first paragraph, the passage states that "in the 1990s, it was discovered that, unlike Earth, Mars no longer possessed a substantial global magnetic field."
   (C) In the second paragraph, the author indicates that two rovers "both discovered geological evidence of past water activity."
   (D) Certain similarities Mars has to Earth were discovered sometime between three centuries ago and 1965, including the length of day, as noted in the second sentence of the first paragraph.
   (E) Certain similarities Mars has to Earth were discovered sometime between three centuries ago and 1965, including the axial tilt of Mars being similar to that of the Earth, as noted in the second sentence of the first paragraph.

9. In the first paragraph, the author most likely mentions the discovery of polar ice caps to suggest that

   (A) until recently Mars's polar ice caps were thought to consist largely of carbon dioxide
   (B) Martian polar ice caps are made almost entirely of water ice
   (C) Mars has many similarities to Earth, including the existence of polar ice caps
   (D) Mars has only a small fraction of the carbon dioxide found on Earth and Venus
   (E) conditions on the planet Mars were once very different than they are at present

This is a specific purpose question that refers back to the second sentence in the first paragraph. The best approach is to determine, using surrounding sentences, what the author's purpose is in mentioning Mars's polar ice caps. The second part of the sentence, "later scientists discovered other similarities to Earth, including length of day and axial tilt," indicates that polar ice caps are introduced as an example of the similarity of Mars to Earth (note the use of the word *other*).

- (A) The passage does not mention the content of the polar ice caps, just that they were observed.
- (B) Again, you do not know, from the passage, the composition of Mars's polar ice caps.
- (C) **CORRECT.** As stated above, polar ice caps are introduced as one of several similarities of Mars to Earth.
- (D) The passage does not indicate the carbon dioxide content of Mars or Earth. It also does not mention Venus.
- (E) While you know from the rest of the passage that conditions on Mars were probably different from what they are now, the author does not mention polar ice caps in order to indicate this.

10. Each of the following can be inferred from the passage EXCEPT

- (A) the presence of certain geological landforms is not definitive proof that there was once life on Mars
- (B) similarities to Earth bolster the idea that a planet might be or have been capable of supporting life
- (C) the absence of a substantial global magnetic field on Mars suggests that it would be difficult to sustain life on Mars
- (D) the presence of water activity on Mars is related to the possibility of life on Mars
- (E) the claim that there was once water on Mars has only limited and indirect support from recent discoveries

An inference question, but an EXCEPT variation. A prediction will not be possible, although if you notice that a choice clearly contradicts the passage, that will be the correct choice. Find each inference that can be defended by going back to the text and does not go far beyond the language in the passage and eliminate those four choices.

- (A) In the second paragraph, the author states that while the presence of geological landforms may indicate the presence of water, it is also possible that these landforms were caused by wind erosion or carbon dioxide oceans.
- (B) The first paragraph describes three similarities between Mars and Earth (polar ice caps, length of day, and axial tilt). The passage then contrasts that evidence: "But" later photos showed a planet "without rivers, oceans, or signs of life." If this later evidence showed no signs of life, in contrast to earlier evidence showing similarities with Earth, then the similarities must support the possibility of life on Mars.
- (C) In the second paragraph, the absence of a substantial global magnetic field is presented as evidence of the lack of life on Mars. Again, note that this answer choice avoids extreme words by using the word *suggests*.
- (D) The first sentence in the second paragraph states that "more recent probes have investigated whether there was once liquid water on Mars." Given this purpose, it is clear that the existence of water is important in order to establish whether or not there was life on Mars.
- (E) **CORRECT.** According to the second paragraph, the "Mars rovers *Opportunity* and *Spirit* . . . have both discovered geological evidence of past water activity." As made clear by the subsequent sentence that "these findings substantially bolster claims," the evidence supporting the claim that there was once water on Mars is substantial. Thus, the passage contradicts the statement that this claim is supported by only marginal evidence.

Unit Two: **Paragraphs and Passages**

11. It can be inferred from the passage that which of the following characteristics of a planet would imply that it might support life?
    Select all that apply.

    - [A] A significant global magnetic field
    - [B] Evidence of liquid carbon dioxide on the planet's surface
    - [C] The average daily level of sunlight reaching the planet's surface

Most of the passage is about what aspects of Mars might or might not imply that it once supported life. Polar ice caps, length of day, and axial tilt are all mentioned to imply life may be possible. The lack of a magnetic field made it impossible, so a magnetic field must be necessary.

- [A] **CORRECT.** The passage says that "Mars no longer possessed a substantial global magnetic field," which led to the disappearance of Mars's atmosphere. This dissimilarity with Earth is used in the passage as evidence against life on Mars. Conversely, therefore, the existence of a global magnetic field would imply that it is possible a planet could support life.

- [B] The passage mentions "carbon dioxide oceans" as a possible cause for certain geological formations. Another possible (and contrasting) cause is liquid water. Since water activity is associated with possible life, and carbon dioxide oceans are mentioned in contrast, carbon dioxide is probably not evidence of life.

- [C] While your general knowledge of the importance of the sun might make it reasonable to assume that the sun would be important on other planets as well, the passage does not discuss this particular issue. The passage does mention "length of day" as a similarity between Mars and the Earth, but length of day does not necessarily mean hours of daylight. A day can also refer to the length of time it takes a planet to rotate on its own axis.

12. Select the sentence in the passage that provides the best evidence that, at the given time, life did not exist on Mars.

The correct answer probably will not be found in the second paragraph, which mostly provides evidence that there *was* life on Mars at one point. In the first paragraph, the third sentence says that in 1965, photos "revealed a Mars without rivers, oceans, or signs of life," providing evidence that life did not exist at that time. The next sentence indicates that the lack of a magnetic field caused some negative consequences incompatible with life. However, this sentence says that there is no longer such a magnetic field, indicating that the field did once exist.

The correct sentence is the third sentence of the first paragraph: "But in 1965, photos taken by the *Mariner 4* probe revealed a Mars without rivers, oceans, or signs of life."

Answers to Passage H: Fossils

Archaeological discoveries frequently undermine accepted ideas, giving rise to new theories. Recently, a set of 3.3-million-year-old fossils, the remains of the earliest well-preserved child ever found, were discovered in Ethiopia. Estimated to be 3 years old at death, the female child was of the *Australopithecus afarensis* species, a human ancestor that lived in Africa over 3 million years ago. "Her completeness, antiquity, and age at death make this find of unprecedented importance in the history of paleo-anthropology," said Zeresenay Alemseged, a noted paleo-anthropologist, opining that the discovery could reconfigure conceptions about early humans' capacities.

Previously, *afarensis* was believed to have abandoned arboreal habitats. However, while the new fossil's lower limbs support the view of an upright stance, its gorilla-like arms suggest that *afarensis* was still able to swing through trees, initiating a reexamination of long-held theories of early human

Chapter 8: **Reading Comprehension Problem Set**

development. Also, the presence of a hyoid bone, a rarely preserved larynx bone that supports throat muscles, has dramatically affected concepts of the origin of speech. Although primitive and more ape-like than human-like, this fossil hyoid is the first found in such an early human-related species.

Upon previewing the questions, here is an example of what you might jot down:

13. Passage org

14. Why quote ZA?

15. Why discovery important?

16. infer: hyoid bone disc.

17. impact disc hyoid bone

18. select: undermine theory

The first question is a twist on a main idea. The remaining questions all provide some context clues to help find the answers, and also set you up to know that the hyoid bone discovery must have been pretty important!

Here is one example of a possible set of notes for this passage:

1. Arch: disc → undermine old, lead to new thry ← main idea
 —e.g., child foss Eth

2. Before: thought af no longer in trees
 BUT disc → reexam old thry
 Also hy bone → Δ thry

Simple Story: New discoveries change old ideas and give rise to new theories. A detailed archaeological example illustrates this overall point. The discovery of a particular skeleton led researchers to reexamine theories about early human life.

---

13. The organization of the passage could best be described as

    (A) discussing a controversial scientific discovery

    (B) contrasting previous theories of human development with current theories

    (C) illustrating a general contention with a specific example

    (D) arguing for the importance of a particular field of study

    (E) refuting a popular misconception

Unit Two: **Paragraphs and Passages**

This question is a variation of a purpose of paragraph question. The correct choice will reflect the purpose of several components of the passage, in order of presentation in the passage. This passage begins by noting that "archaeological discoveries frequently undermine accepted ideas, giving rise to new theories." It supports this statement by relating the impact of one discovery in the field. Thus, your predicted answer will reference both the overall contention and the use of the example.

- (A) This choice omits the phenomenon that the discovery is meant to illustrate: discoveries often give rise to new theories. Also, there is nothing controversial about the described discovery.
- (B) The passage does not focus on the contrast between previous theories of human development and current theories. Rather, it discusses a singular discovery that affects previous theories. The passage would need to outline both previous and current theories of development and then contrast them. Instead, the passage focuses on how one example illustrates a way in which the field of archaeology evolves.
- (C) **CORRECT.** The passage makes a general claim and uses a specific example to support that claim, just as this choice states.
- (D) One might feel that the evolution of theories of human development is a worthwhile object of contemplation, but the *passage* does not argue for the importance of archaeology as a field of study. This answer choice misstates the organization of the passage.
- (E) The passage does not indicate how popular the earlier theories of human development were. Also, the passage provides only one example of a single discovery and its importance. The language employed in the passage does not warrant describing the passage as a refutation of past theories.

14. **The passage quotes Zeresenay Alemseged in order to**
    - (A) provide evidence to qualify the main idea of the first paragraph
    - (B) question the claims of other scientists
    - (C) provide evidence to support the linguistic abilities of the *afarensis* species
    - (D) provide corroboration for the significance of the find
    - (E) provide a subjective opinion that is refuted in the second paragraph

This specific purpose question references the quotation in the first paragraph. That quote highlights the importance of the discovery and is followed by another similar reference. The quotation is used to emphasize the exceptional importance of this find; the correct answer for this Inference question will reflect this emphasis.

- (A) The main idea of the first paragraph is that a new finding can call accepted archaeological theories into question. The rest of the paragraph provides an example of this phenomenon. The quotation emphasizes the importance of the discovery itself, not the example, nor does the quotation qualify or limit the main idea of the first paragraph.
- (B) The passage does not discuss claims of other scientists.
- (C) The discussion of the linguistic ability of the *afarensis* species is in the second paragraph and is unrelated to this quotation.
- (D) **CORRECT.** The point of this paragraph is to illustrate that in archaeology, important factual discoveries lead to theoretical changes. The quotation corroborates the idea that this discovery is in fact a significant one.
- (E) The quotation is offered as corroboration of the importance of the discovery and is not refuted at any point in the passage.

Chapter 8: **Reading Comprehension Problem Set**

15. **Each of the following is cited as a factor in the importance of the discovery of the fossils EXCEPT**

    (A) the fact that the remains were those of a child
    (B) the age of the fossils
    (C) the location of the discovery
    (D) the species of the fossils
    (E) the intact nature of the fossils

On EXCEPT questions, it is typically easier to eliminate incorrect answer choices until only one is left. No prediction will be possible.

(A) The fourth sentence of the first paragraph cites a quotation from a noted paleo-anthropologist that the find of the child fossils was of unprecedented importance due to the child's "age at death." Therefore, the fact that the remains were those of a child was of substantial significance.

(B) The "antiquity" (a synonym for *age*) of the fossils is mentioned in the fourth sentence of the first paragraph as a reason why the fossils were an important discovery.

(C) **CORRECT.** The location of the fossil discovery is mentioned in the first paragraph of the passage. However, the location is not provided as a reason why the fossils are significant.

(D) This choice is tricky. The second paragraph describes what was previously "believed" about *afarensis* and that this evidence "dramatically affected" certain theories about the development of speech in humans. The fossils were of a "human-related species," so the species itself was significant in influencing the theories about human speech.

(E) The fourth sentence of the first paragraph notes that the find was important due its "completeness." The intact nature of the fossils is another way of saying that the fossils are complete.

16. **It can be inferred from the passage's description of the discovered fossil hyoid bone that**

    (A) *Australopithecus afarensis* was capable of speech
    (B) the discovered hyoid bone is less primitive than the hyoid bone of apes
    (C) the hyoid bone is necessary for speech
    (D) the discovery of the hyoid bone necessitated the reexamination of prior theories
    (E) the hyoid bone was the most important fossil found at the site

Unit Two: Paragraphs and Passages

The passage provides the following information about the discovered hyoid bone: It is the oldest ever found, and it is "primitive and more ape-like than human-like." The passage also states that the discovery will impact theories about speech.

- (A) The passage gives no information about the linguistic capacities of *Australopithecus afarensis*. The passage does not give enough information to infer that the species was capable of speech.
- (B) The passage indicates that the discovered hyoid bone more closely resembles those of apes than humans. However, while the passage does generally relate to evolution, the discovered bone is not necessarily less primitive than that of an ape. It could be slightly different in an equally primitive way; not all differences in structure would make a bone more advanced.
- (C) While it can be inferred that this bone has some effect on speech, the passage does not indicate that it is "necessary for speech." It is possible that a species could be capable of speech without a hyoid bone.
- (D) **CORRECT.** The passage states that the discovery of the hyoid bone "has dramatically affected concepts of the origin of speech." Thus, it can be inferred that the discovery made the reexamination of prior theories necessary.
- (E) The passage does not rank the importance of the fossils found; as a result, this choice is not necessarily true. It is possible that other fossils were of equal or greater importance.

17. **The impact of the discovery of the hyoid bone in the field of archaeology could be best compared to which one of the following examples in another field?**

    - (A) The discovery and analysis of cosmic rays lend support to a widely accepted theory of the origin of the universe.
    - (B) The original manuscript of a deceased nineteenth-century author confirms ideas of the development of an important work of literature.
    - (C) The continued prosperity of a state-run economy stirs debate in the discipline of macroeconomics.
    - (D) Newly revealed journal entries by a prominent Civil War–era politician lead to a questioning of certain accepted historical interpretations about the conflict.
    - (E) Research into the mapping of the human genome gives rise to nascent applications of individually tailored medicines.

When you are asked to choose which answer best parallels a part of a passage, be sure that you grasp the nature of the example in the passage before considering the answer choices. This is a variation on the specific purpose question type: Which answer choice contains a statement that would serve a similar purpose?

The passage indicates that the discovery of the hyoid bone "has dramatically affected concepts of the origin of speech." This evidence supports the passage's main point: New discoveries can undermine or call into question existing theories and give rise to new ones.

Chapter 8: **Reading Comprehension Problem Set**

The correct answer will describe a discovery that would have a nearly identical impact in another field.

(A) In this example, the discovery serves to support a widely accepted theory, as opposed to causing a reexamination of that theory.

(B) In this answer choice, the discovery serves to confirm earlier held ideas, as opposed to causing a reexamination of those ideas.

(C) There is no indication that an accepted theory is applicable and being called into question. Further, the "continued prosperity" is not a new discovery or change in the way that things used to be done or viewed.

(D) **CORRECT.** This answer choice correctly describes a discovery that causes a reexamination of earlier ideas. In this case, newly uncovered journal entries spur a reevaluation of certain historical ideas regarding an important conflict.

(E) In this answer, scientific advances in the field of biology give rise to new applications. It does not discuss a discovery that calls accepted ideas into question.

18. Select the sentence that most distinctly undermines an accepted paleo-anthropological theory.

This Select-in-Passage question asks for a specific example of the main idea: a new discovery that undermines or calls into question an accepted theory or idea.

The first sentence of the second paragraph describes a previously accepted theory about *afarensis*. The next sentence describes how this theory was undermined, and it is the correct answer: "its gorilla-like arms suggest that *afarensis* was still able to swing through trees, initiating a reexamination of long-held theories of human development." The example of the hyoid bone mentioned later never describes exactly what theory was undermined by its discovery.

The correct sentence is the second sentence of the second paragraph: "However, while the new fossil's lower limbs support the view of an upright stance, its gorilla-like arms suggest that *afarensis* was still able to swing through trees, initiating a reexamination of long-held theories of early human development."

Answers to Passage I: Chaos Theory

Around 1960, mathematician Edward Lorenz found unexpected behavior in apparently simple equations representing atmospheric air flows. Whenever he reran his model with the same inputs, different outputs resulted—although the model lacked any random elements. Lorenz realized that tiny rounding errors in his analog computer mushroomed over time, leading to erratic results. His findings marked a seminal moment in the development of chaos theory, which, despite its name, has little to do with randomness.

To understand how unpredictability can arise from deterministic equations, which do not involve chance outcomes, consider the non-chaotic system of two poppy seeds placed in a round bowl. As the seeds roll to the bowl's center, a position known as a point attractor, the distance between the seeds shrinks. If, instead, the bowl is flipped over, two seeds placed on top will roll away from each other. Such a system, while still not technically chaotic, enlarges initial differences in position.

Chaotic systems, such as a machine mixing bread dough, are characterized by both attraction and repulsion. As the dough is stretched, folded, and pressed back together, any poppy seeds sprinkled in are intermixed seemingly at random. But this randomness is illusory. In fact, the poppy seeds are captured by "strange attractors," staggeringly complex pathways whose tangles appear accidental but are in fact determined by the system's fundamental equations.

During the dough-kneading process, two poppy seeds positioned next to each other eventually go their separate ways. Any early divergence or measurement error is repeatedly amplified by the mixing

Unit Two: **Paragraphs and Passages**

until the position of any seed becomes effectively unpredictable. It is this "sensitive dependence on initial conditions" and not true randomness that generates unpredictability in chaotic systems, of which one example may be the Earth's weather. According to the popular interpretation of the "Butterfly Effect," a butterfly flapping its wings causes hurricanes. A better understanding is that the butterfly causes uncertainty about the precise state of the air. This microscopic uncertainty grows until it encompasses even hurricanes. Few meteorologists believe that we will ever be able to predict rain or shine for a particular day years in the future.

> **Upon previewing the questions, here is an example of what you might jot down:**
>
> 19. main idea
>
> 20. poppy after mixed
>
> 21. rounding errors
>
> 22. examples of systems
>
> 23. pairs in chaotic sys
>
> 24. author: weather systems
>
> 25. select P2–P3: why misnomer?
>
> The first question will come from your initial read. Many of the other questions offer specific items to keep an eye out for as you create your headline list.
>
> **Here is one example of a possible set of notes for this passage:**
>
> 1. 1960 L: unexp behav in air flow eqs
>
>   Reran model, diff results
>
>   tiny rounding errors blew up
>
>   help dev <u>chaos thry</u>—<u>little to do with randomness</u> ← main idea
>
> 2. Unpredict can come fr determ eqs
>   —non-chaotic: 2 poppy seeds in or on bowl
>
> 3. Dough mixing (chaos): seed movmnt <u>seems</u> random but is NOT
>
> 4. Seeds go sep ways → unpredict, not truly random
>   —weather, butterfly eff
>
> **Simple Story:** Lorenz discovered something about chaos theory (which is not really about randomness). Non-chaotic systems are predictable. Chaotic systems increase initial differences, so even though they are not actually random, they are hard to predict.

Chapter 8: **Reading Comprehension Problem Set**

19. **The main purpose of this passage is to**

    (A) explore a common misconception about a type of complex physical system
    (B) trace the historical development of a scientific theory
    (C) distinguish a mathematical pattern from its opposite
    (D) describe the spread of a technical model from one field of study to others
    (E) contrast possible causes of weather phenomena

The first paragraph introduces chaos theory by describing a historical moment in its development. The main idea comes at the end of the first paragraph: "chaos theory. . .has little to do with randomness." The next three paragraphs focus on further explaining this mystery with analogies involving poppy seeds and bread dough. Finally, as a minor addendum, the last paragraph mentions how this understanding of chaos theory might be applied to the weather, as a possible specific case of a chaotic system.

Taking all of these roles together, the main idea of the passage is an explanation of how chaotic systems *seem* to be random (a common misconception) but actually are governed by very complex equations.

   (A) **CORRECT.** The complicated aspects are the characteristic features of chaotic systems, such as "sensitive dependence on initial conditions and staggeringly complex pathways." The point of the passage is to explain such features.

   (B) The first paragraph, as an introduction, describes a particular milestone in the historical development of chaos theory. However, the passage does not go on to describe other developments of this theory over time.

   (C) Perhaps the behavior of chaotic systems could arguably be described as a "mathematical pattern." However, the passage does not discuss any category of systems that is categorized clearly as the *opposite* of chaotic systems. Certain non-chaotic systems are described in the second paragraph, but it is not clear whether these systems would be the opposite of chaotic systems, or whether *random* systems would be the opposite.

   (D) If chaos theory is the technical model mentioned in the answer choice, the passage never describes how that model spreads from one field of study to any other.

   (E) In the fourth paragraph, the "Butterfly Effect" is mentioned as a popular explanation for at least some hurricanes. However, no other causes of weather phenomena are ever discussed.

20. **In the example discussed in the passage, what is true about poppy seeds in bread dough once the dough has been thoroughly mixed?**

    (A) They have been individually stretched and folded over.
    (B) They are scattered in random clumps throughout the dough.
    (C) They are accidentally caught in tangled objects called "strange attractors."
    (D) They are bound to regularly dispersed patterns of point attractors.
    (E) They are in positions dictated by the underlying equations that govern the mixing process.

Unit Two: **Paragraphs and Passages**

The third paragraph contains this specific detail, describing what happens to these poppy seeds: they "are intermixed seemingly at random." But the positions of the seeds are not random, as the next sentences emphasize. Rather, the seeds "are captured by 'strange attractors,' staggeringly complex pathways whose tangles. . .are in fact totally determined by the system's fundamental equations." Thus, the positions of the seeds are themselves "determined by the system's fundamental equations."

- (A) The passage mentions nothing about any stretching or folding of the poppy seeds themselves; rather, the dough is stretched and folded.
- (B) The poppy seeds are scattered throughout the dough, but not in random clumps.
- (C) The poppy seeds are caught in strange attractors, but there is nothing *accidental* about their capture. Moreover, the strange attractors described in the passage are not physical objects but rather mathematical pathways.
- (D) Point attractors are not mentioned in relation to the dough-mixing process. Also, the poppy seeds, which have been "intermixed seemingly at random," are not placed at regular intervals.
- (E) **CORRECT.** The poppy seeds may seem to be scattered at random, but they follow the pathways of the strange attractors. These pathways, and thus the seeds' positions, have been "determined by the system's fundamental equations."

21. According to the passage, the rounding errors in Lorenz's model

- (A) indicated that the model was programmed in a fundamentally faulty way
- (B) were deliberately included to represent tiny fluctuations in atmospheric air currents
- (C) were imperceptibly small at first, but tended to grow
- (D) were at least partially expected, given the complexity of the actual atmosphere
- (E) shrank to insignificant levels during each trial of the model

Use the key words "rounding errors" and "Lorenz's model" to find the relevant text for this specific detail question. The reference to Lorenz leads to the first paragraph: "Lorenz realized that tiny rounding errors in his analog computer mushroomed over time, leading to erratic results." In other words, the rounding errors started out small but became larger.

- (A) Although these rounding errors are in fact *errors*, nothing in the passage indicates or implies that the model overall was built incorrectly.
- (B) The errors were not deliberately included in the model. The passage's first sentence states that Lorenz found "unexpected behavior" in his model. It may be argued that the role of these errors is similar to the role of "tiny fluctuations in atmospheric air currents"—that is, they both introduce uncertainty that grows over time. However, this answer choice claims incorrectly that the errors were inserted on purpose.
- (C) **CORRECT.** This answer choice corresponds very closely to the statement in the passage. Some synonyms have been used, but the meaning is the same: "were imperceptibly small at first" substitutes for "tiny," and "tended to grow" substitutes for "mushroomed over time."
- (D) The passage indicates that the behavior of the model was *unexpected*. Nothing in the passage indicates that Lorenz expected the errors at all.
- (E) The errors did not shrink, but rather "mushroomed over time."

Chapter 8: **Reading Comprehension Problem Set**

22. **The passage mentions each of the following as an example or potential example of a chaotic or non-chaotic system EXCEPT**

    (A) a dough-mixing machine
    (B) atmospheric weather patterns
    (C) poppy seeds placed on top of an upside-down bowl
    (D) poppy seeds placed in a right-side-up bowl
    (E) fluctuating butterfly flight patterns

The passage mentions several examples of systems, both chaotic and non-chaotic, to illustrate the special characteristics of chaos. This question is an exercise in finding the references to key words contained in the four wrong answers.

(A) A dough-mixing machine is first mentioned at the beginning of the third paragraph as an example of chaos in action: "Chaotic systems, such as a machine mixing bread dough . . ."

(B) Atmospheric weather patterns as a system to be studied are mentioned in both the first and the last paragraphs. In the last paragraph, the passage states that the Earth's weather may be an example of a chaotic system.

(C) Poppy seeds placed on an upside-down bowl are described in the second paragraph as an example of a non-chaotic system that creates divergence.

(D) Poppy seeds placed in a bowl that is right-side-up are described in the second paragraph as an example of a non-chaotic system that creates convergence.

(E) **CORRECT.** Butterfly flight patterns are not discussed as examples of systems themselves. According to the last paragraph, the "Butterfly Effect" is a popular metaphor with a common interpretation, but that is not the same as a literal chaotic system.

23. **It can be inferred from the passage that which of the following pairs of items would most likely follow typical pathways within a chaotic system?**

    (A) Two particles ejected in random directions from the same decaying atomic nucleus
    (B) Two stickers affixed to a balloon that expands and contracts over and over again
    (C) Two avalanches sliding down opposite sides of the same mountain
    (D) Two baseballs placed into a device designed to mix paint
    (E) Two coins flipped into a large bowl

Stripped down to its essence, this inference question asks which of the five choices describes a system that is the most *chaotic*, according to the characteristics of chaos outlined in the passage. The most important proof sentence is at the beginning of the third paragraph: "Chaotic systems, such as a machine mixing bread dough, are characterized by both attraction and repulsion." Thus, look for the system that is the most analogous to the dough-mixing machine. Moreover, the system should contain both attractive and repulsive elements: In other words, the two items embedded within the system should sometimes come near each other and then separate again.

At the beginning of the fourth paragraph, there is a superficially appealing, but ultimately distracting, sentence: "During the dough-kneading process, two poppy seeds positioned next to each other eventually go their separate ways." This sentence could lead you to think that the defining characteristic of chaotic systems is simply that two embedded items move away from each other. The question is asked in such a way as to focus your attention on the two items, so that you might then use this proof sentence alone and choose an incorrect answer. It is better to use the very first sentence of that paragraph that applies to *any* chaotic system for your prediction: "characterized by both attraction and repulsion."

- (A) The two particles ejected from a nucleus do diverge, but they do not approach each other again. Moreover, there is no implication of any activity analogous to mixing bread dough.
- (B) The stickers on the balloon separate and come together repeatedly. This behavior meets the criterion of "both attraction and repulsion." However, there is no mixing, and as a result, the system cannot be said to be analogous to a machine mixing dough.
- (C) As in answer choice (A), the two items in question (avalanches) separate but never draw near each other again. Likewise, there is no mixing in the system.
- (D) **CORRECT.** Two baseballs placed into a device designed to mix paint is analogous to two poppy seeds placed in bread dough being mixed by a machine: Parts of the system are separated, intermingled, and brought back together again in regular, though complex, ways, as determined by the laws of physics. The pathways of the two baseballs will diverge and converge repeatedly, as in any other chaotic system.
- (E) The two coins flipped into a bowl are closely analogous to the example in the second paragraph of the passage of two poppy seeds placed in a bowl and allowed to fall; this system is presented as non-chaotic.

24. **The author implies which of the following about weather systems?**
    Select all that apply.

    - [A] They illustrate the same fundamental phenomenon as Lorenz's rounding errors.
    - [B] Experts agree unanimously that weather will never be predictable years in advance.
    - [C] They are governed mostly by seemingly trivial events, such as the flapping of a butterfly's wings.

This is a Select One or More question of a specific detail variety. It is mostly relevant to the last paragraph of the passage, so take a little time to refresh your understanding of the few sentences devoted to weather systems.

- [A] **CORRECT.** Lorenz's rounding errors are actually found in the first paragraph: "Lorenz realized that tiny rounding errors…mushroomed over time." Similarly, from the final paragraph: "This microscopic uncertainty grows until it encompasses even hurricanes." These are both examples of chaotic systems.
- [B] The last sentence of the passage says: "Few meteorologists believe that we will ever be able to predict rain or shine for a particular day years in the future." The sentence does not indicate that meteorologists are unanimous in this opinion; in fact, "Few meteorologists" indicates that at least one actually believes that such predictions might be able to be made in the future.
- [C] While the passage indicates that the wings of a butterfly can affect weather systems, it does not say that this is the most important contributing factor. Likely, major climatic events are more important than seemingly trivial events, such as a butterfly taking flight.

25. **Select the sentence in the second or third paragraph that illustrates why "chaos theory" might be called a misnomer.**

Misnomer means that something has been given an incorrect or misleading name. The first paragraph states that chaos theory, despite its name, "has little to do with randomness." Look for a sentence in the second or third paragraph that illustrates this point.

The final sentence of the third paragraph uses poppy seeds to show that even the bread-mixing machine, which appears to be mixing things at random (in a "chaotic" manner), is actually moving the seeds through "staggeringly complex pathways whose tangles appear accidental but are in fact determined by the system's fundamental equations." In other words, there's nothing chaotic at all, only a very complex organization. This is a perfect example of why "chaos theory" is a kind of misnomer. (The question's request for an illustration is a good clue that you want an example from the passage.)

Note that the second-to-last sentence of the third paragraph, "But this randomness is illusory," does indicate that chaos theory might be called a misnomer. This sentence, though, does not illustrate *why* this is so.

The correct sentence is the final sentence of the third paragraph: "In fact, the poppy seeds are captured by 'strange attractors,' staggeringly complex pathways whose tangles appear accidental but are in fact determined by the system's fundamental equations."

CHAPTER 9
Issue Essay

In This Chapter...

- Essay in a Nutshell
- Analyze an Issue
- Style Points
- Analyze an Issue Sample Essays
- Notes on Preparation
- Vocabulary Challenge
- Answers and Explanations

CHAPTER 9 Issue Essay

The first part of the exam will consist of one essay, technically called the Analytical Writing Assessment (AWA). The Analyze an Issue essay is to be completed in 30 minutes. The goal of the essay is to discuss a general interest topic. The essay section always comes first before any of the Math or Verbal sections. The essay does not factor into your main GRE score; it is scored on a separate 6-point scale in increments of 0.5 (0 is lowest, 6 is highest). In this chapter, you will learn strategies for practicing, planning, and executing your essay.

Here are your Chapter 9 vocabulary words:

> indefatigable (A)
>
> amalgamate (A)
>
> malleable (E)
>
> veracity (E)
>
> peddle (A)
>
> ubiquitous (E)

Essay in a Nutshell

For those who consider themselves already very good at essay writing and have limited study time, here's the gist:

The Issue essay is very much like every other five-or-so paragraph academic essay you've ever written. Some people have trouble thinking of examples for abstract topics, such as, "Is justice more important in a society than compassion?" But if you feel confident about that, it's likely you won't need much preparation.

When you take practice tests, **do** write the essay, even if you don't need the practice or don't care about the essay score. The extra hour of writing tests your stamina and can tire you out before you reach the multiple-choice sections. Practicing the extra length will make you more indefatigable on test day.

Write a lot. No matter what the official rules say, longer essays get higher scores.

Pay attention to the specific instructions. While the essay prompts will broadly follow the themes mentioned above, each will have slightly different instructions. Responding to everything asked of you in the instructions is a key component of achieving a high score.

How Essays are Used by Graduate Schools

Graduate schools to which you send your GRE scores will be able to read your actual essays. Don't write anything you wouldn't want the admissions committee to read (avoid writing anything offensive or anything with a very political or self-exposing slant).

Unit Two: **Paragraphs and Passages**

The schools are aware of the constraints you are under as you write. In the "Guide to the Use of Scores" that ETS offers to graduate school admissions departments, ETS writes, "A GRE essay response should be considered a rough first draft since examinees do not have sufficient time to revise their essays during the test. Examinees also do not have dictionaries or spell-checking or grammar-checking software available to them."

It is impossible to say broadly how much the essay counts in graduate school admissions; there are simply too many programs and too many schools. Some math and science programs may take little or no account of the essay, and some more writing-intensive graduate programs may consider the essays more carefully. Some schools may use the essays as a screening device (so a very low essay score might keep the rest of your application from being given a serious review). It's also reasonable to presume that your essays are more likely to be taken into account if your undergraduate schooling was done in a language other than English.

The admissions department at the particular graduate program to which you are applying is the best source of information about how the GRE essay will be used. If the admissions department is not forthcoming, you'll just have to do your best, which is a good policy anyway.

Most MBA programs do not weigh AWA scores highly at all. If you are applying to a program that does not heavily weight the AWA, do your best, make sure that the AWA score is respectable, but do not place much emphasis on this element of your GRE preparation! If, on the other hand, you are applying for a PhD or for a master's in a field other than business, ask your desired programs how they weigh the AWA section of the GRE, and adjust your preparation emphasis accordingly.

The Physical Mechanics of Essay Writing

Assuming that you are taking a computer-based GRE (true in the United States and most other countries), you will be typing your essay into a text box. There is no limit to how much text you can enter, but you can only see about 35 lines of what you've written before you have to scroll. The system feels like a clunky, old-fashioned word processing program. You will have "Cut" and "Paste" buttons, as well as an "Undo" button. There is no bold, italic, or underline. There is no tab/indent. The program does not offer any type of spell-check or grammar check.

You will have scratch paper (the same scratch paper you use for the rest of the exam) on which to plan your essay, but you can also outline in the text box (though be sure to delete any notes or outlines before submitting your essay).

Once you've completed the essay and clicked on "Submit," you cannot go back. If you complete the essay before the time expires, you can go immediately to the next section, but you do *not* get to use any extra time on other sections. If you do finish early, consider letting the clock run down and using that extra time to take a mental break. (If you do this, you must remain in your seat, as this is not an official break.)

There is a 1-minute break after the essay; you will then proceed to your first Math or Verbal section.

Essay Length

For each essay, use a five-paragraph structure as a baseline. Sometimes you'll write four paragraphs, sometimes you'll write six, but the basic structure is an intro and a conclusion sandwiching a few main examples or reasons, each in its own body paragraph.

Interestingly, Manhattan Prep's analysis of published GRE essays written by actual students and given real scores shows a very strong correlation between length and score. Let's be very clear: **Even when ETS says that essay length doesn't matter, it does.**

To ensure your essay is long enough, you will have to brainstorm and plan your essay very efficiently (about 3–4 minutes) so that you can get started writing as soon as possible.

Write as much as you can in the time allotted!

Spelling and Grammar

On the GRE, while good spelling and grammar are better than poor spelling and grammar, the ideas you present are far more important.

According to ETS, "Scorers are trained to focus on the analytical logic of the essays more than on spelling, grammar, or syntax. The mechanics of writing are weighed in their ratings only to the extent that these impede clarity of meaning." In other words, as long as the grader can understand you, they are not supposed to count off for minor and infrequent spelling and grammar errors.

Scoring

The essay is scored from 0–6, and is reported separately from your Math and Verbal scores. Scoring is done according to a publicly available Scoring Guide, which will be discussed more fully in the following sections.

Essays are scored by specially trained college and university faculty who will not see your name, gender, geographical location, or any other identifying information. The essay will be read by one human grader and one *e-rater*®, described by ETS as "a computerized program developed by ETS that is capable of identifying essay features related to writing proficiency." If the human grader and the *e-rater*® disagree, another human grader reads the essay, and the two human scores are amalgamated to create your final score for that essay.

It goes without saying that any evidence of cheating, which includes using anyone else's work without citation, will get your GRE score (the entire thing, not just the essays) canceled and your fee forfeited.

Analyze an Issue

For the Analyze an Issue assignment, you will be presented with a statement or a claim. Your job is to agree or disagree with the statement, and then write a compelling essay to support the position you've taken.

The topic that you are given on the real test will be chosen from a list of topics available on the ETS website. Yes, that's right—you can view all of the possible topics ahead of time. There are dozens, so don't spend your time memorizing them, but do use them to get a sense of what you might see on test day.

In the issue essay, you are generally expected to **take a side**. Don't just say, "It depends." Instead, make sure you articulate a particular point of view. You can, and usually should, acknowledge that the other side has some merit, but do so in a way that doesn't hurt your own argument. If you do write a more modified thesis along the lines of "it depends," make sure you clearly explain *what* it depends on, so that your essay seems thoughtful and precise, rather than just indecisive.

Unit Two: **Paragraphs and Passages**

Scoring Guide

According to *The Official Guide to the GRE®*, an essay that scores a 6 generally does the following:

- "Articulates a clear and insightful position on the issue in accordance with the assigned task
- "Develops the position fully with compelling reasons and/or persuasive examples
- "Sustains a well-focused, well-organized analysis, connecting ideas logically
- "Conveys ideas fluently and precisely, using effective vocabulary and sentence variety
- "Demonstrates superior facility with the conventions of standard written English (i.e., grammar, usage and mechanics), but may have minor errors"

As discussed in the previous section, a majority of the scoring rubric is based on the quality of your argument, not the quality of your writing. This section will discuss how to generate strong arguments for the Issue essay. A subsequent section will discuss tips for writing style on the GRE essay.

Essay Instructions

Pay attention to the specific instructions given with the essay as it may affect how much content you have to write about the other side of the argument. ETS lists six different possible ways you might be prompted to respond to a topic. Here they are, from *The Official Guide for the GRE® General Test*:

1. "Write a response in which you discuss the extent to which you agree or disagree with the statement, and explain your reasoning for the position you take. In developing and supporting your position, consider ways in which the statement might or might not hold true and explain how these considerations shape your position.

2. "Write a response in which you discuss the extent to which you agree or disagree with the recommendation, and explain your reasoning for the position you take. In developing and supporting your position, describe specific circumstances in which adopting the recommendation would or would not be advantageous and explain how these examples shape your position.

3. "Write a response in which you discuss the extent to which you agree or disagree with the claim. In developing and supporting your position, be sure to address the most compelling reasons and/or examples that could be used to challenge your position.

4. "Write a response in which you discuss which view more closely aligns with your own position, and explain your reasoning for the position you take. In developing and supporting your position, address both of the views presented above.

5. "Write a response in which you discuss the extent to which you agree or disagree with the claim and the reason on which that claim is based. (NOTE: For this prompt, the claim will be accompanied by a reason why the claim has been made. You'll need to give your opinion on both.)

6. "Write a response in which you discuss your views on the policy above, and explain your reasoning for the position you take. In developing and supporting your position, consider the possible consequences of implementing the policy and explain how these consequences shape your position."

These instructions may seem quite different, but they really fall into three general categories:

1. Pick a side of the prompt and defend it, but explain when the other side might be true or more logical (#1, #2, #3, and #4 from above).
2. Pick a side of the prompt, and also make sure to discuss the reason the author gives in defense of that prompt (#5 from above).
3. Pick a side and discuss the consequences of your opinion (#6 from above).

In the end, you will *always* want to do the following, regardless of the Issue prompt you're given:

1. Take a point of view on the given issue.
2. Support your point of view using relevant and *specific* examples.
3. Acknowledge both sides of the issue and the specific instructions in the question.

Brainstorming

Spend 3–4 minutes brainstorming specific, real-world examples. Let your perspective be malleable: Try to think of examples on both sides of the issue. *Real-world* means some event or phenomenon that actually occurred, whether in history, in your own life, or even in a book that you read. Once you're done brainstorming, pick the side for which you have the best examples; plan for the strongest points on that side to each become a body paragraph and start writing.

Practice it with this topic:

> "The better a new idea is, the greater the opposition to that idea when it is first presented. Only later, usually once the person who had the idea is no longer around to enjoy its success, do we consider the thinker a genius."

First, make a T-chart, like this:

Why brainstorm both sides of an issue? It is often true that the side you don't believe is the easier side to write. Perhaps this is because when you believe in something strongly, it seems obvious to you, and it's harder to come up with concrete reasons or examples to support your opinion. By writing down "For" and "Against," you are setting yourself up to think in each direction. This is especially useful when you are trying to come up with counterexamples.

Write down one-word (or very short) tags for each possible reason or example. On this prompt, for instance, Galileo might pop to mind because he was persecuted for saying that the Earth moved around the Sun, but after his death, his ideas were vindicated, and he was considered a scientific hero. On the other hand, there are plenty of geniuses who were renowned during their own lifetimes (Einstein was quite famous in his own time). Jot these down on your T-chart—Galileo on the left, and Einstein on the right.

Unit Two: Paragraphs and Passages

A good way to get your brainstorming done quickly is to piggyback off examples you already have. Once you've thought of Galileo, can you think of other people like him who were persecuted for their ideas—ideas that are now considered correct? You might think of someone like Nelson Mandela, who spent 27 years in prison. But wait! He was hailed as a hero for so much of his life, and he was the first democratically elected president of South Africa. This is actually a pretty good example for the Against side. (This is why it's good to brainstorm both sides.)

Also on the Against side—once you've thought of Einstein, can you think of other famous geniuses? How about Stephen Hawking? If you run out of steam, think to yourself, "Hmm, Einstein and Stephen Hawking are both scientists. Can I think of the "Einstein" of some other field?" Perhaps someone like W. E. B. DuBois, who was considered a radical in his own time; however, after his death, his ideas were vindicated by the civil rights movement of the 1960s. Hmm, DuBois actually fits better on the "For" side. Is there someone else who was a social activist whose ideas were later vindicated? How about the early feminists, such as Elizabeth Cady Stanton and Lucretia Mott? See, you're on a roll!

Here, the example goes further than it needs to for the sake of demonstrating the brainstorming process. Stop as soon as you have three good ideas for one side.

For	Against
Galileo	Einstein, Hawking, Mandela

Your initial thought might have been that you wanted to argue for, but you've come up with three against examples. Go with it! Your goal is to write the best essay you can as quickly and as easily as possible. You've got what you need to do that, so start writing.

You may have noticed that the previous examples were drawn from history and current events. While personal examples are allowable, they don't tend to make for the most rigorous and persuasive essays. Personal examples can be considered a backup plan for when you get stuck in your brainstorming.

You are *not* required to use example after example in your essay. You are also perfectly welcome to use well-considered reasoning. Some topics lend themselves better to examples, while other topics lend themselves better to argumentation.

Here's another example topic.

> **"Every nation should require students to study at least one foreign language from the elementary school level through the university level."**

Your challenge here is to "divide up" your reasoning into discrete arguments so that your essay doesn't just ramble on without structure.

You might just start with the first thing that comes to mind. For instance, is it equally true in "every nation" that students should be required to study foreign language? Probably not. Jot this down in the Against column.

On the other hand, the world is becoming more connected. Most people who end up conducting international business, or emigrating to new lands, don't know from childhood that they're going to do so. As children, they're not in a position to decide whether to take foreign languages. It would be best to require foreign languages so that they're prepared for whatever happens in their adult lives. This would go in the left column.

One possible thesis might be, "While foreign language study has many benefits, both practical and intellectual, it is going too far to say that such study should be mandatory for every citizen of every nation. Other factors should be taken into account." Those broad factors mentioned (maybe whether the nation's primary language is already an international language, whether the nation's primary language is in danger of dying out, and whether the nation has more pressing concerns) could each become the foundations of one of the following body paragraphs. This thesis clearly takes a stance against the prompt, but it certainly isn't arguing that foreign language study is bad—it is taking a very reasonable, balanced approach.

When a topic is phrased in an extreme way ("everyone should do X"), **don't ignore practical issues**. In some nations, it would be difficult to even find foreign language teachers. Some nations barely have schools of any kind, so foreign language instruction hardly seems like a main priority. And who decides which languages are mandatory? Not all students are the same—maybe most students could be required to take foreign languages, but the few who are having trouble with basic skills that they will need for adult life ought to be waived from foreign language requirements so that they can focus on things they will really need.

Here is a sample T-chart containing some of these ideas:

For	Against
World is more int'l—students don't know what they'll need as adults, so prep them now.	Some nations need f.l. more than others.
	Some nations not practical—schools very basic, no f.l. teachers.
	Which f.l.? Who decides?
	Preserve culture, some nations' languages might die out.
	ALL PEOPLE EVERYWHERE? Too extreme.

It's totally okay to have an unbalanced T-chart. You *want* to use this to pick which side to write on. (Of course, there is no "right" answer to an Issue question, and your personal T-chart might have led you to argue in favor.)

This chart shows five arguments against. You probably won't have time to write an entire body paragraph about each one, and some ideas are really building off of other ones (for instance, it might be hard to write an entire paragraph on the idea "Who decides which foreign languages to take?"). So either pick your three or so strongest arguments, or else *group* your arguments into three or so groups.

Here is what a test-taker might jot on paper next to the chart:

F.l. good but shouldn't be mandatory for all.

    I. Diff countries, diff needs.
    II. Some nations must focus on survival—priorities!
    III. Not practical—some nations can't, what lang? Some want to preserve culture.
    IV. Individual students are diff.

You also want to make sure to **acknowledge the other side** (usually in the introduction, although sometimes in the course of the body paragraphs). This is very easy to do, since you have brainstormed both sides. Just take a point or two from the side you *didn't* pick, and say something like, "While a reasonable person might think X, actually Y is more important," or "While a reasonable person might think X, this is not the case *all of the time*." For instance, on the foreign language topic:

> *While a reasonable person might suggest that because children don't know whether they'll move to other nations or engage in international business as adults, we should prepare them for such experiences now. However, some people will stay in their home countries and work in jobs that don't require a second language. It makes sense to leave decisions about education in the hands of each nation and its school systems.*

Acknowledging the other side is a great way to fill out your introduction or conclusion. Or, if you have a lot to say in rebuttal to an opposing point, you can write a body paragraph of the form "objection → your response → your argument."

In other words, *anticipate counterarguments and respond to them*. This is especially important if you have decided on what you know to be an unusual viewpoint. If your argument is that governments should not provide public schools, you absolutely must address the first thing that may pop into someone's mind: "But what about children whose parents can't afford to pay private school fees?"

Finally, a word about your thesis or main idea: While sometimes it makes sense to simply agree or disagree with the topic, feel free to take a balanced, in-between approach. The graders enjoy nuance. Just be very clear about what you mean. Still, *in between* doesn't mean vague or wishy-washy. For instance, if you want to say that foreign language instruction should be mandatory in some countries and not others, say exactly what should be the deciding factor. A good thesis (for someone who is more on the "for" side of the foreign language topic) might be:

> *Because foreign language instruction is increasingly important in our interconnected world, it should be a priority in school curricula. However, in some nations, foreign language instruction is simply not practical or even possible. Thus, foreign language instruction should be mandatory at all levels of schooling except in nations where such a requirement is impracticable or for individual students whose learning difficulties make the requirement unreasonable.*

Note that this person isn't exactly arguing for the topic as written. But there's no question what the writer's position is. This is a detailed, balanced, and reasonable thesis.

If you do go beyond a simple "agree" or "disagree" thesis, avoid theses that are too extreme, but also those that are too soft and agreeable. An overly extreme thesis might be "*Foreign languages should not be made mandatory for any students, because students should never have to study something they don't want to. Children should always make their own decisions.*" This goes beyond what is required and is difficult to prove. An example of an overly soft or agreeable thesis might be "*Foreign languages can be valuable in certain pursuits. For example, foreign language study can help students become translators, foreign language teachers, or travel writers."* This statement is so mild that it is almost impossible to *disagree* with, and it doesn't confidently answer the instructions.

In sum, your thesis or main idea shouldn't be something so extreme that you can't defend it, but it also shouldn't be something so humdrum and obvious that a reasonable person couldn't take an opposite view. Don't oversimplify the topic. **Pick a thesis you would use to start an interesting, intelligent discussion among reasonable people.**

The brainstorming and planning process above might sound as though it would take a person *much* longer than the 3–4 minutes recommended at the beginning of the chapter. Keep in mind that the sample T-charts contain a bit more information than you would need to write down, since you'll only be writing for yourself. If you write "SH" for "Stephen Hawking," you only have to remember what your abbreviation means for a couple of minutes, so feel free to be brief.

You can write an essay outline, separate from your brainstorming, if you find it helpful. But consider labeling points from your T-chart "I," "II," and "III" to save time, as opposed to rewriting your notes in outline form. Alternatively, you can type your outline on the computer so that you have bits of it to reuse as you write your full essay. Whatever you do, practice your preferred approach so you can confidently implement in the time constraints of the test.

Practice with brainstorming will reveal that the same examples can often be used on a variety of prompts. There's nothing wrong with that! Many topics lend themselves to discussing climate change; for instance, the issue of whether technology/progress/new ideas can have a downside seems to be a common underlying theme. And, of course, write about what you know. If you were a philosophy major, or an environmental science major, etc., feel free to draw disproportionately on those types of examples.

When you practice brainstorming, give yourself plenty of time the first time through—maybe 10 minutes. The next time, cut it down to 8 minutes, then 6, 5, 4…With practice, you will be able to reliably brainstorm in 3–4 minutes or even faster.

Writing the Issue Essay

Structure

Here is a basic structure for the Issue essay:

Introduction: Briefly restate the issue with the goal of demonstrating to the grader that you understand the topic. *Do not simply repeat the prompt* (the grader knows what topic you are writing about). Then define terms (if needed), acknowledge complexity, and establish your "take" or thesis on the issue.

Body: Write two to four paragraphs, each illustrating one of your main points. Keep in mind: *Don't spend too much time making a single point or you will run out of time!*

Conclusion: Re-summarize your position, perhaps acknowledging the other side. An exemplary conclusion adds some final extra insight—a new window to the main idea you've been discussing all along.

Aim for three substantive sentences in your conclusion; these sentences can vary widely in length and content. A relevant quote would be a good way to fill out a conclusion.

A conclusion often ends with a final sentence that either generalizes the situation and makes it more universal or looks toward the future. For instance:

> As our world becomes more interconnected through technology and increasingly global outlooks, we must look for every possible way to prepare the next generation for a more international world—a world replete with possibilities, if we are willing to look beyond our already blurring national boundaries and engage with humanity at large.

Of course, many wind up right near the end of the 30 minutes when it comes down to writing a conclusion. So while a new insight would be nice, it may not realistically happen. Don't stress. In general, if you are running out of time or are stuck for a final concluding sentence, try something along the lines of "In order to have a better world in the future, we must do X."

Trouble Getting Started?

If you freeze when trying to start your introduction, write a different paragraph first! Just pick whichever example seems easiest to write and dive in. You can certainly cut and paste as needed. In the worst case, use a starter sentence to turn the engine over in your mind: "This is a dumb idea because…" or "This is a great idea because…" Just keep an eye on the clock and make sure you leave enough time for both an intro and a conclusion.

A Note on Proofreading

Very few test-takers will have time for significant proofreading. Keep in mind that the graders are aware of your time constraints. They are not judging your spelling or punctuation, except where it muddies your meaning. In fact, the most important part of proofreading on the GRE is to check that you responded to the specific instructions that were presented in the prompt. Beyond that, just try to put yourself in the shoes of the grader, and check that all of your points are stated clearly. Let the commas fall where they may!

Style Points

No, the GRE does not literally award "style points." But, as seen in the citations of the Scoring Guide, an effective and engaging writing style can help you achieve a high score. While the previous sections focused on how you might structure your arguments, this section offers tips for the nitty-gritty of writing your paragraphs and sentences.

General Style Tips

Tone: There's no specific rule against saying "I," but don't be too informal. Avoid conversational asides, and don't try to be funny. Keep the tone serious and academic.

Varied diction: Throughout the essay, you will say the same thing several times. Don't use the exact same words: Paraphrase yourself. If in the introduction, you wrote, "The most important virtue in a leader is a strong sense of ethics," in your conclusion, you might write, "A strong moral framework is paramount for a leader."

However, don't get excessive about it—if you're writing an essay about the environment, you're definitely going to have to use the word "environment" numerous times. It would be great if you could switch up "environment" every now and then with something like "global ecosystem," but don't get too distractingly creative (Mother Earth, the rotating blue orb we call home), and as long as the same exact word isn't too ubiquitous, you've done the job.

Varied sentence structure: Aim for a mix of long and short sentences. Throw in an occasional semicolon, hyphen, colon, or rhetorical question. For example:

> Is it the case that sacrifice is the noblest of all virtues? Even a cursory analysis ought to indicate that it is not; the greatest of all virtues can hardly be said to be the one with, typically, the least utilitarian value.

Make sure you know how to correctly use any punctuation you decide to include.

Vocabulary: Use GRE-type words in your writing, as long as you're sure you can use them correctly. Some good vocabulary words to think about are those about arguments themselves, since those will work in nearly any essay. Some examples are: *aver, extrapolate, contend, underpin, claim, hypothesize, rebuttal, postulate, propound,* and *concur*.

Transitions: A top-scoring essay has body paragraphs that lead logically into one another. You can create this chain of logic by arranging your examples or reasons in a progressive way and by using transition phrases and similar signals. The simplest transitions involve phrases such as "On the other hand..." or "Finally..." A more complex transition might take the following form:

> The obstacles toward international cooperation include not only [the stuff I discussed in my last paragraph], but also [the stuff I'm about to discuss in this paragraph].

Analyze an Issue Sample Essays

> **Every nation should require students to study at least one foreign language from the elementary school level through the university level.**
>
> Write a response in which you discuss the extent to which you agree or disagree with the recommendation, and explain your reasoning for the position you take. In developing and supporting your position, describe specific circumstances in which adopting the recommendation would or would not be advantageous and explain how these examples shape your position.

Foreign language study can be a valuable component of a balanced education. So, too, can poetry, economics, or public speaking. But students are individuals, and live in a wide variety of circumstances around the world. It is going too far to say that every nation should require its students to study foreign languages.

Different countries have different needs and circumstances. While many bemoan the lack of international outlook in the United States, it is reasonable to note that most Americans do just fine speaking only one language. Of course, universities, prep schools, and other institutions are still free to make foreign language instruction mandatory, as many do now. In Sweden, however, it is a sound policy to make foreign language mandatory for nearly everyone; Sweden has an excellent school system, free through the university level, and it is clear that Swedish is a minority language, and English has actually become the language of international business in Sweden and throughout Europe. Sweden currently mandates the teaching of English, as it should. If the government did not compel students to learn English, they would struggle to compete in the global job market.

While Sweden has one of the highest standards of living in the world, many nations simply have no ability to provide foreign language instruction, nor does it seem as though such instruction should be the top priority. In many countries, primary schools cost money, and many girls don't get to go to school at all, or must drop out due to lack of funds, early marriage, or their families' needing them to work. If female students in Afghanistan are to receive only a few years of education in their entire lives, it seems absurd to mandate that they learn foreign languages, as this would be a waste of their time and effort. Individual schools and teachers should be free to decide how to best use the limited time available.

Finally, not only are nations different from one another, but so are students. Many students have learning disabilities that make foreign language learning virtually impossible. Even those who don't have such disabilities have individual differences and interests that should be respected. A scientific prodigy who may go on to cure cancer or AIDS ought to be permitted to focus solely on science at least at certain levels of his or her education. For every hour spent learning a foreign language, there is an opportunity cost: something else not being mastered.

Of course, virtually everyone is in favor of a more global outlook, and virtually no one thinks that foreign language study is bad. However, making foreign language instruction mandatory in every nation, at every level of schooling, is unjustifiable. Different nations have different needs, and different individuals have their own capacities and goals. Foreign language study can truly open the world to those who partake, but there are many reasons not to mandate it.

Comments:

This is a moderately lengthy, argument-based essay that takes the somewhat obvious tack of disagreeing with an extreme topic.

The essay contains good transitions at the top of the third and fourth paragraphs, linking a discussion of Sweden to a discussion of poorer nations, and then linking differences among nations to differences among individuals. The examples progress in a logical way.

The language and ideas are clear, and the essay persuades by acknowledging common beliefs on the topic ("virtually everyone is in favor of a more global outlook, and virtually no one thinks that foreign language study is bad") and addressing those beliefs ("there are many reasons not to mandate it"). Also, the essay responds to the specific instruction to describe how the mandate would be advantageous (as in Sweden's case) or not advantageous (as in the case of the United States, learning-disabled children, etc.).

The previous essay is not perfect, but even if it had contained several typos, misspellings, or grammar errors, it would likely receive a strong score of 5 to 6.

> **Strong beliefs prevent people from thinking clearly about issues.**
>
> Write a response in which you discuss the extent to which you agree or disagree with the claim. In developing and supporting your position, be sure to address the most compelling reasons and/or examples that could be used to challenge your position.

The phrase "strong beliefs" may bring to mind images of heroes, people who have fought valiantly for what they knew to be right, or it may bring to mind images of tyrants, people whose beliefs were so strong (if misguided) that they were able to commit atrocities without regard for others. Whether such figures fall on the right side of history or not, strong beliefs often brook no adjustment and permit no new information to be considered. However, some beliefs are strong for good reason—who is not possessed of a strong belief that the earth is round, for instance? Strong beliefs do prevent people from thinking clearly about issues when those beliefs are based on emotion, group loyalty, or tradition;

however, strong beliefs need not cloud our thinking when those beliefs are a genuine product of a logical, ongoing search for truth that is open to revision and new evidence.

Seventeenth-century Italian astronomer Galileo Galilei alleged that the Earth moved around the Sun, rather than the reverse; for this heliocentric theory he was tried by the Catholic Church, convicted of heresy, and placed under house arrest for the rest of his life. Leaders of the Church held the strong belief that the Earth must be at the center of the universe. When presented with evidence that the orbits of the planets seemed to go every which way in this model (yet Galileo's model showed the planets moving, more sensibly, in ellipses), the Church did not admit this new evidence into its thinking. Of course, Galileo himself was possessed of strong beliefs, and although he was forced to publicly recant, he did not actually change his view. Yet Galileo's belief was not dogmatic; it was based on years of astronomical observation and careful calculations. Furthermore, Galileo, a Catholic, began with a geocentric worldview; his very heliocentric position was proof of his willingness to change his mind in the face of new evidence.

While Church leaders possessed strong beliefs that brooked no adjustment, Rene Descartes was a devout religious thinker whose strong beliefs did not cloud his thinking. The purpose of Descartes's famous "I think, therefore I exist" was to create a system of logic that would allow him to clear away that which he only thought he knew (but didn't actually know for sure) so he could logically build a case for his religious belief. Adopting a position of ultimate skepticism, Descartes asserted that all he really knew was that he existed. He then reasoned, logically, from that point. Whether one agrees with Descartes's conclusions, his "Meditations" is a masterwork of clear and rigorous thinking.

Just as Descartes was willing to toss aside all he thought he knew in pursuit of verifiable truth, thinkers on moral issues, such as slavery, have demonstrated that strong beliefs cloud our thinking if we don't admit of new evidence, but can be a force for good if we do. In the United States prior to the Civil War, pro-slavery forces argued that the great society of ancient Athens had been built on a framework of slavery. When presented with new information—such as that Greek slavery was very different from the slavery practiced in the United States or Sojourner Truth's poignant "Ain't I a Woman?" address, reprinted across the nation—many did not change their minds. Of course, some did, and the North had no shortage of outspoken abolitionists. The Civil War was a war of strong belief against strong belief; the side most willing to change its mind in the face of moral argument was, rightfully, the side that won.

All people are created equal, but all strong beliefs are not. Strong beliefs based on evidence and logic are strong beliefs that are nevertheless changeable, and need not muddy our thinking. It is dogmatism that is the enemy, not strength of conviction.

Comments:

This is a lengthy, example-based essay that gives a balanced, nuanced position on the topic. "Strong beliefs prevent people from thinking clearly about issues" is a fairly extreme statement, so a more nuanced thesis here is a good strategy. The introduction is long in order to give time to develop that thesis: "Strong beliefs do prevent people from thinking clearly about issues when those beliefs are based on emotion, group loyalty, or tradition; however, strong beliefs need not cloud our thinking when those beliefs are a genuine product of a logical, ongoing search for truth that is open to revision and new evidence."

The first body paragraph is sophisticated—it actually gives two intertwined examples by showing that the Church's strong belief was indefensible, but Galileo's strong belief was justifiable.

The second body paragraph is somewhat weaker, but there is a nice transition between the two paragraphs ("While Church leaders possessed strong beliefs that brooked no adjustment, Rene Descartes . . ."), and the writer balanced out an example about religious belief gone wrong with an example of religious belief the writer thinks falls on the other side of the thesis.

The third body paragraph is fine, although it doesn't seem to fit the topic as well as the first two; the writer makes no distinction between "new information" such as astronomical observation and "new information" in a moral sense. However, the slight shift in emphasis allows the writer to incorporate other examples recalled from his or her college course on pre–Civil War U.S. history.

The conclusion flows nicely from the third example (although this is not necessarily expected in an essay). It is brief and to the point and restates the thesis in different words.

Though this essay does not take an overarching stance for or against, it succeeds at explaining *why* the statement might sometimes be true, and other times untrue. It makes clear what the strongest arguments both for and against the prompt are, and provides an argument for when each side applies. This is an example that succeeds adequately in addressing the specific instructions, even without a declarative "for" or "against" thesis.

The writer's language and main ideas are clear. The second and third examples are not as strong as the first, but this essay's main strengths are its well-developed main idea and sophisticated attempt to validate a two-part thesis with relevant examples.

The previous essay is also not perfect, but would likely receive a strong score of 5.

Notes on Preparation

For more sample Issue essays, with comments provided by the people who grade the real GRE, check the ETS website or the *Official Guide* Analytical Writing chapter.

Now that you know the ins and outs of the GRE essays, here are some final notes on how to finish your preparation:

1. Read the GRE's official sample essays.
2. Brainstorm examples for a large number of topics from the published topic pool on the ETS website.
3. Write several practice essays under timed conditions, also using topics from the topic pool. Don't select the topics you most *want* to write about—just scroll down the list and do the first topic you land on, or ask someone else to assign you a topic. Write your practice essays on a computer, using only the functions available to you on the real exam (i.e., turn off spell check and grammar check).
4. Take several full-length Manhattan Prep GRE practice exams, and don't skip the essay section!

Vocabulary Challenge

> Did you spot these vocabulary words? If not, go back and find them in context! (The word may be in a different form than listed here— "digressing" instead of "digress," for example.) Write your own definitions based on the evidence in the chapter.

1. indefatigable (*adj.*), p. 301
2. amalgamate (*v*), p. 303
3. malleable (*adj.*), p. 305
4. veracity (*n*), p. 313
5. peddle (*v*), p. 313
6. ubiquitous (*adj.*), p. 319

Answers and Explanations

Vocabulary Challenge

1. indefatigable (*adj.*): untiring, not able to become fatigued
2. amalgamate (*v*): blend, merge, or unite
3. malleable (*adj.*): able to be bent, shaped, or adapted
4. veracity (*n*): truthfulness, accuracy; habitual adherence to the truth
5. peddle (*v*): travel around while selling; sell illegally; give out or disseminate
6. ubiquitous (*adj.*): existing everywhere at the same time

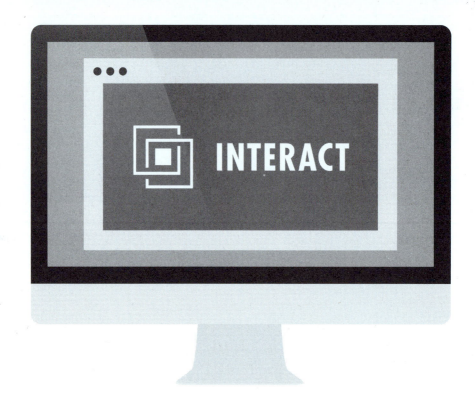

NEED MORE THAN BOOKS? TRY INTERACT™ FOR GRE®!

Interact for GRE is an on-demand, adaptive learning experience made by Manhattan Prep's 99th-percentile GRE instructors. It's like having a GRE teacher with you anywhere you are. Interact adapts to your performance by providing you with prompts and delivering customized feedback based on your responses. This branching video technology makes Interact personalized to your skill level, so you'll never feel left behind.